Double Particularity

Double Particularity

Karl Barth, Contextuality, and Asian American Theology

Daniel D. Lee

Fortress Press
Minneapolis

DOUBLE PARTICULARITY

Karl Barth, Contextuality, and Asian American Theology

Cover design: Alisha Lofgren

Hardcover ISBN: 978-1-5064-1852-0

Paperback ISBN: 978-1-5064-2335-7

eBook ISBN: 978-1-5064-1853-7

The paper used in this publication meets the minimum requirements of American National Standard for Information Sciences — Permanence of Paper for Printed Library Materials, ANSI Z329.48-1984.

Manufactured in the U.S.A.

This book was produced using Pressbooks.com, and PDF rendering was done by PrinceXML.

For my parents,
Young Keun Lee
and
Jeong Ja Lee

Contents

Acknowledgments

My tortuous journey to develop a Barthian methodology for Asian American theology goes much further back than my Fuller years. However, the encouragement and support of Dr. Howard Loewen, my *Doktorvater*, was crucial to finally bringing this study to fruition. Without his pastoral and insightful guidance, I would not be where I am as a theologian today.

I am also grateful to all the teachers whom I have had over the years. In the process of researching this project and constructing my arguments, the wisdom of Dr. Veli-Matti Kärkkäinen, Dr. Paul Louis Metzger, and Dr. Darrell Guder have been instrumental in my creative and analytical process. My reading of Barth has taken shape during the four years of attendance at Dr. George Hunsinger's Barth reading groups at Princeton Theological Seminary. Dr. Hunsinger's words about the various patterns and motifs of Barth's theological imagination still echo through my head whenever I read the *Church Dogmatics*. Dr. Bruce McCormack's challenge to read Barth for myself, from my perspective as an Asian American, spurred me on. Dr. Mark Kinzer and Dr. Richard Harvey were excellent guides in my exploration of the connections between the Jewish flesh of Jesus and contextual theology. I also would like to acknowledge Dr. Joel Green, Fuller's CATS Director, who encouraged me to pursue a more "practical" research project and fully engage with the Asian American theme all through my work, instead of relegating it to a small section.

There are other colleagues who have journeyed with me in this process. Dr. Ken Fong, who served as my Th.M. thesis advisor and who has been instrumental in the development of Fuller's Center for Asian American Theology and Ministry, has been a constant source of support. I have also enjoyed the camaraderie and scholarly fellowship of Dr. Jennifer Rosner, Dr. Michael Jimenez, and David Hunsicker, all students of Dr. Howard Loewen.

I must also thank my good friends, Joshua Ritnimit, Sam Bang, and Joseph Lee, all of whom affirmed the importance of my research for the broader church, served at various times as sounding boards, and believed in me. Good friends are rare. Therefore, I treasure their friendship in my life.

Special thanks go to my beloved wife, Judy, who has supported me throughout this project and throughout my academic journey for over fifteen years. She has been—and still is—my "Samwise Gamgee" through all the rejections, failures, and discouragement that I endured over the years. This work is the fruit of our partnership in the gospel. I also thank my three precious daughters—Annabel, Priscilla, and Teresa—who, at various times, prayed for Daddy's dissertation.

Finally, this study is dedicated to my late father, Young Keun Lee, and my mother, Jeong Ja Lee. I learned to appreciate the life of the mind through my father. I know that he would have relished this accomplishment with me. My mother has been my first and primary spiritual mentor all my life. Her faith still challenges me to stay rooted in the church and connected to God with a humble heart.

Introduction

The present work is a constructive proposal for theological methodology addressing the Asian American context using the resources and trajectory of Karl Barth's theology. While it hopes to contribute to the field of Barthian studies and of Asian American theology, this work is not an exhaustive analysis of either field. Rather, it focuses primarily on employing Barth's theology to develop a methodology for engaging the Asian American context. This methodological focus means that it is an integrative and synthetic work, bringing seemingly disparate thoughts and concepts together. We should note that the Asian American context serves as an example or a case study because the methodology that is proposed here translates to other contexts.

With the center of worldwide Christianity moving to the global South, and even as American Christianity becomes more reflective of immigrant populations, the theological need for a deeper engagement with context is more urgent than ever before. Karl Barth offers much wisdom and insight for the churches of the majority world and for these ethnic churches, even though he is often seen as just a figure in the Western historical tradition. Barthian reception in the Anglo-American context as well as Barthian studies bear some guilt for this narrow perception. And even in recent years, while genetic-historical research has done so much to recover the "contextual" Barth, excavating Barth's interaction with his context has more often been the main focus, often lacking constructive proposals for extending

Barth's thought to contemporary issues and challenges, especially regarding cultural plurality. This work is a contribution to the development of a connection between Barth and contextual theology, to the stimulation and enrichment of both.

One clear proof of the need for such a work, not just in the Asian American context, but worldwide, lies in the discrepancies between contextual theology and lived Christianity in the global South and in minority communities in the USA. On the one hand, postcolonial theology, with its liberationist rubric, gives voice to the majority world and the minority Christianities in the USA. On the other, the grassroots Christianities of these segments often remain disconnected from these often academic representations. Speaking from the Asian context, Simon Chan has articulated this exact dynamic in his recent methodological proposal to theologize from the ground up, starting with grassroots faith.[1] Chan rightly critiques academic theologies with their elitist agendas for their disconnection from the people on the ground, and thus, his contribution is welcome.

As a so-called modern day church father, Barth's wisdom and influence cannot be ignored. However, for the most part, he has not been considered a source of insights and inspiration for the task of contextual theology or theology explicitly situated in context. Partly, the disconnection between Barth and contextual theology arises from the state of contextual theology and its methodological presuppositions that do not adequately recognize the dangers of cultural captivities and domestications of the Word. We should note that while we use the term "contextual theology," we admit that it is highly problematic because every theology is contextual, whether consciously or not. What our global context requires is a shift from "contextual theologies" to the "contextuality" of all theology. In fact, the truth that every theology is contextual is now universally acknowledged. However, it often remains merely a simple undeveloped assertion. The contextuality of some theologies might

1. Simon Chan, *Grassroots Asian Theology: Thinking the Faith from the Ground Up* (Downers Grove, IL: InterVarsity Academic, 2014).

be explicit and developed, while the contextuality of others might remain implicit and even unconscious, and thus, even more vulnerable to cultural captivity.

When engaging the context means capitulating to it, Barth's approach cannot but be seen as purely anticontextual. According to still-lingering conventional wisdom, Barth represents a way of doing theology that simply says "*Nein*!" to any constructive engagement with the context. Of course, such a view, albeit still popular, misses a much more nuanced truth of Barth's contextuality, the nature of Barth's theological interaction with the context. To many who have only known his *Nein*, the wisdom of looking to Barth for insights concerning contextuality will seem very suspect. Therefore, we begin with a short *apologia* for looking to Barth for wisdom about contextual theology.

Why Karl Barth?

While there are many works throughout his theological career that we can highlight, the most significant articulation of Barth's contextual theological approach is found in a very short letter that was published posthumously. In this letter in *The South East Asian Journal of Theology*, Barth exhorts non-Western theologians to engage in the task of theology concretely in their "new, different, and special situation with heart and head, with mouth and hands."[2] Overall, Barth does two things in this letter. He describes what his constant theological agenda has been throughout his career, and he also offers some advice for these Asian theologians.

In describing his work, Barth first provides "two small criteria," which would enable them "to judge whether [they] had understood what [his] concern in theology has been, and is."[3] First, theology should be free from all "Babylonian captivities," that is, cultural or contextual strictures to the freedom of God. Whether this concern was expressed

2. Karl Barth, "No Boring Theology! A Letter from Karl Barth," *The South East Asian Journal of Theology* 11 (Autumn 1969): 3–5. This letter was penned by Eberhard Busch, Barth's last assistant, and approved by Barth. See Eberhard Busch, *Meine Zeit mit Karl Barth: Tagebuch, 1965-1968* (Göttingen: Vandenhoeck und Ruprecht, 2011), 677.
3. Barth, "No Boring Theology!," 4.

as the "infinite qualitative distinction" between God and humanity, the "Godness of God," the Wholly Otherness of God, the *Realdialektik*, the precedence of the divine Subject, asymmetric dialectic, actualistic ontology, or any number of *simuls* found throughout his works, Barth sought to remain faithful to the freedom of God from the context.

Second, "Yes" should be the dominant note. "No boring theology! No morose theologians!" exclaimed Barth.[4] Barth's doctrine of election with its universal implications brought the Yes to the forefront, making it explicitly dominant. Joy is a recurrent theme that occurs throughout the *Dogmatics*.[5] So, in these two criteria, we have the controlling foundation of Barth's contextuality.

In addition to these self-reflections, Barth also offers "two friendly suggestions." First, he encourages these Southeast Asian theologians to "say that which [they] have to say as Christians for God's sake, responsibly and concretely with [their] own words and thoughts, concepts and ways!"[6] Barth reminds them that they "truly do not need to become 'European', 'Western', not to mention 'Barthians', in order to be good Christians and theologians."[7] This explicit call to contextuality is not simply a kind word to "contextual theologians" in some "pagan" land. Rather, it is the same calling that Barth himself sought to live out, using his own words and concepts—indeed, his philosophical tools—to speak of God as he has described above. This is his understanding of his own vocation as well.

Second, Barth admonishes these Asian theologians to remember that we all need "to believe, to trust and to obey only one Spirit, one Lord, one God," and to proclaim "the one event" of Jesus Christ.[8] This point, along with the first one, constitutes Barth's *double particularity*, which will be discussed further in chapter 2: The particular Word of that one event speaks to all of us in our particular contexts. In *CD* IV/1, Barth states the same concern this way:

4. Ibid.
5. See John Mark Capper, "Karl Barth's Theology of Joy" (PhD diss., Cambridge University, 1998).
6. Barth, "No Boring Theology!," 5.
7. Ibid.
8. Ibid.

> Christians will always be Christians first, and only then members of a specific culture or state or class or the like. . . . Christianity exists in Germany and Switzerland and Africa, but there is no such thing as a German or Swiss or African Christianity (IV/1, 703).[9]

In this letter, written three weeks before he died, Barth outlines not only the kernel of his theological concern but also a rough outline of theological contextuality.[10] Using this letter as a signpost, it is possible to tease out the evidence of this contextual sensibility in various parts of Barth's vast corpus.

This letter is not the only reason why Barth should be considered a major source for wisdom about theological contextuality. We will later examine various works that have highlighted Barth's theology as missional or as a theology of mission.[11] Moreover, we will delve into the way Bruce L. McCormack's seminal work with its genetic-historical approach shifted the direction of Anglophone Barthian studies toward Barth's contextuality.[12]

In the latest example of such research, David Congdon theorizes that Barth's break with liberalism was fraught with missiological import. In fact, Congdon argues that we see Barth's "dialectical theology from the outset as a theology of mission, understood as a theology concerned with critically interrogating the relation between gospel and culture."[13] A careful study of Barth's early interest and engagement with missiology reveals that his rejection of liberal theology also meant the denial of "an imperialist and colonialist form of mission."[14] While

9. In terms of allegiance and the danger of ideological cooptation, Barth is right to argue for us being a Christian first. However, given that there is a pervasive and assumed European and white normative of Christianity, this argument would need to be decolonized before it can be of benefit to Christians of every background.

10. The letter is dated November 19, 1968. Barth died on December 10, 1968.

11. See John G. Flett, *The Witness of God: The Trinity,* Missio Dei, *Karl Barth and the Nature of Christian Community* (Grand Rapids, MI: Eerdmans, 2010); and Darrell L. Guder, ed., *Missional Church: A Vision for the Sending of the Church in North America* (Grand Rapids, MI: Eerdmans, 1998).

12. See Bruce L. McCormack, *Karl Barth's Critically Realistic Dialectical Theology: Its Genesis and Development 1909–1936* (Oxford: Clarendon, 1995).

13. David W. Congdon, "Dialectical Theology as Theology of Mission: Investigating the Origins of Karl Barth's Break with Liberalism," *International Journal of Systematic Theology* 10, no. 4 (October 2014): 390–413.

14. Ibid., 391.

Congdon's short article cannot cover the whole extent of his proposal, his overall interpretative vision is this:

> Barth's career can and should be understood as the consistent attempt (a) to critically oppose the church's capitulation to a culturally captive Christianity and (b) to construct a positive alternative account of knowing and following God that is not liable to such captivity and is, for that reason, a theology of mission. Put another way, a theology is genuinely *missionary* if it makes the crosscultural movement of the gospel internal to its message and logic–that is, if it funds the freedom of the gospel for new situations. Seen from that perspective, Barth is a profound theologian of mission from the beginning.[15]

No doubt, the genetic-historical approach has prompted a more careful and accurate reading of Barth. However, McCormack critiques those who mistakenly saw his approach as "an exercise in historical theology and nothing more," missing its "constructive level" and "what this implies for theology *after* Barth."[16] This present work is an attempt to build upon the genetic-historical research and insights to construct an Asian American theology, with much broader implications for global theology.

The idea of seeking after a theology *after* Barth is, in fact, very Barth-like. Barth made it very clear that he himself was not a Barthian. He was a fine example of how to move beyond his teachers as a student. Whether as a student of John Calvin or Wilhelm Herrmann, Barth believed that just repeating their words as his own or making their views his was not truly learning from them.[17] As a matter of fact, "those who simply echo Calvin are not good Calvinists, that is they are not really taught by Calvin."[18] Rather, being "taught by Calvin means . . . doing our best to follow him and then–this is the crux of the matter–making our own response to what he says."[19]

There are those who find Barth so brilliant a teacher that they feel

15. Ibid., 407.
16. McCormack, *Karl Barth's Critically Realistic Dialectical Theology*, vi.
17. Karl Barth, *Theology of John Calvin* (Grand Rapids: Eerdmans, 1995), 4–5, 71. Karl Barth, "The Principles of Dogmatics According to Wilhelm Herrmann," in *Theology and Church, Shorter Writings 1920-1928* (New York: Harper and Row, 1962), 238–39.
18. Barth, *John Calvin*, 4.
19. Ibid.

they cannot disagree with him and attempt to move beyond him.[20] Surely, a theologian's call to move beyond his or her teachers is not just a matter of ability, insight, or inspiration, but is a matter of faithfulness to the present moment as well. Dialogue with a teacher such as Calvin "may end with the taught saying something very different from what Calvin said but that they learned from or, better, through him."[21] Just like the Israelites in the wilderness, who could not live on old manna but had to gather it each day, we must listen for the Word of God *here* and *now*. Of course, this attention to encountering the Word in our own particularity is exactly what Barth taught as a teacher. This Word is never simply a repetition of past encounters. This way of learning to move beyond is what Barth says of Herrmann as a teacher:

> I let Herrmann say to me one essential truth. This truth, followed out to its consequences, later forced me to say almost everything else quite differently and finally led me to an interpretation of the fundamental truth itself which was entirely different from his. And yet it was *he* who showed me that truth.[22]

No such radical diversion from Barth's theology will be found here, but there are places where we forge paths that Barth never did. For those constructive attempts at contextual faithfulness, we offer no apology to Barth or to any others.

In sum, Barth's self-aware contextual dynamic, missional outlook, and proper theological pedagogy are reasons why he has so much to contribute to our rapidly globalizing situation and why he should be studied for deep wisdom about contextual engagement.

20. Torrance states, "Barth is not a theologian one can criticize [*sic*] until one has really listened to him and grasped his work as a whole and discerned its place in the history of theology." While I agree with the general tenor of Torrance's statement, I wonder if this is the path to becoming a Barthian, rather than a student of Barth (Thomas F. Torrance, *Karl Barth: An Introduction to His Early Theology 1910-1931* [London: SCM, 1962], 7–9).
21. Barth, *John Calvin*, 4.
22. Barth, "The Principles of Dogmatics According to Wilhelm Herrmann," 239.

Layout of the Study

The method of this study can be described as constructive-integrative. The overall movement is to appropriate key theological insights and elements from Barth's theology—such as actualistic ontology, threefold doctrine of reconciliation, radical Christocentricity, ecclesial orientation, and rejections of abstractions and of natural theology—to use as building blocks for understanding contextuality. Moreover, the Asian American context will serve as the concrete setting for demonstrating this new understanding of contextuality. Engaging the Asian American context will involve an integrative dimension of incorporating social sciences and church praxis with theological contextuality.

This work integrates research and insights from three primary fields: 1) Barthian studies, focusing on the contextual nature of Barth's corpus and his theological treatment of culture, as well as missiological insights from his doctrine of vocation, 2) works on contextual theology, intercultural theology, and global theology, and 3) various proposals for Asian American theology. Therefore, the pattern of engagement and development for every chapter will be to proceed first by discussing Barth; then, general contextual concerns; and finally, Asian American theology. This threefold synchronic structure of each chapter guides our agenda to employ Barth's theology for the development of contextuality in general, and of Asian American theology in particular.

The argument of the book will develop as follows:

Chapter 1 begins the study by proposing a new way to define or frame the particularity of a context. By exploring Barth's thoughts on Jesus's Jewish flesh and its connection to Israel as God's elect, we sort out exactly where cultural/ethnic particularity fits into the context for receiving God's Word. Next, we bring these ideas into conversation with the works of J. Kameron Carter, Willie Jennings, and Kathryn Tanner, covering race, identity, and culture. We argue that in receiving God's Word, the context must be understood as concrete, enveloping all aspects of cultural/ethnic particularities; however, these particularities must be dealt with in a nonessentialist fashion, meaning that they must not be treated as being constitutive in a changeless manner. This dialectical position of being concrete, yet nonessentialist in defining the context is the key argument of this chapter.

Looking to the Asian American context, we critique three representative methodologies of Asian American theology using this concrete, yet nonessentialist definition of the context. Acknowledging the weaknesses of these methodologies, we introduce the Asian American Quadrilateral (AAQ) as a working definition of the Asian American context that incorporates the four intersecting spheres of Asian heritage, migration experience, American culture, and racialization. The rest of the chapters build upon this new framework for understanding the Asian American context and developing an Asian American theology.

Chapters 2 and 3 make up the heart of this book, showing what theological contextuality meant for Barth and what it can mean for our current situation, the former chapter addressing the *formal* questions, and the latter, the *material* ones. Chapter 2 explains the theological and *formal* bases and dynamics of contextuality through Barth's actualism, which means that God is continually and always the Subject of divine revelation even when God becomes the Object of our knowledge. This actualism is the engine that runs the Barthian theology that engages his contemporary context. It is the logic of Barth's contextuality. Highlighting this actualism explains how Barth was both a theologian of the Word, as well as a highly contextual theologian. At its heart, Barth's contextuality is rooted in the God who is alive and present in the world. This presence is the justification for the contextuality of all theology; we must listen for God's Word here and now.

We describe the outworking of Barth's actualism, or the truth of this living God, in terms of *double particularity*, *God's counter-questions*, and the *universal-particular dynamic*. These three concepts will be unpacked in depth later, but here, we offer a teaser to whet the appetite. *Double particularity* refers to the place of theology that must account for the particularity of revelation and the particularity of our context. *God's counter-questions,* which challenge our questions, are what distinguishes Barth's method of correlation from Paul Tillich's, for example. The *universal-particular dynamic* refers to how the universal gospel must be mediated via particular expressions, and to how these particular expressions of the gospel must be in service of the universal church. The complex dynamics of these concepts are articulated, and then, illustrated in Barth's understanding of the nature of the Reformed confessions. These concepts can serve as interpretative tools for all theologies in engaging their context.

Moving to the Asian American context, we propose three crucial theological tasks for any Asian American theology: knowing the context, critically engaging the context, and remaining in communion with the one universal church. We should note that these tasks are critical in all theologies. They protect the Asian American theologian from various dangers and distortions when navigating the universal-particular dynamic. Moreover, these three tasks reside at three different levels of theological reflection: the methodological, ecclesial, and personal levels. While the academic disciplines of systematic and practical theologies are considered distinct, they cannot be separated if the context is taken seriously—as it is here. Each of these levels of theological reflection addresses the various theological tasks that are needed in the church.

Chapter 3 focuses on the *material* concerns of what engaging the context concretely means. After evaluating various approaches to understanding Barth's theology of culture, we propose a new way of dealing with culture by drawing from his doctrine of reconciliation. Incorporating the idea of *participatio Christi* (participation in Christ) from Barth's view of election as universal and christological, we present a triadic cultural reconciliation as an interpretive rubric, where the justification, sanctification, and vocation aspects function together to engage various dimensions and trajectories of culture. Interacting with Niebuhr's typology and drawing from the critique and insights of Kathryn Tanner, John Howard Yoder, and Lesslie Newbigin, this reconciliation rubric is envisioned as a grammar to judge, transform, and call for divine purposes any aspect of culture, while remaining dynamic, dialectical, and nuanced.

We bring this triadic grammar to bear upon each of the four aspects of the AAQ: Asian heritage, migration experience, American culture, and racialization, displaying the strength of its dynamic, dialectical, and nuanced features. Our goal here is to demonstrate the power and versatility of using this reconciliation-themed grammar. What we propose is that this discernment work will occur at the three different levels of theological reflection—the methodological, ecclesial, and personal levels—by Christians of divergent heritages, generations, and situations, as a guide to hear God's Word clearly and live it out boldly.

In chapter 4, we propose an Asian American ecclesiology, which draws from the christological rubrics and insights of Barth. Barth uses the Chalcedonian categories to evaluate ecclesiological distortions. For example, churches can be docetic and ebionitic, depending on the embodiment of the theological and sociological realities of their communities. We delineate the salient features of Barth's ecclesiology—for example, the precedence of the theological over the sociological and the ecclesiological movements of gathering, upbuilding, and sending—for the purpose of funding the construction of an Asian American ecclesiology. Then, we evaluate and critique Church Growth ecclesiology and multiracial ecclesiology, both of which have had a significant influence among Asian Americans, using the Chalcedonian categories. We find that both ecclesiologies have fallen into the trap of theological abstraction.

Moving on, Barth's christological logic and the triadic aspects of gathering, upbuilding, and sending become the building blocks to construct an Asian American ecclesiology. This ecclesiology proposes that Asian American churches be *contextual, transitional, missional,* and *liberational* communities corresponding to the four aspects of the AAQ.

Finally, the conclusion offers some reflections about the future of Barthian studies and theological contextuality, as well as possible trajectories for further research in Asian American theology.

1

Particularity: Defining the Context

One of the critical challenges of Asian American theology is the difficulty of defining a context that is extremely diverse and complex. Not only do the aspects of multiple ethnic heritages and generations pose challenges, the overall context itself is in flux amid changing global forces and cultural shifts. As postcolonial studies argue for an anti-essentialist hybridic identity for subalterns, this hybridity applies just as well to Asian Americans who must negotiate various aspects of their bicultural identity. Essentialism refers to stereotypical and homogenizing representations of a social group, usually by the colonializing power or the majority culture, representations that disregard this group's internal diversity and shifting nature, and hold hegemony over it. Avoiding this problem, and proceeding in a nonessentialist fashion, is one of our key tasks.

This conundrum of Asian American identity becomes apparent when the label "Asian American" is often used in an ethnically specific and narrow manner to functionally refer to first-generation Korean Americans in the works of Jung Young Lee or Sang Hyun Lee, for example.[1] A different ethnic center is adopted for the term "Asian American" in the works of Japanese American or Chinese American theologians.[2] This kind of ethnic and generational monopolizing of the term "Asian American" exacerbates matters by confusing identity and contextual framing. For example, what does Confucianism have to do with South Asian Americans, or is marginality really experienced similarly among various generations, or in what sense is the Chinese Exclusion Act or Japanese internment significant to other communities?

Considering the size of Asia, the term "Asian American," properly speaking, includes those of East Asian, Southeast Asian, and South Asian heritages at the very least. The peoples covered by this broad category do not share any single cultural heritage, history, immigration narrative, or even skin color. While the concept of marginality in some shape or form is often used to circumvent this diversity issue, such a strategy results in ignoring each person's cultural heritage and dulling the particularity that is so crucial for any theology that takes context seriously.

Regarding this issue of context and ethno-racial identity, a cursory look at Barth's works yields scant resources, except for his condemnations of *Blut und Boden* (Blood and Soil) ideology and its theological counterparts. However, such a judgment belies the rich potential in his insights and nuances present in his understanding of *Volk* (peoplehood or nationhood). Although Barth does not always develop his insights fully or in the direction that is required for the task of Asian American theology, it would certainly be a mistake to think that constructive wisdom about defining contexts and identities is absent altogether in his work.

As we have discussed in the introduction, the goal here is not so much to be faithful Barthians, but to honor Barth as a teacher by continuing his theological trajectory, as Barth does with John Calvin and Wilhelm Herrmann. Therefore, Barth's ideas presented here, as

1. Jung Young Lee, *Marginality: The Key to Multicultural Theology*, (Minneapolis, MN: Fortress Press, 1995); and Sang Hyun Lee, *From a Liminal Place: An Asian American Theology* (Minneapolis, MN: Fortress Press, 2010).
2. David Ng, ed., *People on the Way: Asian North Americans Discovering Christ, Culture, and Community* (Valley Forge, PA: Judson, 1996).

in the later chapters, will be extended and also critiqued at times for our purposes. However, we will follow closely Barth's deep theological conviction of respecting divine precedence in all matters in an attempt to avoid Babylonian captivities of every kind.

With these reflections in mind, Barth's affirmation of the Jewish flesh of Jesus, the implications of election for Israel and the Jews, and his connection of these insights to the general concept of peoplehood are fruitful groundwork for defining, developing, and engaging with contexts for Asian American theology. In the flow of argument from the Jewish flesh of Jesus to general peoplehood, Barth avoids the abstract nationalism that so plagued his contemporary political and ecclesial situation, while allowing for the affirmation of nationhood or peoplehood as a concrete context for receiving God's Word for discipleship. The key lies in avoiding essentialism, in a sense, and asserting that peoplehood as a context is reversible, fluid, and removable.[3] The limits of Barth's insights will be noted in time; however, the crucial idea is that by rejecting an essentialist definition of the context, it does not become a straitjacket or a form of Babylonian captivity for the Word.

As proposed in the schema delineated in the previous chapter, we proceed first by discussing Barth, then, general contextual theology, and finally, Asian American theology. Our argument begins with Barth's rejection of abstract nationalism while retaining a sense of peoplehood, which he exposits in the "Neighbors Near and Far" section in §54 of the *Church Dogmatics* III/4.[4] This section represents Barth's mature thought regarding the idea of peoplehood, where he explores the relationship between Israel and the nations. In order to understand the wider background to this relationship between Israel and the nations, the election of Jesus Christ and of Israel is addressed.

3. Barth does not use the word "essentialism," which has been developed within postcolonial studies. However, Barth's articulation of cultural boundaries resonates closely not only with Tanner's description of the postmodern notion of culture, but also with postcolonial insights into hybridity.

4. Carys Moseley, *Nations and Nationalism in the Theology of Karl Barth* (New York: Oxford University Press, 2013). Moseley addresses this dynamic of Barth's rejection of nationalism while affirming nationhood. While we do not follow the logic of her argument, we are indebted to her for exploring Barth's wider engagement with these concepts throughout his career.

Moreover, the ways Israel and the nations relate to the doctrine of creation and providence are explored. The concluding point is that peoplehood boundaries matter for theology, but with significant qualifiers.

Second, continuing Barth's flow of thought, peoplehood as a concrete context, yet in a nonessentialistic manner, is articulated. Barth's affirmation of Jesus's Jewish flesh and the fluidity of peoplehood as a context are extended by putting them in conversation with the works of J. Kameron Carter, Willie Jennings, and Kathryn Tanner.

On the one hand, the Jewish flesh of Jesus is significant for the discussion of the context's concreteness. In his provocative work, *Race*, Carter recovers the covenantal flesh of Jesus to dismantle the racist structures of modernity.[5] Also, Jennings, in his *Christian Imagination*, argues that this covenantal flesh lays aside essentialist differences to achieve true intimacy as the body of Christ.[6] As we will argue below, however, this definition of Jewish flesh as covenantal appears too narrow as it does not take seriously the fullness of this flesh, thus exposing it to a docetic reduction and losing the concreteness of carnal election, as Michael Wyschogrod argues. Jewish flesh is not just a theological or spiritual reality; it is an embodied reality that can be expressed as peoplehood with its particularities. This carnal election means that cultural or ethnic identity is theologically significant—a point that Carter and Jennings undervalue.

On the other hand, this cultural or ethnic concreteness is not an essentialist aspect of the context, which means it is not an unchanging, homogenous stereotype. Contextual particularities matter in the concrete situations of discipleship; however, they are ultimately reversible, fluid, and removable. In this sense, Barth's insights resonate closely with Kathryn Tanner's postmodern notion of culture as a dynamic and porous phenomenon.[7]

Finally, this notion of nonessentialist concreteness of the context is

5. J. Kameron Carter, *Race: A Theological Account* (New York: Oxford University Press, 2008).
6. Willie J. Jennings, *The Christian Imagination: Theology and the Origins of Race* (New Haven, CT: Yale University Press, 2010).

used to critically evaluate the theological adequacy of Asian American theologies and also to dynamically define the Asian American context. While there are various approaches to Asian American theologies, we suggest that at least three main methodologies are significant: the cultural, marginality, and postcolonial approaches. Our goal is to expose their weaknesses and affirm their strengths regarding their methods. Offering a constructive proposal, the Asian American Quadrilateral (AAQ) represents a new way of defining the context as the intersection and the interaction of four layers: Asian heritage, migration experience, American culture, and racialization. This dynamic and multilayered approach seeks to take the concrete particularities seriously without essentializing them.

Now that we have laid out a map for the rest of this chapter, we begin by looking at Israel and the nations within Barth.

Jesus the Jew, Israel, and the Nations in Barth's Theology

Barth's exposition of the concept of *Volk* (peoplehood or nationhood) is important for contextual theology because he explicitly affirms the importance of taking one's immediate and concrete situation seriously in both theological work and discipleship. This simple but significant point is lost to many who only hold shallow stereotypes of Barth. Of course, Barth often made this methodological move implicit, simply assuming it. In our discussion of actualism in the next chapter, we will more deeply explore Barth's stress on the present particular situation. We should also note that Barth's contemporary political situation, in which *Volk* and *Rasse* (Race) were essentialized to the point of idolatry, made him wary of the overemphasis, or misplaced emphasis, on essentialism in theology.

To get a good grasp of the development of Barth's thought, including his rejection of nationalism and affirmation of nationhood, we will cover three key themes in this section: Jesus as a Jew, the election of Israel, and the nations in light of Israel. The goal here is not a

7. Kathryn Tanner, *Theories of Culture: A New Agenda for Theology* (Minneapolis, MN: Fortress Press, 1997).

systematic study of Barth's Israelology, which goes beyond the scope of this study, but rather, the construction of an argument that reveals the connection between these three themes, leading to an understanding of nationhood or peoplehood.[8] Affirming the Jewishness of Jesus first debunks any form of nationalism. Jesus's Jewishness is, of course, vitally connected to the election of Israel, which serves as a larger context for the christological election. The chosen nation then serves as a center from which to understand the basis and destiny of all other peoples.

Jesus the Jew and the Election of Israel

In December 1933, as Hitler's first year as chancellor came to a close, Barth preached a sermon on Jesus as a Jew at Schlosskirche in Bonn.[9] Based on Romans 15:5–13, Barth argued that

> Christ belongs to the people (*Volk*) of Israel. *This* people's (*Volk*) blood was in his veins, the very blood of God's Son. *This* people's (*Volk*) way of life he took on by taking on humanity, not for the sake of this people (*Volk*) or from a preference for this people's (*Volk*) blood or race, but rather for the sake of truth, that is, for the sake of demonstrating the truthfulness and faithfulness of God.[10]

Barth explicitly subverted Nazi ideology of German Christians, in which Jesus was seen as an Aryan, even as a leader of an anti-Semitic crusade.[11] Barth's bold claims led many in the congregation to walk out in protest.[12] However, in the larger context of this sermon, Barth stresses the Jewishness of Jesus to communicate the *extra nos* (outside

8. For the place of Israelology in the broader discipline of systematic theology, see Arnold G. Fruchtenbaum, *Israelology: The Missing Link in Systematic Theology* (Tustin, CA: Ariel Ministries, 1994).
9. Karl Barth, "A Sermon about Jesus as a Jew," in *Preaching in Hitler's Shadow: Sermons of Resistance in the Third Reich*, ed. Dean G. Stroud (Grand Rapids, MI: Eerdmans, 2013), 64.
10. Ibid., 68.
11. The view of Jesus within Germany at the time was complex. There were some who rejected the Jewish Jesus as having impure blood. However, the German Christianity viewed him as an Aryan or a Teutonic Jesus, who was a warrior opposing the Jews. Thus, this anti-Semitic Jesus led the way for Hitler to assume the role of a spiritual leader in the same tradition. See Mark R. Lindsay, *Covenanted Solidarity: The Theological Basis of Karl Barth's Opposition to Nazi Antisemitism and the Holocaust* (New York: Peter Lang, 2001), 199–200.
12. Karl Barth, "A Sermon about Jesus as a Jew," n18.

of us) character of the gospel, its unmerited nature and the fact that salvation does not come from us, but from outside, even from the Jews. Moreover, as a result, the church is unlike a nation and is created out of a disparate heterogeneous mix of people.[13]

With such rhetoric and theological assertions, Barth made a stand against the nationalistic idolatry and its co-option of the creation order doctrine. However, Barth's Christology did not always affirm the Jewish flesh of Jesus. In chapter 2, drawing from the watershed work of Bruce McCormack, we will discuss the progressive development of Barth's theology from the harsh diastasis of the *Römerbrief* to the *Humanity of God,* recovered through his doctrine of election.[14] Here, however, we simply highlight the important moments in Barth's changing thoughts on the historical particularities of revelation in Jesus Christ.

At the beginning of his theological career (1916–20), when he broke radically with the liberal tradition that subsumed revelation into history, Barth firmly believed that God as "Wholly Other" must be protected in order for God to be God and not just a projection of humanity.[15] While God's revelation in Christ occurred *in* history, it could not be *of* history. This revelation was a pure event, only limited narrowly to the crucifixion and resurrection but not including the person of Jesus Christ in his entirety.[16] Correspondingly, there was little room for the humanity of Jesus to be significant, nor for the historical particularity of Jesus as Jewish.[17]

Continuing his dialectical conviction and retaining the all-important diastasis between God and humanity, Barth made a significant breakthrough by recovering anhypostatic-enhypostatic Christology during his Göttingen years (1921–24). On the one hand, the anhypostatic side stated that the human nature of Christ had "no independent existence before its union with the divine Logos . . . [and]

13. Moseley, *Nations and Nationalism*, 114.
14. Bruce L. McCormack, *Karl Barth's Critically Realistic Dialectical Theology: Its Genesis and Development 1909-1936* (Oxford: Clarendon, 1995).
15. Lindsay, *Covenanted Solidarity*, 202.
16. Ibid., 204.
17. Ibid., 201.

safeguarded revelation from historicization."[18] History would neither become a straitjacket of revelation nor would it replace it. On the other hand, the enhypostatic side affirmed that "the Godhead included all the (perfected) human attributes," allowing Barth to be "insistent that the fully divine Christ is also fully human and, thus a specific historical reality."[19] In this sense, in *CD* I/1, Barth followed the Chalcedonian insight and rejected both ebionitism and docetism—the first, a heresy that historicizes revelation, and the second, one that denies historic specificity.[20]

So far, Barth has arrived at the notion that Jesus's historic specificity matters; however, that specificity could be theoretically generically human. In a sense, Jesus's Jewishness could be merely accidental. In the 1930s, opposing Nazism and German Christianity through various political writings, Barth came to stress that salvation comes from the Jews and that Jesus was Jewish, as we saw in his sermon of 1933. Furthermore, Barth established the necessity of Jewish flesh dogmatically in his doctrine of election.

The innovation in Barth's doctrine of election lies in his understanding of Jesus Christ the God-man "as both the subjective and objective ground of our election . . . at once the electing God and the elected man."[21] Moreover, Barth avers that this election is supralapsarian and universal. Focusing on the object of election, the chosen are not some abstract human beings, but rather, the particular man, Jesus of Nazareth and the people who are in him.[22] That historic particularity, and that particularity as Jewish flesh, was established before creation.

In his postwar years, Barth would stress Jesus's ethnic identity explicitly, saying that his Jewish flesh is something "we must emphasise especially [because it] is often overlooked. . . . It is not taken

18. Ibid., 203. See Karl Barth, *The Göttingen Dogmatics: Instruction in the Christian Religion* (Grand Rapids, MI: Eerdmans, 1991), 152.
19. Lindsay, *Covenanted Solidarity*, 203.
20. Karl Barth, *The Doctrine of the Word of God*, vol. I/1, *The Church Dogmatics* (Edinburgh: T&T Clark, 1956), 399–403. Hereafter, references to the *Church Dogmatics* will take the form: Barth, *CD* I/1, 399–403.
21. Lindsay, *Covenanted Solidarity*, 214.
22. Ibid. See *CD* II/2, 8.

seriously or seriously enough."[23] Only in his Jewish flesh is Jesus the savior of the world because his Jewishness is necessary to confirm God's election of and faithfulness to Israel.[24]

Through the election of Jesus Christ, we have arrived at the election of God's people. For Barth, the election of God's people takes two forms—Israel and the church. Because Jesus Christ is *the* reprobate and *the* elect in Barth's christological rendering of the doctrine of election, Barth extends this logic to explain the place of Israel and the church without falling into supersessionism or anti-Semitism:

> Israel is the people of the Jews which resists its election; the Church is the gathering of Jews and Gentiles called on the ground of its election. This is the formulation which we have adopted and this or a similar formulation is necessary if the unity of the election of the community (grounded in the election of the one Jesus Christ) is to remain visible. We cannot, therefore, call the Jews the "rejected" and the Church the "elected" community. The object of election is neither Israel for itself nor the Church for itself, but both together in their unity.[25]

These two forms of election—Israel and the church—united in the one covenant of grace, both witness to the person of Jesus Christ. For that reason, Barth rejects mission to the Jews because they are already witnesses as "to divine judgment, to the promise as heard, and to the humanity that is passing away."[26] The church, on the contrary, witnesses "to God's mercy, to the promise as believed, and to the humanity that is to come."[27] In its witness, Israel has a legitimate

23. Ibid, 212. Quoted from *CD* IV/1, 166–17.

24. Ibid. See *CD* IV/1, 168, 170, and Karl Barth, *Evangelical Theology: An Introduction* (London: Collins, 1965), 27–28. We note that Barth's own rhetoric regarding Israel, i.e., "Synagogue of death" (CD II/2, 264), paints a much more ambivalent picture. To make matters worse, Barth acknowledged that he struggled with "a totally irrational aversion" in his personal encounter with Jews. See Karl Barth, *Letters, 1961-1968* (Grand Rapids, MI: Eerdmans, 1981), 262. Also, Sonderegger underscores Barth's anti-Judaism, not anti-Semitism; see Katherine Sonderegger, *That Jesus Christ Was Born a Jew: Karl Barth's Doctrine of Israel* (University Park, PA: Pennsylvania State University Press, 1992). For a more negative assessment of Barth's views of the Jews, see Stephen R. Haynes, *Reluctant Witnesses: Jews and the Christian Imagination* (Louisville, KY: Westminster John Knox, 1995), 64–89.

25. Barth, *CD* II/2, 199.

26. Eberhard Busch, "Indissoluble Unity: Barth's Position on the Jews during the Hitler Era," in *For the Sake of the World: Karl Barth and the Future of Ecclesial Theology*, ed. George Hunsinger (Grand Rapids, MI: Eerdmans, 2004), 68, 70. This idea of Israel as "the humanity that is passing away" and representing divine judgment is clearly problematic. It is debatable if the dualistic notion of Israel and church can overcome its tendency toward anti-Semitism even as Barth seeks to avoid it.

27. Ibid., 71. See *CD* II/2, 195–305.

place alongside the church, opposing any form of supersessionism that replaces it with the church. In fact, in God's faithfulness, Israel, even after its rejection of Christ, remains the first and original people of God:

> Without any doubt the Jews are to this very day the chosen people of God in the same sense as they have been so from the beginning, according to the Old and New Testaments. They have the promise of God; and if we Christians from among the gentiles have it too, it is only as those chosen with them; as guests in their house, as new wood grafted onto their old tree.[28]

As these two forms of election bear witness to different aspects of Jesus Christ, they also differ in the sense that Israel is a "people" (*Volk*), in which membership is through birth, whereas the church is an "assembly" or a "gathering" (*ecclesia*), in which the members are those called by God.[29] Closely relates to the idea of Israel as *Volk*, Barth observes rightly that the church is composed of both Jews and Gentiles.

However, more surprisingly, Barth also states that Jews in the church, like Paul, might not "abandon Judaism because of their faith in Christ, but [remain] Jews, loyal and obedient members of Israel, the eternally elect people."[30] This idea of Jews within the church, who remain faithful Jews, will prove to be a significant point later. Barth does not develop this idea of faithful Jews within the church any further; however, he states their role as the church's "secret origin, as the hidden substance which makes the Church the community of God."[31] From this perspective, the creation of the one new humanity in Christ would not mean the dissolution of Jewish peoplehood (Eph 2:15). However, just what does this "peoplehood" mean?

In his doctrine of providence, Barth lists the history of the Jews as a sign and witness of divine providence, even as he puzzles over defining the Jewish *Volk*.[32] In terms of race, speech, culture, religion, and even

28. Karl Barth, "Jewish Problem and the Christian Answer," in *Against the Stream: Shorter Post-war Writings, 1946-52* (London: SCM, 1954), 200, as quoted in Michael Wyschogrod, *Abraham's Promise: Judaism and Jewish-Christian Relations* (Grand Rapids, MI: Eerdmans, 2004), 220.
29. Busch, "Indissoluble Unity," 67n49.
30. Ibid., 67. See *CD* II/2, 235, for this idea of Israel in the church. Also see Mark S. Kinzer, *Postmissionary Messianic Judaism: Redefining Christian Engagement with the Jewish People* (Grand Rapids, MI: Brazos, 2005), 176.
31. Barth, *CD* II/2, 201.

history, Barth sees no unifying commonality that can define the Jews as a single people. For example, there is no such a thing as pure Jewish blood or even particular physical features. Hebrew continues to serve as a cultic language, but the people of the Jewish diaspora speak many languages as their mother tongues.[33] In terms of culture, again, their diasporic reality has led to various levels of assimilation and exchange with various national cultures throughout Europe. In terms of religion, a person is still a Jew, whatever his or her religion might be. Finally, the history of Jewish people is fragmented, again because of their diasporic dispersion. Ultimately, rather than any external features, it is only the singular electing love of God that holds them together and sustains them.[34] Jewish identity is a riddle biologically, but is a witness to God's providence theologically.

Despite all these ambiguities, the Jews still exist as a people and will continue to exist as a witness to God's faithful election. Moreover, their eternal election provides a way to understand their place in relation to all the other peoples on the earth.

Israel, the Nations, and the Context of Discipleship

Beginning from establishing the Jewishness of Jesus as a necessary aspect of his historic specificity, we then situate the election of Israel within the broader soteriological context. We are now finally ready to see the place of Israel in respect to the nations and to define one's cultural/ethnic context theologically, looking at Barth's exposition of "Near and Distant Neighbours" in *Church Dogmatics* III/4.[35]

In regard to the election of Israel and the role of the nations, Barth's line of thought moves from revelation, creation, and reconciliation. In this whole discussion, Barth seeks to reject the natural theology of the *Deutschen Christen* (German Christian), while finding the proper place of *Volk* within theology.

32. Barth, *CD* III/3, 210–26.
33. This is not true of the state of Israel where Hebrew also functions as the mother tongue of its citizens.
34. Ibid., 221.
35. Barth, *CD* III/4, 285–323.

First, to think properly about the nations theologically, Barth begins with the reminder that revelation is primarily and centrally about the covenant and with special history. The nations and world history can only be secondary and peripheral:

> Neither the history of humanity nor that of the nations is the true theme of the biblical message. The most to be said is that it is always a subsidiary theme. . . . The main theme is the history of the covenant between God and man which secretly begins in and with creation, is revealed in the election and calling of Abraham, is fulfilled in the coming of Jesus Christ and is shown in His promised return to be the meaning and purpose of all creaturely occurrence.[36]

Submitting to revelation with special history at the center means taking the doctrine of election as the basis for theological reflections on general history. Thus, the election of Jesus Christ and the one community of Israel and the church determine how we are to understand the nations.

Second, based on revelation, Barth rejects *Volk* or *Rasse* distinction as an order of creation. The idolatry of the German Christians claimed "people[hood] and nationality as the creation of God" and that the "distinctive nature of each nation is a special creative thought of God."[37] However, Barth finds that in the creation accounts in Genesis, there is no creation of the nations, let alone their histories. From Genesis 1–9, there is no account of the relationship of near and far neighbors, or of the place of these nations in respect to God:

> It seems obvious that nations were actually there. But it is hard to find any concrete indications. The narrators obviously wish to conceal the fact, to push it into the background. . . . As His will as Creator it is obviously not bound in [any ethically significant] way in these chapters.[38]

In a way, the place of the nations is a matter of providence, not of creation proper. Furthermore, these nations cannot be understood independently of the covenant, Christ, or revelation.

36. Ibid., 309.
37. Ibid., 307.
38. Ibid., 311.

Third, when the nations are included in Genesis 10 and 11:1–9, they serve as a transition to the beginning of the covenant of grace and the calling of Abraham in Genesis 12. Like the two accounts of creation, Genesis 10 and 11:1–9 provide two distinct accounts of the separation of the people.[39] On the one hand, the Table of the Nations in Genesis 10 provides this separation or differentiation in a neutral, matter-of-fact way, without judgment. This differentiation is under divine providence and must be accepted in obedience. However, Barth avers that based on this account, there cannot be any "abstract internationalism and cosmopolitanism," nor "abstract nationalism and particularism" because there is no justification for that kind of assertion.[40] On the contrary, the tower of Babel narrative in Gen 11:1–9 recounts this separation, not as a simple differentiation, but rather, as a scattering, as a work of divine wrath. Barth interprets the tower as an expression of religious hubris and the scattering as not only judgment, but also an act of grace in order to thwart greater human rebellion.

As stated at the beginning of this discussion, these two accounts of peripheral world history in Genesis 10 and 11:1–9 must be understood in light of the central special history in Genesis 12, the election of a particular people who will bring all these nations back together again. The calling and election of Israel, fulfilled in the person of Jesus Christ the Jew, establish the place of the nations and give them a *teleological* movement toward becoming the one people of God.[41]

Looking to the New Testament, in the miracle of Pentecost in Acts 2, the Spirit works in and through Israel as a bridge people to overcome the separation between the nations. Barth stresses that the multinational crowd at Pentecost was "the universal Israel," meaning faithful Jews and proselytes from all over the world. Also, the disciples represent the Israel in its impure Galileans, who are "halfway already

39. See Hunsberger's analysis of various interpretations of these two passages in regard to cultural diversity. He labels Barth's view as a dialectical assessment that still has a negative view of this diversity, and prefers the progressive assessment of Newbigin. See George R. Hunsberger, *Bearing the Witness of the Spirit: Lesslie Newbigin's Theology of Cultural Plurality* (Grand Rapids, MI: Eerdmans, 1998), 244–55.
40. Barth, *CD* III/4, 312.
41. Ibid., 320.

to the Gentile world outside . . . the Israel of the frontiers."[42] So, as a bridge people, Israel holds a sacramental role in bringing the nations together again:

> It is in this one people that the expansion and universalisation takes place. The new language is spoken by Israel, even if only border Israel. And it is heard and understood by Israel, even if only the Israel of the dispersion.[43]

Barth stresses that this is a divine work, not the work of Israel, but it is a divine work *in* and *through* Israel, the one people of God called out of the many nations.[44]

Barth's teleological perspective of human differentiation assesses the separation as something that is overcome eschatologically in Jesus Christ. However, the call of one people of God does not mean the dissolution of all particularities. As noted above, Barth allows for the distinction between the Jew and Gentile even in the church, which is God's eschatological community. Jesus Christ himself remains a Jew forever and never loses his cultural/ethnic particularity because of its soteriological significance. The Jews are forever God's chosen people because God keeps God's promises. Given that truth, are the Gentiles simply generically gentile, lacking any particularity?

In protecting against distortions of a creation order basis for ethnic/cultural particularities, Barth appears to overreact and sound more philosophical than biblical as though there are no nations in the eschaton, contra the biblical witness (Rev 7:9, 21–22). Of course, as Barth has noted, cultural/ethnic distinctions are so fluid that they cannot be essentialized or divinized. However, they are a part of who we are as human beings, if we are not to end up with a gnostic anthropology. Even in the eschaton, with all the dividing walls broken

42. Ibid., 322.
43. Ibid., 323.
44. Hunsberger notes that, for Barth, the original unity that exists before Genesis 10 and 11 is "ultimate," because Barth believed that the "present diversity as only provisional and as an interruption of the ideal," and thus, "cultural plurality can only then be seen in an ultimately negative light" (Hunsberger, *Bearing the Witness of the Spirit*, 248). However, as discussed in the previous section, Barth's idea of "faithful Jews within the church," who do not simply lose their particularity offers another possible perspective within his theology, even if he did not develop it further. See *CD* II/2, 235.

down by Christ and united into his one Body, these particularities cannot disappear if we are truly human and not simply spirit. Given his political context, it might be understandable, but Barth did not develop these pressing issues as Lesslie Newbigin did, for example.[45]

In any case, whatever his eschatological perspective on cultural/ethnic particularities was, Barth firmly asserted that particularities are a part of the concrete context in which we encounter God's Word. We locate Barth's view about nationhood/peoplehood as a context for discipleship under the command of God within the doctrine of creation.

For Barth, the command of God assumes the dialectical union of dogmatics and ethics. There exists an "inseparability of indicative and imperative," meaning that in encountering God, we are summoned under divine lordship.[46] This command means "permission, 'the granting of a very definite freedom'" in which we are free to be who we really are.[47] Because our true identity is found in Christ, God's command "in effect, says not only: This is what you must do! But also: This is who you are!"[48]

Peoplehood is the particular context in which God's command is received. God's command, his call to freedom, comes in the context of fellowship with others, in the encounters between men and women, between parents and children, and between neighbors near and far. In his discussion of "Near and Distant Neighbors," Barth positively as well as critically addresses the issue of belonging "to a larger group which forms a more or less recognizable totality."[49] Barth affirms the rightful need for contextualization, while claiming that the gospel is beyond every context.

More specifically, Barth positively affirms our cultural context, and yet, gives it critical limits. At a "lower level" from the standpoint of our

45. As Newbigin was a missiologist, especially in a country as diverse as India and later on in multicultural England, addressing cultural diversity was a core aspect of his calling. See Newbigin's discussion of this theme in Lesslie Newbigin, *The Gospel in a Pluralist Society* (Grand Rapids, MI: Eerdmans, 1989).
46. John Webster, *Karl Barth*, 2nd ed. (New York: Continuum, 2004), 154.
47. Ibid., 155. Quoting from Barth in *CD* II/2, 585.
48. Ibid., 156.
49. Barth, *CD* III/4, 287.

experience, the "wider blood-relationship and biological particularity, . . . speech and customs, and perhaps a common geographical location" in their totality provide a sense of belonging, a home for us.[50] It is in this place or space that we hear God's Word, the divine command. These particular places "acquire for [a person] the character of an allotted framework in which he has to express his own distinctive obedience."[51]

In our own language, geographical location, and history, we do hear and obey God's command. Barth notes that these three examples of cultural context are not meant to be exhaustive. They are merely examples to show that in every way, our context is to be taken up in our response to God's command. Regarding our cultural contexts, "it is not accidentally or in vain but meaningfully and purposively that God has called himself and the men of his people to serve Him in this determination and with this outlook, background and origin."[52] Within the context of the divine command, our cultural context is "not mere disposition of nature or fate," but "really is important, and has therefore to be honoured and loved."[53]

However, at a "higher level" from the direction of God's command, even this context must submit to divine lordship and must be dealt with critically.[54] All these aspects of cultural context must be "absolutely subordinate" to the purposes of the divine command.[55] They must not be an end in themselves.[56] Barth state his chief concern thus:

> Again everything hinges upon the preservation of the right super- and sub-ordination in this decision. The command of God must be *master*, and all historical interpretations and notions, all other considerations, all economic, political, social, cultural and even religious evaluations of the situation must *be mastered and not try to play the master*.[57]

50. Ibid.
51. Ibid., 288.
52. Ibid., 292.
53. Ibid., 293.
54. Ibid., 287.
55. Ibid., 290.
56. Ibid.
57. Ibid., 296. Emphasis added.

In fact, those three examples, along with every other aspects of our cultural context are reversible, fluid, and removable.

The opposition between people from different cultural contexts is *reversible* and *reciprocal*. This relationship is not a naturally ordered one, not part of the created order. Also, our cultural distinctives are *fluid*. The boundaries of culture are not so sharply defined. While cultural boundaries might exist, there is also engagement, exchange, and connection across different cultural contexts. Moreover, the cultural boundaries are *removable*. Languages die. People intermarry. Nations break apart, and new ones form.

Because these cultural contexts are reversible, fluid, and removable, they cannot constitute a permanent division between fellow human beings. Moreover, they cannot become the criteria to which the command of God must conform: "There is obviously no special form of the command of God in respect of the existence and relationships of peoples."[58] We must understand that Barth is not rejecting the significance of our cultural context. Rather, he is setting proper limits upon them so that they do not become idols.

In this section, we covered much ground to see the vital connection between Jesus the Jew, God's election, Israel, the nations, and the concrete context for discipleship in the theology of Karl Barth. The question of cultural/ethnic particularity is not a marginal matter, but rather, lies at the heart of Christianity with the identity of Jesus Christ. In the next section, we see how Barth's concerns and ideas resonate closely with the contemporary developments in reflections about identity and culture.

Non-Essentialist Concreteness of the Context

The insights of Barth presented above serve as the raw material for this section, which steps back toward more general concepts for contextual theology. In conversation with contemporary theologians, we argue that the context is *concrete*, yet *nonessentialist*.

58. Ibid., 303.

In developing the *concreteness* of the context, we examine the "new black theology" (Willie James Jennings, J. Kameron Carter, and Brian Bantum) to engage the Jewish flesh of Jesus as it relates to the problem of race. However, instead of race, our concern is cultural particularity. Critiquing their racial framework and looking to the insights of Michael Wyschogrod, we argue that in order to avoid docetic anthropology or discipleship, cultural particularities must be engaged.

We draw the concept of context as *nonessentialist* from Kathryn Tanner's postmodern notion of culture that poses context as dynamic, conflicted, and porous. The concrete context previously affirmed is a contested space as well as a nonstatic one. Therefore, ethnocentricity or identity politics of boundary-keeping or purity-seeking is not allowed theologically. Rather, in this hybrid space as postcolonial theology as stated, we are constantly negotiating and discerning the context.

Concreteness of the Context

Barth developed a doctrine of election of a Jewish Jesus and of Israel, and further connected this doctrine vitally to the place and role of the nations. These same themes are at play in the so-called new black theology of Jennings, Carter, and Bantum, which is framed within questions about race and colonialism.[59] For our purposes, we will limit our discussion to Jennings and Carter alone because they represent the core arguments of this "new" theology. Our concern is the connection that is made between the Jewish flesh of Jesus and the nations or cultural diversity.

In *Race*, J. Kameron Carter theorizes "that the modernity's racial imagination has its genesis in the theological problem of Christianity's quest to sever itself from its Jewish roots."[60] This supersessionism led to the concept of whiteness, which allowed Europeans to transcend the

59. Jonathan Tran, "The New Black Theology: Retrieving Ancient Sources to Challenge Racism," *The Christian Century*, January 26, 2012, http://www.christiancentury.org/article/2012-01/new-black-theology. See Carter, *Race*, Jennings, *Christian Imagination*; and Brian Bantum, *Redeeming Mulatto: A Theology of Race and Christian Hybridity* (Waco, TX: Baylor University Press, 2010).
60. Carter, *Race*, 4.

particularities of their identity toward an enlightened universality of this general whiteness, unlike other races that were still stuck in their ethnic distinctiveness.[61]

In this paradigm of whiteness, Jesus is not Jewish but simply a transcendent or abstract human figure. Moreover, as Christ's wisdom moves beyond the crude laws of the Old Testament, it ironically represents "a purer form of . . . the wisdom of the Greek philosophers."[62] This denial of Jewish particularity, Carter elaborates, is gnostic, neo-Marcion, and docetic; furthermore, it denies the body and establishes a racism that is deeply rooted in the modern situation.[63]

To counter this rejection of the concrete particularity in favor of abstract universality, Christ's flesh as Jewish, covenantal flesh must be recovered. This covenantal flesh constitutes—instead of some ethnocentric affirmation of identity—"a social-political reality displayed across time and space into which the Gentiles are received in praise of the God of Israel."[64] For Carter and Jennings, the concept of identity is problematic because of its ethnocentric nature. They are seeking to establish a particularity, or a "social-political reality displayed across time and space" that does not succumb to ideological co-option and become a theological abstraction. Avoiding identity and its temptation toward purity, Carter argues that Christ's flesh is "mulatto" in that it is multiracial and "*intra*racial," continually intersecting and being "contaminated" by God's disruptive presence and the inclusion of Gentiles.[65]

Carter states that this "mulatto" reality is Pentecostal in that different bodies are "no longer within an order of tyrannical division [as in the Tower of Babel] but, rather, in an order of 'peaceful difference,' the one-many structure of creation."[66] Thus, particular bodies are made one without being confused, "without a loss of what is distinctive regarding the many as to 'language, places, and customs'"[67]

61. Ibid., 89.
62. Ibid., 117.
63. Ibid., 107.
64. Ibid., 30.
65. Ibid.
66. Ibid., 351.

Just as the true meaning of Israel's election is "to be a nonnationalistic nation, a different kind of people" with a nonsolipsistic destiny, all the peoples in Christ are to have their identities "dispossessively" with an openness and vulnerability to others.[68]

Whereas Carter situates his argument about racism within the intellectual framework of modernity, Jennings looks to colonialism as the culprit. However, there is much in common between Jennings and Carter, such as their focus on the Jewish flesh of Jesus, the connection between supersessionism and contemporary racism, and the problem of abstract universalism.

Jennings bemoans the colonialist mindset that made "theology as the catalyst for cultural recapitulation. Theology invited peoples to look culturally inward in search of a theological reiteration of the collective self."[69] For example, looking at the gospel translation theories of Lamin Sanneh and Andrew Walls, Jennings observes that both mission historians miss the supersessionism embedded in their ideas about the universal gospel transcending the Jewish particularity. Thus, they both fail to seriously account for the colonialist sensibility even as they affirm indigenous culture. In a sense, the problem of Christianity in context can be posed in christological terms, that is, as docetism and adoptionism:

> Unfortunately, the universal (bound up in docetism) and the contextual (bound up in adoptionism) are currently the dominant options for the contemporary theological imagination. They are two sides of the same coin, the one enabling the other, and neither finding its way to a Christian theology that of necessity creates intimacy [between peoples].[70]

Determining a theological basis for establishing this elusive intimacy amid the division is the agenda of Jennings.

Jennings believes that the key to a necessary intimacy between diverse peoples is found in the election of Israel, more particularly in "Jesus' own trajectory toward the many in Israel and through Israel to

67. Ibid., 364.
68. Ibid., 309.
69. Jennings, *Christian Imagination*, 154.
70. Ibid., 167.

the many in the world."[71] In his work of reconciliation, Jesus, through his death and resurrection, creates a new people out of both Jews and Gentiles through which their hostilities are broken down by his peace. The peace of Christ moves beyond "the binary of adherence or betrayal of culture, nation, or people" and creates a "people defined by their cultural differences yet who turn their histories and cultural logics toward a new determination, a new social performance of identity."[72]

Carter and Jennings display such creative reframing and innovative resourcing of tradition. Through affirming the Jewish flesh of Christ and christological dangers of docetism and adoptionism, they powerfully address the problem of abstract universality and divisive identity politics. Our flesh in its particularity—in other words, the concreteness of our context—matters though it cannot be seen as closed or pure.

However, in the midst of this talk about interracialism, not just multiracialism, and about overcoming divisions caused by cultural nationalism, is cultural difference itself seen as something negative? In the case of racism, theological whiteness, colonial sensibility, and cultural difference per se are all perceived as oppressive, or at most, neutral, never positive.[73] The difference is what separates us from each other, making intimacy between us so difficult and even threatening.

This exact point is what concerns Néstor Medina about the proposal of Carter and Jennings:

> Despite their best intentions, their insistence on the "disarticulation" of ethnic and cultural identity inevitably leads toward a "universal" rearticulation as children of the covenantal relationship ironically under the particular Jewish Jesus (Carter and Jennings). Their proposal, then, quickly and dangerously turns into a kind of universalizing theological shift within which people's actual ethnocultural identities are neutralized if not disposed, and are seen to bear no impact on their experiences and expressions of faith.[74]

71. Ibid., 265.
72. Ibid., 273.
73. According to Hunsberger's categories, Carter and Jennings appear to fit into a negative view of cultural diversity. See Hunsberger, *Bearing the Witness of the Spirit*, 244–55.
74. Néstor Medina, "Transgressing Theological Shibboleths: Culture as Locus of Divine

As noted above, the understanding of cultural differences in the works of Carter and Jennings is nuanced. However, ultimately these differences seem merely to be obstacles to overcome or challenges to endure, without offering any significant or positive contribution to faith. Possibly, Carter and Jennings denigrate cultural differences as a result of their racial framing. Medina points to the "narrow black-white framing" as the straitjacket that hampers a fuller and varied articulation of cultural diversity. Moreover, cultural heritage simply is not a topic that is pressing for the African American context, unlike the Hispanic or Asian American contexts.

How does all this fare with Barth's view, as presented above? Although Barth does not fully develop these connections and implications, we can see how his insights about the Jewishness of Christ and the election of Israel and his rejection of supersessionism resonate closely with Carter and Jennings. Without the Jewish flesh of Christ, Christianity loses its scandal of particularity and its *extra nos* nature, the fact that the gospel does not come from us, nor from our people, but from the Jews. Affirming the election of Israel and God's continual faithfulness to this people displaces any other nation's effort to take up this chosenness in some form of manifest destiny. On the one hand, the nations, which have their meaning in and through Israel, come together at Pentecost and resolve their differentiation. This point resonates closely with the views of Carter and Jennings. On the other hand, Barth stressed that the nations do serve as the context of discipleship and therefore must be engaged with, even though never idolized. This point is somewhat marginalized in the works of these two theologians.

Like Carter and Jennings, Barth struggled to affirm a positive stance in his dialectical view of cultural plurality. However, there is an interesting kernel left in his view of the relationship between the church and Israel that we have noted above. Barth could talk about Jews in the church, who "remained Jews, loyal and obedient members

(Pneumatological) Activity," Paper presented at the annual meeting of the AAR/SBL, Baltimore 2013.

of Israel, the eternally elect people."[75] For Barth, Christ's creation of a new people out of Jews and Gentiles does not mean that their cultural particularities are marginalized. For Barth, Jesus's flesh is Jewish, not "mulatto" because Barth's concern is the historical Jesus and the *Totus Christus* (the whole Christ). Is the eclipse of the historical by the ecclesiological body of Christ theologically appropriate? Even if the church as the body of Christ is made of many peoples, in what sense can we say that Christ's flesh is interracial? Herein lies our concern.

Contra Carter and Jennings, Barth's view of the election of Israel is not just theological or covenantal, but rather historical, in the sense of cultural or ethnic as well. Whereas Jennings, for examples, pits the ethnic Israel opposed to the covenantal Israel, Barth retains both. Otherwise, even if Israel apart from church is allowed, Israel within the church would cease to exist since a new people have already been created in Christ.

Enriching our discussion, Michael Wyschogrod stresses this very point about the election of Israel being not just covenantal, but "corporeal" in its physical bodies in their cultural, ethnic particularity.[76] The covenantal and carnal are not pitted against each other, and "the bifurcation of spirit and matter" is rejected.[77] The meaning of this carnal election is that God embraces "a people in the fullness of its humanity, and in this way to confirm the human creature as it was created to live in the material cosmos."[78] The issue here is God's election creating "a people that is in God's service in the totality of its human being."[79]

This carnal election makes sense within Judaism, but if this election is carnal through family lineage, how would it relate—if at all—to the radical inclusion of Gentiles in Christ? Wyschogrod's response is to point to the problem of law observance in Christianity. Although many Christians have held a narrow antinomian view that rejects the law as

75. See Barth, *CD* II/2, 235.
76. Michael Wyschogrod, *The Body of Faith: God in the People Israel* (Lanham, MD: Jason Aronson, 1996), xxxiii–xxxiv.
77. Ibid., 177.
78. Wyschogrod, *Abraham's Promise*, 10.
79. Ibid.

bestowing death because it leads to guilt, many passages in the New Testament affirm a positive view of the law.[80] More specifically, in the early church (Acts 15), the problem of the full inclusion of Gentiles into a predominately Jewish-believing community is resolved by only posing the Noachide obligation (Genesis 9) for the Gentile believers. Thus, the witness of early church is the crucial point:

> It is quite clear, however, that both factions in Jerusalem agreed that Jews, even after Jesus, remained under the prescriptions of the Torah. If the Jesus event had changed Jewish Torah obligation, then it would hardly make any sense to argue whether non-Jews required circumcision and Torah obligation. The debate concerned gentiles; both sides agreed about the Torah obligation of Jesus-believing Jews.[81]

This law observance means that "Jews retaining their separateness, even in the Church."[82] The Christian doctrine of election cannot be "a demythologization of the Jewish doctrine of election" where carnal particularity gives way to universal abstraction.[83]

In making sense of the ethnic/cultural aspect of this carnal election, Wyschogrod observes that in the call of Abraham, he is initially led to leave his family and his people, signifying that natural relations are set aside. However, Abraham and his family are reinstated and taken up for divine purposes. Thus, God "does not, therefore, destroy the natural but confirms it by placing it in its service."[84] Relating this to the cultural national identity, Wyschogrod states that

> To believe that the individual can be lifted out of his nation and brought into relation with God is as illusory as to believe that man's soul can be saved and his body discarded. Just as man is body and soul, so man is an individual and member of a nation. . . . The national election of Israel is therefore again a sign of God's understanding of human predicament and the confirmation of and love for that humanity. By sanctifying the nationhood of Israel, God confirms the national order of all peoples and

80. It is helpful to note that the Reformed tradition, in general, seeks to assert a positive use of the law as primary, and Barth specifically claimed the law as another form of the gospel throughout his *Church Dogmatics*.
81. Wyschogrod, *Abraham's Promise*, 163.
82. Ibid., 183.
83. Ibid., 184.
84. Wyschogrod, *Body of Faith*, 67.

> expresses his love for the individual in his national setting and for the nations in their corporate personalities.[85]

This is the core element of Néstor Medina's critique of Carter and Jennings and their negative view of the ethnocultural dimension because

> to remove ethnic and cultural identity out of the theological equation is to engage in a kind of docetism that denies the impact and contribution of the human ethnocultural dimension to our understanding of the reality of the divine, and to our expressions and experiences of faith. Otherwise the historical Jesus is not historical at all. If Jesus was indeed fulfilling Israel's covenantal relationship with YHWH, he did so as an ethnically and culturally Jewish man from Nazareth.[86]

Ultimately, theological affirmation of a culture and ethnicity is rooted in the Jewish flesh of Jesus and in the election of Israel. Against all docetic and abstract universality, the doctrine of election establishes the concreteness of the context in theology and discipleship.

Contextual Particularities as Nonessentialist

While our assessment found Carter and Jennings to be too negative in their view of cultural difference and still too docetic in their Christology and anthropology, they rightly raise concerns about the idolatrous role of essentialism and pure identity, as noted above. In the name of cultural integrity, identity can become a basis for segregation and ethnocentricity, neither of which has a place within the church. Therefore, we must echo what has been argued by Carter and Jennings and aver that contextual particularities are nonessentialist and have no creational foundation. We further elaborate on this point through the work of Kathryn Tanner and from insights of postcolonial theologies.

While Barth's relativizing of cultural boundaries was considered anthropologically naive and missiologically negligent within the

85. Ibid., 68.
86. Medina, "Transgressing Theological Shibboleths."

modern understanding of culture, postmodern developments have affirmed the general contours of his views. Precisely at these limiting critiques of the cultural context, Barth resonates with the postmodern notion of culture as presented by Kathryn Tanner.[87]

The modern idea of culture, which has a complex relationship to Western colonialism, developed to mean "a group-differentiating, holistic, non-evaluative, and context-relative notion."[88] This notion of culture focused on internal organization, seeking a meaningful coherence of cultural elements. Also, it emphasized a synchronic perspective, tending to downplay human agency and the internal dynamics of change. The result was an understanding of culture as something static with sharp boundaries, boundaries that must be respected.

The postmodern developments, while not rejecting this modern definition, critique its inattention to historical process. Culture cannot be seen as "a given, as something already formed and finished."[89] Culture is continually and constantly being negotiated, even when it is being passed down through practices and traditions. There exists within every cultural context its own internal dynamics of change, conflict, and contradictions, regardless of external influences.

As a result of these more recent insights, cultural contexts can no longer be defined as "sharply bounded, self-contained units."[90] Ultimately, as "change, conflict, and contradiction are now admitted *within* culture, the anthropologist has no reason to insist on a culture's sharp boundaries" as was done previously.[91] Ironically, what postmodern cultural theorists are stating—that cultural contexts are reversible, fluid, and removable—Barth had already argued theologically in the early twentieth century.

Connecting back to the "Near and Distant Neighbors" (*CD* III/4) section in *Church Dogmatics*, Barth accepts our context, even with all

87. Tanner, *Theories of Culture*.
88. Ibid., 24.
89. Ibid., 40.
90. Ibid., 53.
91. Ibid.

these fluidities, as the place or space to hear God's command and make discipleship concrete. In a sense, Barth is taking the context provisionally, whatever form it is in at that particular moment. In that sense, if we are to take seriously Tanner's point about culture changing over time and also having internal conflict and contradictions, our description of a context's concreteness cannot result in constancy or homogeneity. Moreover, the theological apparatus to engage this context must also be complex enough to be adequate for the dynamic task. In chapter 3, we use Barth's doctrine of reconciliation to engage the context in a dialectical fashion that is nimble and nuanced enough to recognize its disparate edges and trajectories. With its dialectic complexity of justification, sanctification, and vocation, Barth's doctrine of reconciliation offers a multiplex cultural engagement pattern without falling into a single type.

Now, turning to postcolonial theology, we focus the theme of identity, specifically the concept of hybridity. However, unlike the postcolonial assessment of this hybridity as wholly a result of colonial oppression, we will also affirm Tanner's insight about the fluidity and complexity of any cultural identity, even apart from external forces.

Postcolonial theology is, in a sense, the latest development of liberation theology, and resides "within the force field of" it.[92] Its agenda is to do theology while "highlighting the historical effects of the European empires, with both their settlers and exploitation colonies" and to propose a way to move beyond their oppression.[93] Postcolonial theology derives its theoretical core from the works of French poststructuralists and targets "*the idolatry of identity* . . . at which the *difference* of identity separates and hardens into *an essentialist sameness*."[94]

Resisting this essentialist view of identity, postcolonial theology focuses on hybridity and the complexities of in-between belonging.

92. Catherine Keller, Michael Nausner, and Mayra Rivera, eds., *Postcolonial Theologies: Divinity and Empire* (St. Louis, MO: Chalice, 2004), 6.
93. Ibid., 7.
94. Ibid., 12. These themes were already mentioned in the works of Jennings and Carter, discussed above.

This hybridity is "produced by empire: by direct invasion, violation, and rape, or by the indirect subjection that stimulates survivalist strategies of mimicry and appropriation."[95]

This wholly oppressive explanation of hybridity, however, is questionable, if we consider Tanner's insights about the dynamics and contradictions of any culture. Without denying the influence of empire, hybridity is, to some degree, the characteristic of every living culture that interacts with others. Postcolonial theology will be discussed a bit further in the next section as a methodology for Asian American theology.

Incorporating this insight from postcolonial theology, we propose that the context in which we encounter God's Word is a hybrid space of multiple layers and conflicting parts. If we are ignorant of its structural powers and disparate aspects, we will become victims and slaves to their subterranean influences. As noted previously, Barth was constantly concerned about various Babylonian captivities that distort and domesticate the gospel. Thus, Barth posed that we begin at the beginning with God's Word, again and again. However, without a deep awareness of these contextual aspects, they will distort even our reading of Scripture.

In the next section, we will review various methodological strategies toward Asian American theology, and then, propose a new way to describe the Asian American context in its fluidity, complexity, contradiction, and hybridity.

Defining the Asian American Context

In this section, we move on two fronts—one critical and one constructive—in our effort to focus on the Asian American context. We critically review three methodologies for Asian American theologies that well represent the current landscape: the *cultural* approach, the *marginality* approach, and the *postcolonial* approach. They will be evaluated for their criterion, orientation, and contextual definition.

95. Ibid., 13.

Constructively, a new defining rubric will be proposed using the fourfold approach labeled the AAQ, which will seek to frame the context with concreteness, but avoid essentialism.

Review of Asian American Theological Methodologies

For the Asian American churches, most of which are evangelical or conservative in theological orientation, the pressing need for contextual theological reflection is apparent.[96] Most works on Asian American mainline theology so far have largely been ignored as being of little relevance to the Asian American church. And as Amos Yong laments, "Asian American evangelical theology has yet to get off the ground even at the beginning of the twenty-first century."[97]

In order to understand the current state of things before seeking a path ahead, this study presents a critical analysis of three significant theologians, each representing an important approach to Asian American theological methodology: C.S. Song for a *cultural* approach, Jung Young Lee for a *marginality* approach, and Wonhee Anne Joh for a *postcolonial* approach.[98]

C.S. Song's third-eye methodology represents a way of approaching Asian American theology from the perspective of Asian indigenous sources.[99] As a first-generation Asian theologian working in the context

96. The sheer number of immigrant churches and Asian American campus ministries point to a need for critical reflection upon their ministry praxis. Also, the presence of various pastoral and popular works on contextual ministry and discipleship is a sign of this need as well. See Jeanette Yep et al., *Following Jesus without Dishonoring Your Parents* (Downers Grove, IL: InterVarsity, 1998); Peter Cha, S. Steve Kang and Helen Lee, ed., *Growing Healthy Asian American Churches: Ministry Insights from Groundbreaking Congregations* (Downers Grove, IL: InterVarsity, 2006); M. Sydney Park, Soong-Chan Rah, and Al Tizon, eds., *Honoring the Generations: Learning with Asian North American Congregations* (Valley Forge, PA: Judson, 2012).

97. Amos Yong, *The Future of Evangelical Theology: Soundings from the Asian American Diaspora* (Downers Grove, IL: InterVarsity Academic, 2014), 120.

98. It should be noted that the delineation of these theologians and their methods into these discrete categories is limited. These approaches are not necessarily separate from each other, but rather, function as different components that sometimes work together even within the works of a single theologian. However, as a heuristic tool to understand the task of Asian American theology, distinguishing these three approaches is helpful for critical analysis.

99. Song has been one of the most prolific Asian/Asian American theologians, producing over ten books. Technically speaking, Song considers himself an Asian theologian, not an Asian American one. However, for our purposes, he serves as a type of theological engagement of an important aspect of the larger Asian American experience. For our concerns, we will primarily focus on his *Third-Eye Theology*, which lay out his methodological agenda. Choan-Seng Song, *Third-Eye Theology:*

of emerging liberation theologies around the world, Song's work must be read alongside theologians such as James Cone and Gustavo Gutiérrez. All of them had to fight for the acceptance of their contextual work as a legitimate form of theology within a Western theological hegemony. Also, even though some loosely consider him an Asian American theologian, Song referred to himself a diasporic Chinese, not an Asian American, and worked to develop an authentically Asian theology.[100]

At the foundation of Song's agenda is his call for a "third-eye theology." Using a Zen Buddhist idea of a third eye that connotes spiritual insight, Song argues for the contextual nature of every theology. Third dimensionality is contextuality, to "see Christ through Chinese eyes, Japanese eyes, Asian eyes" just as Western Christians have done from their own standpoints in the past.[101] Just as "no artist has been able to capture the *whole* Christ, the *true* Christ, Christ as he was and is," all theologies, speaking from their contexts, will together represent the fullness of what Christianity truly is.[102]

Song's methodological content focuses on Asian culture and is expressed in his "story theology" notion, which has two aspects. On the one hand, "story theology" is a catch-all phrase that seeks to use all kinds of personal and communal stories of Asia as sources of theology. On the other hand, "story theology" means that Song does his theology through storytelling. In contrast to "the conceptual and rationalistic approaches" of the West, Song seeks to approach theology intuitively.[103] Theology here is not a science, but wisdom with an emphasis on praxis. This narrative approach, which is fraught with ambiguities, makes the particularities of Song's theology difficult to tease out. However, this lack of precision is part of his Asian agenda.

The specific features of Song's proposal are as follows: First, a

Theology in Formation in Asian Setting, rev. ed. (Maryknoll, NY: Orbis, 1991). See Choan-Seng Song, "Five Stages toward Christian Theology in the Multicultural World," in *Journeys at the Margin: Toward an Autobiographical Theology in American-Asian Perspective*, ed. Peter C. Phan and Jung Young Lee (Collegeville, MN: The Liturgical, 1999), 1–21.

100. Peter C. Phan, Jung Young Lee, eds., *Journeys at the Margin*, xxi.
101. Song, *Third-Eye Theology*, 28.
102. Ibid.
103. Ibid., 62.

universalism through christological abstraction works as a theoretical foundation. Similar to Tillich's method, for Song, the meaning of the incarnation can be abstracted as an idea, particularly as the love of God.[104] By making Jesus Christ a "direct and complete embodiment of God's saving love," Song makes a way to identify similar Christ-like "redemptive quality" in Asian culture and history.[105] Second, corresponding to this christological abstraction, Song argues that theology must begin with humanity and end with God. This radical approach *from below* is stated in incarnational language. Because Jesus is the love between God and humanity, he can only be encountered in the neighbor.[106] Third, just as revelation and context are merged together, Western tradition and Scripture are also conflated. Song decries the Constantinian bondage of Western theology and its oppressive impact upon non-Western churches.[107] So although it might appear that he is able to make a distinction between Christianity and the West, Song pits "Christian" against "Asian," accepting this cultural captivity as a given.

Song's theology appears to have had prescient insights into the problems of the Western tradition. Many of Song's arguments and assertions about the contextuality of theology, made decades ago, have now become generally accepted. Song's accusation that Western theology is entangled in a conceptual and rationalistic framework has also been a recent topic of Western theologians.

Of course, there are some serious concerns with Song's work as well. While "story theology" as a way to engage culture can be valuable, storytelling as a form of theological discourse lacks theoretical rigor, leaving too many ambiguities in Song's proposals. Using Asian folktales to interact with Confucianism is creative; however, does that kind of interaction necessarily exclude a conceptual discourse about the interaction of theology and Confucianism? Song's reactive stance

104. Later in his trilogy, Song also uses the reign of God to mean the incarnation. Either way, the incarnation is a symbol for an abstract concept.
105. Song, *Third-Eye Theology*, 133.
106. Ibid., 113.
107. Ibid., 20.

toward the Western tradition commits him to a false and unnecessary bifurcation. Also, Song's attempt to emphasize Asian culture through a conflation of context and revelation is problematic. Song makes Jesus Christ into an abstract concept of liberation that can be identified within Asian culture, albeit in indefinite form.[108] Moreover, Song's assessment of the Western tradition is contradictory because even as he talks about it as someone else's tradition, he nevertheless is a part of it and works within it, using its sources. This issue of Western tradition is closely related to Song's conception of Asian and Christian. At times, Song can pit the two against each other, meaning that Christianity is a Western entity. But Song actually does not work from this understanding, because if he did, he would not be able to judge Western distortions of Christianity—that is, Constantinian subjugation.

With Jung Young Lee's marginality, we have a theological reflection upon the Asian American immigration experience and its ensuing marginalization.[109] In Song's work, Asian Christians are trying to make sense of their rich cultural heritage while questioning the relevance of an equally rich Western tradition. In Lee's work, Asian Christians find themselves in a foreign land, beset with structural racism that pushes them to the margins of American society. Lee's theology begins with his biography and uses the sociological concept of marginality to develop a whole theology for Asian Americans with liberationist tones.

Lee begins his *Marginality* with a statement that "theology is autobiographical, but it is not an autobiography"[110] If theology is to be contextual, the primary context for theology is one's life. Lee believes that this is the reason "why one cannot do theology for another."[111] This sentiment echoes C.S. Song's rejection of the universality of Western theology for him and for Asia. Lee's particular life story that

108. In Chan's assessment, this preoccupation with spiritually discerning the context proves to be exceedingly difficult, if not all together quixotic. Simon Chan, "Future of Global Theology from an Asian Perspective" (A guest lecture at Fuller Theological Seminary at the release of the *Global Dictionary of Theology*, Pasadena. October 23, 2008).

109. It should be noted that Lee, like Song, wrote works focusing on Asian culture. However, due to the limitations of this present study, his influential work on marginality is the exclusive focus.

110. Lee, *Marginality*, 7.

111. Ibid.

situates his theology is his immigration and the subsequent marginalization within American society.

While previous generations of immigrants from Europe have been able to assimilate into "a melting pot" of sorts, Asian Americans have found themselves unable to fully belong, like many post-1965 immigrants from outside of Europe. However, the promise of America as a land of immigrants moving toward Martin Luther King, Jr.'s integrative dream has emboldened Asian immigrants to claim America as their home, along with all other immigrants. Lee reflects theologically upon this experience.

Lee describes how Asian American identity itself is an oppressive American social construct. As a Korean American, Lee must accept the fact that to many white Americans, all East Asians are indiscriminately grouped together in whatever category the former find accessible. For example, to some, he, a Korean American, becomes a "Chinaman."[112] In a racialized society, which sees only colors, particular ethnicities become blurred and inconsequential. However, this blurring of ethnicity must be accepted as a part of our "Asian American" experience.

In order to deal with the unwieldy and diverse concept that "Asian American" is, Lee narrows his topic down to East Asian Americans from China, Japan, and Korea who have a great deal of cultural heritage in common and with whom he most closely identifies.[113] These immigrants have not only found themselves carelessly grouped together by mainstream society, but they are also unable to be fully accepted as Americans, regardless of their cultural assimilation. Lee succinctly summarizes the problem that while "culture is mutable, race is immutable."[114] Asian Americans, therefore, are marginalized, belonging to neither Asia nor America, but standing "ambivalently between two worlds."[115]

Lee builds his whole theology upon this concept of marginality in

112. Ibid., 26.
113. Ibid., 8.
114. Ibid., 35.
115. Ibid., 43.

two moves. First, Lee distinguishes among three definitions of marginality: the classical "in-between," the contemporary "in-both," and his own proposal of "in-beyond."[116] The classical definition of marginality as "in-between" framed the experience negatively, as something that only exists in the nexus of the worlds, belonging to neither the Asian nor the American worlds. The contemporary, multicultural definition of "in-both" is mainly positive, arguing that the marginal person belongs to both worlds, which is even better than belonging to just one. Bringing these two perspectives together, Lee posits his "in-beyond," which is both positive and negative, holding both dimensions together simultaneously. The strength of this new definition is that the new marginal person can "*live in both of [the worlds] without being bound by either of them.*"[117]

Second, this new marginality becomes a christological concept by defining "Jesus Christ as a new marginal person *par excellence*."[118] In a limited analogical way, the incarnation is a "divine marginalization," through which "God emigrated from a heavenly place to this world."[119] Building upon this foundation, Lee develops his view of discipleship, the church, and transformation, which follows closely the typical contours of liberation theology with its "preferential option for the poor, the weak, the powerless, and other marginalized people."[120] Also, like other liberation theologies, Lee's theology is oriented toward praxis, although the issue here is about marginalization.

Lee's work is an American theology of liberation from an Asian perspective and bears much in common with black theology. However, in contrast to African Americans who have endured inexpressible violence, injustice, and dehumanization, the Asian American problem has been one of inability to assimilate into American society, remaining perpetual foreigners, and becoming invisible in the black-white binary paradigm. Because of the special social location of many

116. Ibid., 57–64.
117. Ibid., 63.
118. Ibid., 71.
119. Ibid., 83.
120. Ibid., 117.

East Asian American as socioeconomically well-off but racially discriminated against, Lee differentiates his theology from a "liberation theology" that focuses exclusively on justice. Rather, Lee believes that justice and love must belong together if his theology is not to create another center–margin oppression.[121]

It is hard for Asian Americans to ignore Lee's contribution to the incipient field of Asian American theology. Lee's work resonated profoundly among first-generation Asian American theologians, becoming a widely referred-to text, because it provided the language and the grammar to theologically express what they had experienced, which was a particular expression of racism distinct from what African Americans have faced. By addressing his particular life journey, Lee, in turn, articulated the experience of countless others who emigrated from Asia to America. Even for the second and third generations, the theme of marginality has continued to inform their experience.

There are two key weaknesses in Lee's proposal. First, Lee's work seems to reduce theology to sociology, with marginality becoming a sort of a straitjacket for all theological reflection. The problem with Lee's social analysis is that it practically frames oppression in black-and-white terms, and therefore, cannot account for all the shades of gray including intra-Asian American forms of oppression. Second, we must ask whether Lee assumes a static or a monolithic view of America. Without a doubt, the white majority still controls the power and the social discourse in America. However, the experience of Asian Americans diverges radically, depending on the particular part of the USA. The experience of being the only Asian American in a small Midwest town is going to be worlds apart from that of living among a sizable Asian American community in Los Angeles County.

Wonhee Anne Joh's methodology, as demonstrated in her *Heart of the Cross: A Postcolonial Christology,* represents the latest postcolonial development in Asian American theology.[122] Joh continues the liberationist trajectory of Song and Lee, while including and expanding

121. Ibid., 73.
122. Wonhee Anne Joh, *Heart of the Cross: A Postcolonial Christology* (Louisville, KY: Westminster John Knox, 2006).

both of their concerns and reflecting the present globalizing world with its attendant phenomena such as transnationalism. One of the most significant developments in the work of Joh and other postcolonial theologians is the affirmation of hybridity to address the ambivalences of identity. The ability to account for multiple themes with significant nuances is the strength of Joh and others in this postcolonial approach. The basic foundation of Joh's theology is also liberationist, and we could ask similar questions that we have asked in evaluating the works of Song and Lee.

While postcolonial sentiments of the non-West, asserting selfhood have existed since post-World War II, by the 1990s, the binarism of liberation theology became complicated by a number of issues: "the oppressive dynamics internal to oppressed communities; the ambiguous and shifting complexities of national, cultural, even sexual identities; and the difficulties of creating sustaining coalitions."[123] Therefore, Joh understands her project "as a supplement to the liberation tradition," in a way, taking Song's concern for Asian cultural sources and Lee's Asian American experience of marginality together with feminist theology and postcolonial theory, thereby creating her own unique theological vision.[124]

The Korean American experience of dislocation with its hybrid identity serves as a point of departure for Joh's theological method. Joh accepts that racism and its resulting marginality are key issues for Asian American theology. In order to articulate a hermeneutical rubric fitting for this context, she looks to Korean cultural ideas of *han* and *jeong* and to postcolonial theory. Like Minjung theologians, Joh accepts the Korean concept of *han* as crucial, a concept meaning deeply rooted suffering due to oppression. However, Joh argues that this liberationist *han* was originally closely tied to *jeong*, which means love and relationality. *Jeong*, previously ignored as a theological concept, is able to address the feminist and postcolonial nuances that *han* neglected.

123. Keller et al., *Postcolonial Theologies*, 5.
124. Joh, *Heart of the Cross*, xxi.

Han and *jeong* are then brought together with postcolonial theory via hybridity, mimicry, and interstitial space. *Hybridity* describes how identity can be a product of multiple agencies with "power [that] flows in multidimensional directions."[125] Not only does the dominant group press for assimilation, the oppressed group resists "by refusing to 'fit' into established categories."[126] *Mimicry* functions closely with hybridity as a subversive and transformative dynamic to repeat the colonizers' ways, while reinterpreting them. These two closely related dynamics occur within the *interstitial third space* that rejects binarism, essentialism, and homogenization. These three ideas together allow for Asian American identity to be dynamic, ambiguous, and yet, subversive. Indeed, Joh considers "postcolonial theory [to be] necessary for doing Korean American theology" because it is able to address the complexities of identity and location.[127] Joh uses postcolonial theory critically, as her basic framework is the experience of Korean Americans. She notes that postcolonial theory appears to fuse race and ethnicity, merging Asians of divergent ethnicities into one homogenized group.[128]

Ultimately, Joh begins with the concept of *jeong* and reads it into the biblical narrative, and finally, into Christology. Methodologically, *jeong* is a preconceived notion that functions in an *a priori* manner, as a given that it is radically embedded within the Korean psyche. *Jeong* is accepted side by side with the biblical narrative. Moreover, the scriptural witness functions as a prop for this Korean concept by affirming its theological legitimacy. Although *jeong* is more of an abstract concept than a story, Joh is following Song's convictions, by asserting that *jeong* is an equal-level dialogue partner with Scripture and tradition.

The chief strength of Joh and other postcolonial theologians is their corrective to liberation theology. Liberation theology has suffered from its blindness to internal oppressions and has also been firmly

125. Ibid., 53.
126. Ibid.
127. Ibid., 70.
128. Ibid., 69.

vested in binarism, separating the oppressor and the oppressed in a static fashion. For example, Joh takes to task Jung Young Lee for his center–margin binarism based on race because it suffers from a myopic view of oppression, blind to class or gender oppressions within the racial separation. The multifaceted nature of postcolonial theory challenges the simple binary distinctions based on race or nationality, opening up seemingly inexhaustive possibilities for recognizing discursive oppression.

Also, as acknowledged at the beginning of this chapter, postcolonial theory's questioning of homogenizing essentialism and its related affirmation of hybridity brings much-needed subtlety. For example, Song slights the continuing relevance of the Western tradition to Asian Christians by calling it someone else's tradition. Since Joh's use of hybridity and mimicry creates an active and nimble Asian American identity, the Western tradition can be critically accepted as a part of her tradition as well. Also, although Joh deals with Korean American identity, Namsoon Kang has argued that hybridity applies to Koreans as well.[129]

Now, turning to some of the questions, we must ask if this postcolonial rejection of essentialism is not thoroughgoing enough. The postcolonial ambivalence over essentialism constitutes a tension between its theory and practice. Because essentialism enables oppressive binarism, it must be repudiated in theory. For example, the subaltern and the colonizing power can be seen in a homogenous, stereotypical fashion without being subject to any internal development or external influence. However, without some general description, oppression cannot be adequately diagnosed and opposed. Thus, the adoption of "strategic essentialism," as Joh proposes, addresses the problem in a provisional way, but nevertheless divides humanity, based on some criteria. This division is a carryover concept from liberation theology that postcolonial critique is reluctant to leave

129. Namsoon Kang, "Who/What is Asian? A Postcolonial Theological Reading of Orientalism and Neo-Orientalism," in *Postcolonial Theologies*, ed. Keller et al., 100–117.

behind, but it makes postcolonialism susceptible to the same problems in liberation theology that it has sought to avoid.

Also, we wonder if the biblical narrative is ultimately at the mercy of Joh's postcolonial apparatus. As with other liberation-oriented theologies, does Joh's postcolonial proposal introduce an arbitrary, foreign criterion that takes precedence over the text? For example, is *jeong* as an *a priori* category becoming correlated with Christ's love on the cross? Joh argues that *jeong* is an "all-pervasive concept that has been the life force of Korean people."[130] But this argument is a mere assertion with no support; based on Joh's use of hybridity, how would she support this statement? Indeed, Namsoon Kang, a Korean feminist postcolonial theologian, rejects such essentializing use of arbitrary Korean cultural concepts altogether as oppressive forms of "neo-orientalism."[131]

Song, Lee, and Joh all contribute to the development of Asian American theology by addressing different aspects of the Asian American experience and proposing ways to engage them. Whatever critique we have for them, their insights and courage in forging new paths for Asian American theology are deeply appreciated. Their works serve as catalysts for further development of Asian American theology. Therefore, in that vein of gratitude, we offer this analysis. Because they all generally share a liberationist foundation, albeit in different forms, they are vulnerable on three fronts, regarding the criterion, orientation, and context of their theologies, although Joh's vision is clearly the most nuanced.[132] Weaknesses on these three fronts correspond to theological decisions about Scripture, the church, and the world.

First, we address their theologies' *controlling passion*. As we have seen above, Asian American theology developed under the genre of liberation theology, sharing its basic methodological presuppositions. One of the key implications of this developmental pedigree was the

130. Joh, *Heart of the Cross*, 128.
131. Kang, "Who/What is Asian?," 113.
132. These evaluative categories were adopted from that of Hunsinger. See George Hunsinger, *Disruptive Grace: Studies in the Theology of Karl Barth* (Grand Rapids, MI: Eerdmans, 2000), 42–59.

establishment of liberation in some form as the core criterion of theological discourse.

Song's theological discourse is narrative in style, eschewing "abstruse theological statements, complicated arguments, and difficult metaphysical propositions" as disconnected from life.[133] Thus, the technical aspect of his methodology can be somewhat veiled. However, as we see in his argumentation, it is clear that Asian stories and biblical stories together function as sources of theology, taking justice for and the liberation of Asian people as the criterion with which to judge both. Lee's methodological criterion is more explicit. His marginality rubric assumes the liberation of Asian Americans as the *telos* of his theology, even as he affirms love along with justice. Joh's postcolonial approach adds another dimension to the liberationist critique, to acknowledge the complexities of oppressor–oppressed dynamics. Nevertheless, she stands within the liberationist rubric, as she clearly states. The controlling passion is still cultural, sociological, and/or political liberation, which evaluates Scripture, tradition, and theology.

In his *Exclusion and Embrace*, Miroslav Volf points out the problems inherent in such an oppression/liberation schema. The language of this schema tends "to undermine the operation of human agency and disempower victims . . . and to imprison them within the narratives of their own victimization."[134] Also, Volf argues that "more often than not, conflicts are messy," meaning that "clear narratives of blame and innocence" are difficult, while opportunities for "ideological self-deception" abound.[135] If the oppressed finally get their liberation, what will happen to the former oppressors? Within this schema, the answer would have to be the "liberation of the oppressors" since there are no other categories. In the end, an oppression/liberation schema fails to take into consideration the guilt of all parties involved *coram Deo* and the need for reconciliation of all peoples in God's presence.

The postcolonial approach comes close to recognizing these issues

133. C.S. Song, *Theology from the Womb of Asia* (Maryknoll, NY: Orbis, 1986), xii.
134. Miroslav Volf, *Exclusion and Embrace: A Theological Exploration of Identity, Otherness, and Reconciliation* (Nashville, TN: Abingdon, 1996), 103.
135. Ibid.

and tries to address them with its attack upon essentialism. However, this trajectory ends up as a dead end with an internal contradiction because it still holds onto the oppression/liberation schema. The lingering "strategic essentialism," is the culprit in this unsatisfactory solution. A full rejection of essentialism would lead to abandoning the oppression/liberation schema since no binary division of humanity is possible. Yet, even without this strategic essentialism, systemic and societal sins with their attendant oppressions could be recognized in a theological manner.

Instead of liberation, which is inadequate as the chief criterion, we argue that biblical narrative must be recovered as the foundational touchstone for Asian American theology. While agreeing with Kwok Pui-lan about the need for the "decolonizing of the mind" from Western hegemonic discourse, we also maintain the need for Scripture's role in "colonizing the mind" with a Theo-drama that controls all whole reality.[136]

One of the reasons Scripture cannot function this way for these contextual theologians is that they have a tendency to fuse Scripture with the Western tradition. As a result of this fusion, Asian and Christian become dichotomous because Christianity is regarded as a Western entity. While cultural captivity to Western Christianity is a dire challenge, this fusion concedes too much to the Western tradition. With this move, these theologians end up robbing themselves of the use of Scripture, as if it is a foreign thing.

By recovering the biblical narrative as the main criterion, which would include crucial issues of justice and liberation, Asian American theology will be able to not only throw off Western hegemony, but also be wary of its own proclivity toward cultural reduction of the gospel. Simon Chan points out that a "serious grappling with Scripture and the Christian tradition . . . provides a wider horizon for evaluating the complex human condition in Asia, whereas a theology reduced

136. Kwok Pui-lan, *Postcolonial Imagination and Feminist Theology* (Louisville: Westminster John Knox, 2005), 22; and Ellen T. Charry, *By the Renewing of Your Minds: The Pastoral Function of Christian Doctrine* (New York: Oxford, 1997), 19.

to a political ideology often ends up quite blind to the dangers from below."[137]

As Lindbeck contends, Asian American theology should redescribe "reality within the scriptural framework rather than translating Scripture into extra-scriptural categories. It is the text, so to speak, which absorbs the world, rather than the world the text."[138] It should not matter if Western tradition has failed to do this, if that indeed is the case. This intertextuality should be the vocation of Asian American theology.

Second, the *orientation* of Song's, Lee's, and Joh's presented theologies must be clarified. Along with this liberation criterion, these theologians have oriented their theologies external to the church, rather than engaging in theology within the community. For instance, Song believes that the Western tradition is too church-centered, arguing instead that the Asians should seek a direct experience of Jesus that bypasses the church.[139] Of course, as we have noted above, this direct experience of Jesus ends up being not much more than an abstract idea of love. Lee's work focuses on experiences external to the Asian American community, experiences of oppression and discrimination in white churches. Lee nowhere addresses concerns and problems within the Asian American community, such as Confucian patriarchy, for example. Joh's work also is generally oriented toward the external oppression of colonialism.

This oppression/liberation schema creates an us-versus-them binarism as well as a sociopolitical emphasis. Thus, these theologies become externally oriented, marginalizing the church as well as the spiritual dimension of Christianity. In black theologies of liberation too, this problem of marginalizing the church is evident. Dwight Hopkins states that the challenge for black theology today is to "view reality as both internal and external," perceiving pressures that exist

137. Simon Chan, "Evangelical Theology in Asian Contexts," in *Cambridge Companion to Evangelical Theology*, ed. Timothy Larsen and Daniel J. Treier (Cambridge: Cambridge University Press, 2007), 230.

138. George A. Lindbeck, *The Nature of Doctrine: Religion and Theology in a Postliberal Age*, 25th anniversary ed. (Louisville, KY: Westminster John Knox, 2009), 104.

139. Song, "Five Stages," 5.

inside the African American community as well as those coming from outside.[140] Hopkins also indicates that black theology must engage individuals as well as the churches at the spiritual level. Surely, this advice can benefit the wellbeing of Asian American theologies as well.

Song correctly assesses the academic captivity by Western theology, and yet, by ignoring the church, his theology also suffers from a similar disconnection. Simon Chan retorts that despite all the talk of being *from below*, this kind of theology bypasses "the living tradition or ecclesial experience" to become an abstract speculation of specialists.[141]

An ecclesial mediation roots the Asian American theologian in a community beyond her own autobiography to encompass a larger scope of experience. This mediation possesses at least two facets. On the one hand, the ecclesial orientation provides a hermeneutical trajectory to interact with the Western tradition. If the tradition is understood as a hermeneutical community, then Western theologians will be judged upon their faithfulness to Scripture, just as Asian American theologians must be.[142] Thought of in this way, the Western tradition is not someone else's heritage, contrary to what Song believes. This hermeneutical community across time and space constitutes ecclesial ecumenicity, in which the Asian American faithfulness can be compared with and corrected by a multicultural body.[143]

On the other hand, through this ecclesial catholicity, Asian American theology would avoid cutting itself off from others by claiming unique beliefs for itself. Volf defines this catholicity as the assertion that "no church in a given culture may isolate itself from other churches in other cultures declaring itself sufficient to itself and to its own culture."[144] This is the true implication of the hybrid identity, that Christians belong together in a larger community of God.

140. Dwight N. Hopkins, *Introducing Black Theology of Liberation* (Maryknoll, NY: Orbis, 1999), 195.

141. Chan, "Future of Global Theology from an Asian Perspective."

142. Stanley J. Grenz and John R. Franke, *Beyond Foundationalism: Shaping Theology in a Postmodern Context* (Louisville, KY: Westminster John Knox, 2001), 119.

143. Volf, *Exclusion and Embrace*, 53.

144. Ibid., 51.

Ultimately, the church mediates our witness to the world by embodying life in an alternative kingdom. An ecclesial orientation in Asian American theology would engage the world as the church, instead of bypassing the church.

Third, we must examine the adequacy of these theologies in *defining their context*. The problems of the oppression/liberation schema, essentialism, and an external orientation all contribute to misinterpreting the Asian American context through homogenization. Therefore, Asian culture, Asian American identity, and American society all tend toward relatively static categories. This problem has been identified within Joh's postcolonial approach, but no convincing solution arises because the foundation of this approach is still liberationist with its accompanying essentialism, albeit as a toned down version.

Regarding Asian culture, Song assumes its importance, but he fails to make a distinction between Asian culture and Asian heritage. Asian culture is a dynamic, hybrid entity, continually negotiating itself in a world of ideas. As Edward Said warns, no one has the authority to describe a culture without doing some violence to its dynamic nature.[145] However, the Asian cultural heritage in its historic nature is something that is more accessible for description. For example, Confucianism as a historic tradition can be described, although its present-day appropriation is more challenging because everyone relates to this historic heritage differently. There will always be cultural mavericks as well as staunch traditionalists. An essentialist view of a culture usually tends to consider cultural innovators as inauthentic sellouts. While much more nuanced, Joh does not vary too far from Song. Her belief in the importance of *han* and *jeong* for Korean Americans could be interpreted as an essentialist conclusion. This is Kang's point: as a modern Korean, she does not find traditional cultural categories to be helpful theological tools.[146]

If Asian culture is essentialized by these theologians, American

145. Edward W. Said, *Orientalism*, 25th anniversary ed. (New York: Vintage, 1994), 331.
146. Kang, "Who/What is Asian?," 112.

culture does not fare much better either. Lee's and Joh's views of American society tend toward being static and uniform, and they fail to see the conflicts and diverse trajectories within it. Lee's focus on racism is correctly perceived by Joh to be deficient, but her solution of simply adding more layers of oppression is still questionable.

David Hollinger's *Postethnic America* posits that multiculturalism has run its course and proposes a postethnic perspective that "promotes multiple identities, emphasizes the dynamic and changing character of many groups, and is responsive to the potential for creating new cultural combinations."[147] Hollinger's thesis is that instead of "identity," which "implies fixity and givenness," "affiliation" should be the main focus of American discourse concerning diversity.[148] Given the rising numbers of mixed-race people of Asian descent in America, this affiliation framework allows for a much wider scope of ethnic realities in ways that Song, Lee, and even Joh cannot encompass.

For Asian American theology to be faithful to the tasks of theology as well as be appropriate for its own Asian American context, it must reestablish a new beginning that takes Scripture, the church, and the changing world seriously.

Awareness of the Asian American Quadrilateral (AAQ)

Now, the constructive task lies before us. The methodologies presented above displayed efforts at securing contextual concreteness, yet they also raised questions because of their various expressions of essentialism. Moreover, this essentialism meant that the context became the *de facto* authority, even ruling over Scripture since it could not critique the context. Furthermore, the essentialized context too easily became a straitjacket for theology, limiting revelation by human experience. All these lessons from the limitations of the approaches previously discussed will be incorporated here.

Our proposal for contextual description focuses not on *identity*, or *affiliation*, but *awareness* or "critical consciousness," as Paulo Freire

147. David A. Hollinger, *Postethnic America: Beyond Multiculturalism* (New York: Basic Books, 2000), 3.
148. Ibid., 7.

would say.[149] Freire sought a liberative pedagogy via conscientization, based on post-Marxist critical theory. While similar to his, our agenda is not liberation from oppression, but submission to revelation, which incorporates liberation from oppression, but is also much broader and more theologically rooted. Through critical awareness of contextual undercurrents, various Babylonian captivities can be thwarted. Also, this awareness can also lead to the hearing of God's Word for the specific situation at hand.

With this awareness, the Asian American context is defined as the intersection of four contextual elements of the AAQ: Asian heritage, migration experience, American culture, and racialization. Because of its liminal state of being betwixt and between, the Asian American context is difficult to outline. Also, there are other minorities in America who exist in similar liminal states, so identifying the uniqueness of the Asian American context can be perplexing. However, by identifying these four main intersecting elements that make up this bicultural context, we can frame it in its unique particularity, distinct from the contexts of other peoples in America. Depending on one's ethnic heritage, migrant generation, location in America, and many other particularities, the ways Asian Americanness is experienced can vary widely. We introduce these four themes, therefore, as tools to discern and articulate one's situation concretely, but still in a nonessentialist fashion.

Properly speaking, the AAQ does not mean that there are four distinct quadrants. Rather, the term simply notes that there are four elements to the Asian American experience. AAQ could be understood and used in two closely related ways, as personally oriented layers of existence and as externally focused hermeneutical lenses with which to interpret experience and praxis. Both of these ways are important because of the intensely personal—or biographical (as noted above)—nature of the task of Asian American theology. Self-awareness impacts positively or negatively our faithfulness to God's Word.

149. See Paulo Freire, *Pedagogy of the Oppressed*, 30th anniversary ed. (New York: Bloomsbury Academic, 2000).

However, because the Asian American community is more complex and broader than anyone's personal experiences or identity, the use of interpretive lenses is required. We now turn to describe each of the four elements.

The first element of AAQ is the Asian cultural, religious, and philosophical heritage that is shared with contemporary Asians, many of whom, like Asian Americans, must also negotiate between this heritage and Western/global influences. This theme describes the various social, political, and religious traditions, with their long development and many interpretations and embodiments, which function implicitly as well as explicitly within the Asian American context. These traditions include Confucianism, Taoism, Buddhism, Shinto, Shamanism, Hinduism, and folk religions, among others.[150] Also, the preference for using Asian heritage acknowledges that because of globalism, hybridity exists in contemporary Asian culture already.

An important detail here is to employ archetypes instead of stereotypes in considering this Asian heritage as a way of understanding Asian American experiences. An archetype, used here, means a symbol or a pattern that exists within and asserts its influence over a given context. How this archetype manifests itself would be open for discernment and discussion. Moreover, it is possible that the archetype may only provoke reactive responses, lacking any affirmative expressions. A stereotype, on the contrary, is an assumption about characteristics held common by a particular group. As a much blunter concept, stereotypes focus merely on external expressions and miss the deeper undercurrents and reactive responses. In a sense, the problem is that such assumptions so often work out of expressions of essentialism.

For example, there exists a Confucian archetype of a father who is authoritarian and emotionally aloof and who embodies the cosmic moral principle within the familial context. This archetype asserts its

150. See Jung Young Lee, *The Trinity in Asian Perspective* (Nashville, TN: Abingdon, 1996) and the "Inculturation" section of Peter Phan, *Christianity with an Asian Face* (Maryknoll, NY: Orbis, 2003), 75–248.

influence varyingly in the traditionally Confucian communities of East Asia. Using the archetype, we might be able to discern reactive parenting strategies among fathers, and deeply rooted anxieties even among those fathers who do not express this archetype. However, a stereotype would assume that all or many East Asian fathers embody these characteristics, which would be an essentialist overstatement. In sum, the archetype category allows a way to concretely identify a specific aspect of a cultural heritage, while at the same time, leaving room for diversity of receptions and manifestations.

The migration experience is the second element. This theme deals with migration and its related phenomena such as the acculturation/enculturation process, intergenerational conflict, trauma, and identity formation. These issues are shared with a wide range of immigrants, from Hispanics to Irish, and Germans although, because of their external distinguishing physical features, Asian Americans face unique challenges that complicate their experience. See for example, how Peter Cha highlights the intersection of identity formation and church involvement among second-generation Asian Americans.[151] Also, Sang Hyun Lee, in his search for theological meaning in the experience of migration, offers the concept of pilgrimage.[152]

We must stress that while immigrants from Asia share many commonalities with immigrants from elsewhere, their experiences are filtered through their Asian heritage, and as we shall see, are impacted by their racialization. In this sense, we must keep in mind that all of these four elements influence and color the others, thus creating a distinctive context for Asian Americans. Also, the narrative and trauma of this transitional experience may leave residual effects on the generations that followed the first immigrants, For example, the Chinese Exclusion Act of 1882 and the Japanese internment during

151. Peter Cha, "Ethnic Identity Formation and Participation in Immigrant Churches: Second-Generation Korean American Experiences," in *Korean Americans and Their Religions: Pilgrims and Missionaries from a Different Shore*, ed. Ho-Youn Kwon, Kwang Chung Kim, and R. Stephen Warner (University Park, PA: Pennsylvania State University Press, 2001), 141–56.

152. Sang Hyun Lee, "Pilgrimage and Home in the Wilderness of Marginality: Symbols and Contexts in Asian American Theology," in *Korean Americans and Their Religions: Pilgrims and Missionaries from a Different Shore*, ed. Ho-Youn Kwon, Kwang Chung Kim, and R. Stephen Warner (University Park, PA: Pennsylvania State University Press, 2001), 55–70.

World War II must be approached from the theme of migration as well as racialization and American culture.

Immigration does not fittingly describe what many Southeast Asians underwent, as they escaped the horrors of war and genocide as refugees to finally settle in the USA. Given its traumatic nature and intensity, the impact of this relocation may overshadow other AAQ elements. We are reminded here that the ways the four AAQ elements are negotiated and expressed depends upon each community and person. However, the element that appears to the most significant could be overshadowing a deeper and most influential element. Therefore, the full awareness of all four elements in the AAQ is required.

The third element is American culture. The American pluralistic post-Christendom context in general, and the evangelical movement in particular, serve as the situation in which many Asian Americans find themselves. This element encompasses not only the multicultural contemporary American culture in which Asian Americans actively participate, but also the Western intellectual tradition and missionary history in Asia of which Asian Americans are heirs. As a result, Asian American Christianity is heavily influenced by the Enlightenment's rationalistic influence, as well as by the Puritanism and revivalism of evangelicalism. Of course, as a part of American society, the church's contemporary struggles with the postmodern and post-Christendom situations apply to Asian Americans as well.[153] Moreover, Asian Americans are also culture-makers who are co-creating contemporary American popular culture in every media and venue.

Finally, racialization is the fourth element. This theme articulates the particular form of racism and discrimination that Asian Americans face as people of color. Asian Americans are beneficiaries and heirs of the long struggle and its resulting accomplishments, in which African Americans have engaged for common equality and dignity. While all minorities face interpersonal and structural racism in various

153. See Elaine Howard Ecklund, *Korean American Evangelicals New Models for Civic Life* (New York: Oxford University Press, 2008); and Rebecca Kim, *God's New Whiz Kids: Korean American Evangelicals on Campus* (New York: New York University Press, 2006).

expressions and degrees, Asian Americans' experiences of racism might be best summed up as their "perpetual foreigner" status, where the Americanness of their identity is not recognized. Asian American manifestations of liberation theology, resonating with Latino Americans, African Americans, and even feminists, address the sociopolitical dimensions of racial injustice and discrimination. Jung Young Lee's *Marginality* is a classic example as we have discussed above.[154]

Under this racialization element, colonialism and Orientalism assert Western culture, heritage, and values over Asian ones. When internalized by Asian Americans, this denigration of Asian heritage, culture, and physical features leads to mimicry or self-hatred, a familiar trope often discussed in Asian American studies and theologies. The Model Minority myth and acceptance as "honorary whites" are also notable aspects of the struggle of Asian Americans as a racial minority.

As stated above, these four spheres or perspectives are interrelated and overlapping. They are also constantly changing in the tumult of globalization. In Asia, especially in urban settings, the cultural heritage is continually being reinterpreted in light of Western influences. More and more, America is embracing its multiethnic reality. Immigrants assimilate to the mainstream culture and later generations sometimes return to look for their heritage roots. Racialization is a function of the slow pace of change in the way America perceives its identity.

Furthermore, the epistemological vector of the communities and individuals is also moving. The direction of one person or a community might be toward American culture to escape the externalism and hierarchy of Asian heritage. However, another person or community might move in the opposite direction, returning to Asian culture to reject the individualism and the lack of community in American culture.

Because of this fluidity, complexity, and dynamic of the Asian American experiences and context, we have focused on *awareness*

154. Lee, *Marginality*.

rather than *identity*. A continual journey of critical awareness will better serve the theological task of hearing God's Word in a concrete situation without absolutizing the context—in other words, free from all Babylonian captivities. Our hermeneutical task in this process of conscientization is to shape a working language and grammar from various interdisciplinary resources so that we can articulate the Asian American experience and critically analyze it in light of the gospel. We must offer not only critical analysis, but also various constructive experiments and creative proposals for the development of contextual theology and ministry in order to stimulate insightful discussion and fruitful research. The later chapters will continue to engage and employ this AAQ way of grasping the context and building upon it to develop an equally fluid and complex theological method.

Conclusion

In this chapter, we covered much ground in an effort to develop a new way to express the particularity of the context. From Barth, we analyzed the affirmation of Jesus's Jewish flesh and its wide implications for the election of Israel and the *telos* of the nations. These topics and ideas helped flesh out the cultural/ethnic particularity as a context of discipleship responding to God's Word. Then, building upon Barth, we introduced how his ideas resonate closely with current contextual agendas, by putting them in conversation with the works of J. Kameron Carter, Willie Jennings, and Kathryn Tanner. Through this engagement, we proposed that the context must be concrete, enveloping all aspects of cultural/ethnic particularities, and yet, be nonessentialist—that is, never absolutized. Contextual essentialism is rejected for the sake of the freedom of the people in that context as well as for the freedom of God's Word. Finally, the last section critiqued three representative methods for Asian American theology, and then, introduced the AAQ as a tool for defining the context. In each of the later chapters, Barth's ideas, concepts, and insights will be developed for the purpose of engaging the Asian American context as defined by the AAQ.

In this chapter, our task was to establish the particularity of the context as concrete yet nonessentialist. The next chapter will explore the dynamics of contextuality, or what it means to encounter God's Word in a particular context.

2

Contextuality: The Logic of Contextual Engagement

The[1] last chapter began with the dynamic and fluid manner in which Barth perceived his context and the importance of his approach as a model for addressing the crisis of theological reflection in Asian American contexts. Also, in reviewing the existing Asian American theological literature, our evaluation was that many scholars lacked a sufficiently robust theological basis for their contextual methodology, in their liberationist and postcolonial approaches, along with their pitfalls. Moreover, the authors of these works struggled to account for the complexity and diversity of the Asian American situation, often falling into essentialisms and stereotypes. By incorporating Barth's insights, a new approach toward Asian American theologies was introduced, with the Asian American Quadrilateral (AAQ) as an

1. A significant part of this chapter was incorporated into a paper presented at the 2016 L.A. Theology Conference, entitled, "Reading Scripture in Our Context: Double Particularity in Karl Barth's Actualistic View of Scripture." This paper will be published in Oliver Crisp and Fred Sanders (eds), *The Voice of God in the Text of Scripture* (Grand Rapids, MI: Zondervan, 2016).

interpretative framework with which to exegete the wider diversity of Asian American contexts.

This chapter builds upon the last one by providing a functional logic for fleshing out the contextuality of Barth's theology and again drawing out its implications for Asian American theological reflection. It has become a mere truism to state that all theology is contextual.[2] However, the understanding or articulation of this contextual nature varies significantly. Many so-called "non-contextual"—often Western—theologians have yet to give a conscious and explicit account of their interaction with their context. Therefore, their articulations reflect a default, pseudo-universal stance. This pseudo-universalism has now been exposed for its colonial and Eurocentric presuppositions. While it would be too easy simply to accuse the Western theological tradition, the fact is that "non-contextual" theologies exist in non-Western contexts as well. Moreover, contextual theologies often themselves fall into myriad forms of cultural captivity. Therefore, the question of contextuality is a pressing one for all theologies in our globalized world. What is required is not just a simplistic assertion of being contextual, but rather, a technical and theologically rigorous articulation of the reality of contextuality in all theology.

Contextuality asks in what manner might a theologian *consciously* and *deliberately* interact with his context. For example, among European theologians, Jürgen Moltmann is a forerunner in framing his work with a clear and explicit articulation of his contextuality, especially since the publication of his systematic works.[3] In comparison to Moltmann, Barth's articulation of his contextuality is scant. However, as we saw in his letter in the *South East Asia Theological Journal*, discussed in the Introduction, Barth was indeed fully aware of these

2. Bosch observes that all theology "is, by its very nature, contextual." See David J. Bosch, *Transforming Mission: Paradigm Shifts in Theology of Mission* (Maryknoll, NY: Orbis, 1991), 423.
3. Using different terminology, Moltmann describes the three possible dimensions of contextuality as "1. contextual, 2. determined by its *kairos*, and 3. related to its own community." By "contextual," Moltmann is referring to the way in which language and culture become the media for theological work. The *kairos* describes the sociopolitical situation that presses for theological reflection. Finally, the community refers to the affiliations and location of the theologian. These are the various dimensions of what contextuality means. Jürgen Moltmann, *Experiences in Theology: Ways and Forms of Christian Theology* (Minneapolis, MN: Fortress Press, 2000), 59–60.

matters even if he did not always express them explicitly. Conscious, deliberate, and explicit awareness of engagement with the context is what distinguishes the idea of contextuality from merely interpreting theologians within their own contexts.

In this chapter, our argument uses Bruce McCormack's research to articulate the inner logic of Barth's contextuality in terms of his actualism. What McCormack identifies as the *Realdialektik* provides the actualistic logic of how Barth's theology interacts with his context and how this aspect is at the heart of his overall theology. This *Realdialektik* affirms an engagement with the context while also guarding against the encroachment of the context upon divine revelation.[4] In other words, McCormack's *Realdialektik* is another phrase for God's sovereign freedom to cross that "infinite qualitative distinction" between God and humanity. In the discussion below, we will show that Barth's understanding of contextuality is not just a certain methodology, but a central aspect of his theology, his understanding of the *living* God to whom we must attend in our particular contexts. This acknowledgement and incorporation of the living God's active and present action is what sets Barth's contextuality apart from other methodologies.

The rest of the chapter will proceed as follows. The first section will unpack Barth's actualistic contextuality. A brief survey of literature interacting with Barth's engagement with his context will be organized into three groups: the political approach, the missiological approach, and the actualistic approach. While the three approaches with their various representatives highlight different aspects of Barth's multifaceted theological framework, the actualistic approach will be presented as the most basic one, upon which the other approaches are based.

In that sense, the work of Eberhard Jüngel—and more specifically,

4. McCormack describes the *Realdialektik* as "the motor which drives Barth's doctrine of analogy and makes it possible" in Bruce L. McCormack, *Karl Barth's Critically Realistic Dialectical Theology: Its Genesis and Development 1909-1936* (Oxford: Clarendon, 1995), 18. The point is that this ontic dialectic is about the fundamental difference between God and humanity that cannot be bridged without a divine act.

that of McCormack—will be the sources for our view of Barth's contextuality. Drawing upon McCormack, we argue that the inner logic of Barth's contextuality is in his *Realdialektik*, an ontological dialectic rooted in God's complete otherness. Unpacked as an actualistic indirect identity, the *Realdialektik* provides the functional logic of Barth's contextuality so that even as Barth interacts with the context reciprocally, the controlling criterion remains God's revelation.

In the second section, the implications of Barth's insights for theological contextuality are explored. Barth's contextuality is able to move from the Word to the world and from the world to the Word, or *from above* and *from below*. *From above*, revelation, with its historic particularity in Jesus Christ, speaks to its receivers in their particular situations. Therefore, it moves from historic particularity to contemporary particularity. The latter particularity is the contextuality of God's Word in our situations. The task of theology is then a secondary reflection upon these primary encounters with the Word. As such, this theological task is engaged in a vernacular, provisional manner, which is also an important aspect of contextuality.

From below, with Barth's christocentric basis, is affirmed his version of a "method of correlation," where the questions and concerns of the world are addressed, but only through the means of God's counter-questions. Also, because the world is *in* Jesus Christ by the eternal election of God, God can employ anything in creation to witness to the one true Light. This movement from below is positive or constructive in its role in helping us to hear the Word come alive for the contemporary situation.

This ordered reciprocal relationality between the Word and the world is closely related to how theology in its universality is applied to its particular expressions. Correctly relating the universal–particular dynamic protects theological discourse from cultural captivities as well as from unexamined contextuality. Finally, the nature of Reformed theology as *reformata semper reformanda secundum verbum Dei* illustrates how all these dimensions come together.

The third section discusses the three levels at which Asian American theological reflection must occur: the methodological, ecclesial, and personal levels. Asian American theology at the methodological level works like this present work, where interpretative frameworks for exegeting the context and the grammar for engaging it are presented. However, God encounters us in our particular situations—which means at the ecclesial and personal levels, with very specific negotiation of the Asian American experience. Concrete theological reflection must occur at the local level in faith communities and in personal discipleship situations.

Barth's Actualistic Contextuality

This section presents the theoretical foundation for the contextuality of Barth's theology. First, a review of significant literature detailing three main approaches to deciphering Barth's contextuality will be presented. Second, the nature of Barth's actualistic contextuality will be outlined through the work of Jüngel and McCormack.

Brief Review of the Significant Literature

Reflecting a widely accepted sentiment in America, Tillich complained that Barth's "neo-orthodox" method sought "to derive every statement directly from the ultimate truth" instead of engaging with the situation apologetically.[5] However, Tillich also believed that Barth indeed "corrects himself again and again in light of the 'situation' and . . . [yet] did not realize that in doing so he ceases to be a merely kerygmatic theologian."[6] Tillich accuses Barth of being naively unaware of his contextuality or of failing to address it in his methodology. In response, Barth noted that Tillich seemed to believe that he "has been asleep since 1920" with no development beyond the "'infinite qualitative difference' between time and eternity" of the second edition of his *Romans.*[7] Tillich's caricature of a contextually

5. Paul Tillich, *Systematic Theology*, vol. 1 (Chicago: University of Chicago Press, 1951), 5.
6. Tillich, *Systematic Theology*, 5.
7. Eberhard Busch, *Karl Barth: His Life from Letters and Autobiographical Texts* (Grand Rapids, MI: Eerdmans, 1994), 437.

oblivious Barth is what remains in the mind of many. As we have noted above, Barth's reflection upon his own contextuality is limited, which has not helped to shed light on this important aspect of his theology.

In contrast to this insufficient depiction of Barth, over the years at least three main perspectives have developed, considering how Barth engages the context consciously: the political, the missiological, and the actualistic.

Friedrich-Wilhelm Marquardt best represents the political perspective of Barth's contextuality. In 1972, Marquardt proposed that Barth's socialist concerns drove his theology, and even, at its very core, his doctrine of God.[8] From this perspective, Barth's theology "must be understood as the conceptual side of a lifelong socialist engagement."[9] George Hunsinger summarizes Marquardt's proposal thus:

> The picture which emerges from Marquardt's work is that Barth, from his earliest essays to final volumes of dogmatics, desired above all else to work out a viable theological solution to the problem of theory and praxis—including political praxis. It was, in fact, the *political* question of theory and praxis which ultimately precipitated Barth's break with liberalism—not merely the theoretical inconsistencies of liberal theology which disturbed him so much in themselves. A look at the chronology of Barth's development in its political context will substantiate this claim.[10]

Marquardt also asserts that Barth's "*Dogmatics* is *also* a commentary on contemporary history"[11] The key insight—or more correctly, recovery—in this interpretation of Barth is that Barth has "always been interested in politics" and he considers "that it belongs to the life of a theologian."[12] Even while political connections were not always made explicit, they consciously impacted Barth's theological project throughout his career.

However, Marquardt's contribution to understanding Barth's

8. Friedrich-Wilhelm Marquardt, *Theologie und Sozialismus: Das Beispiel Karl Barths* (Munich: Chr. Kaiser, 1972).
9. George Hunsinger, *Karl Barth and Radical Politics* (Philadelphia, PA: Westminster, 1976), 9.
10. Ibid., 18.
11. Friedrich-Wilhelm Marquardt as quoted in Timothy J. Gorringe, *Karl Barth: Against Hegemony* (Oxford: Oxford University Press, 1999), 18. Friedrich-Wilhelm Marquardt, *Theologie und Sozialismus: Das Beispiel Karl Barths* (Munich: Chri. Kaiser, 1972).
12. Hunsinger, *Radical Politics*, 182.

contextuality is not without its problems. George Hunsinger avers that Marquardt "reduces Barth's doctrine of God to its political function" when he argues that Barth "conceives of God as praxis, power, this-worldliness and in this sense a reality," and when he reductively formulates "God's being *as* his act, not in his act."[13] Thus, within Marquardt's interpretative framework, Barth's theology is subsumed under his contextuality, making his doctrines a predicate of his political concerns.[14] Given Barth's caution and rejection of Babylonian captivities of every kind, such a proposal is untenable. Indeed, Jüngel rightly orders the relationship when he states that "politics was a predicate–the 'political side'–of his theology, but his theology was never a predicate of politics."[15]

While Marquardt's political interpretation of Barth is overstated, his work stimulated much research on Barth's contextuality in Germany and elsewhere.[16] For example, Timothy Gorringe proposed that from first to last, Barth's work is "against hegemony," against the use of ideological power against human freedom.[17] Barth as "a theologian actively [sought] to respond to the events of the day."[18] In a letter written in 1957, Barth describes just such an interaction:

> I used what I thought I had learned and understood so far to cope with this or that situation, with some complex of biblical or historical or doctrinal questions, often with some subject presented to me from outside, often in fact by a topical subject, e.g. a political issue. It was always something new that got hold of me, rather than the other way around.[19]

Others have also pursued this political aspect of Barth's theology.[20]

13. Ibid., 189.
14. Ibid.
15. Eberhard Jüngel, *Karl Barth: A Theological Legacy* (Philadelphia, PA: Westminster, 1986), 41.
16. McCormack, *Karl Barth's Critically Realistic Dialectical Theology*, 26–27.
17. Timothy J. Gorringe, *Karl Barth: Against Hegemony* (New York: Oxford University Press, 1999), 1.
18. Ibid., 16.
19. Busch, *Karl Barth*, 420.
20. Paul Chung states, "Barth's theology (critical, dialogical, open to the world) is inherently related to the concrete contextuality of his life setting." Chung concludes his research by musing about Barth's contextuality for the concerns of religious pluralism. Paul S. Chung, *Karl Barth: God's Word in Action* (Eugene, OR: Cascade, 2008). Also, Carys Moseley framed Barth's theology in terms of resisting the powers of ideological nationalism. Carys Moseley, *Nations and Nationalism in the Theology of Karl Barth* (New York: Oxford University Press, 2013). Political theologians in South Africa have also engaged Barth and drawn inspiration from his work with the Barmen Declaration

All these works address the question of Barth's contextuality in engaging the *kairos* moment, using Moltmann's term, focusing more specifically on the political dimension of his theology. The missiological perspective addresses more of the social and cultural situation.

From early on, missiologists such as Hendrik Kraemer and Lesslie Newbigin began to apply Barth's stance against natural theology and against the idea of *point of contact* to their tasks on the field and to ecumenical endeavors. Kraemer believed that Barth's "great service" to the world was reminding us "of the real meaning of revelation" with "its special and *sui generis* quality and significance."[21] Developing this insight into what he called "biblical realism," Kraemer proposed a prophetic and revelatory biblical hermeneutic centered on Christ. In Kraemer's mind, this hermeneutic served as a critical paradigm for the purification of Western Christianity, and as a basis for a radically discontinuous engagement of revelation with world religions.

Also, Lesslie Newbigin observed the way Barth's judgment of religion protested against the forcing of the gospel into the plausibility structures of modernism:

> Either one can take the general religious experience of mankind as the clue for our understanding of the human situation, and then seek categories with which to fit Jesus into this understanding; or one can take Jesus as the absolutely crucial and determinative clue for all understanding and then try to understand the rest of human experience from this centre. This, of course, is the issue which Karl Barth pressed relentlessly in all his writing.[22]

In Newbigin's application, conversion becomes a "paradigm shift" where the old plausibility structure is demolished and the new paradigm of the upside-down Kingdom is embraced.[23]

While these examples are missiological applications of Barth, Darrell

in their struggle against apartheid. Charles Villa-Vicencio, ed., *On Reading Karl Barth in South Africa* (Grand Rapids, MI: Eerdmans, 1988).

21. Hendrik Kraemer, *The Christian Message in a Non-Christian World* (New York: IMC, 1947), 122.
22. Lesslie Newbigin, *Context and Conversion* (London: Church Missionary Society, 1978), 3.
23. Lesslie Newbigin, *Foolishness to the Greeks: The Gospel and Western Culture* (Grand Rapids, MI: Eerdmans, 1986), 148.

Guder has shown that Barth himself is a missional theologian, by stressing that his "theological project is located in the context of the decline of Western Christendom."[24] In his doctrine of reconciliation, Barth makes this post-Christendom context explicit by stressing the importance of mission in Christian vocation. Guder argues that the whole of Barth's doctrine of reconciliation must be read with this missional character in mind. Also, like Kraemer and Newbigin before him, Guder demonstrates the potent relevance of Barth's insights about Christendom and modernity for mission, especially in North America.[25] Again, along with the political side, the missional dimension of Barth's theology as it engages the social and cultural context of post-Christian modernism is often ignored in Barthian studies.[26]

The actualistic perspective looks to the heart of Barth's theological method as it arises out of his doctrine of God. Those approaching Barth's contextuality from the political aspect also note this actualism, but its broader implications are often missed. In his *God's Being Is in Becoming*, Eberhard Jüngel articulates the relationships between God and the world and between God and history, and thereby engages the contextuality question within an ontological framework.[27] Entering a conversation in which Helmut Gollwitzer defends God's objectivity and God's being as "*in-and-for-himself,*" *contra* Rudolf Bultmann's subjectivity of God, Jüngel proposes that in the triune being of God, the divine self is both objective and subjective.[28] In Jüngel's view, in divine revelation, "God's Word is identical with God Himself" or "the *being of God* comes to the word."[29] Therefore, divine objectivity and subjectivity are not antithetical to each other. Yet, God remains God in this event,

24. Darrell Guder, "Mining Barth's Dogmatics for a Missional Ecclesiology," in *Dogmatics after Barth: Facing Challenges in Church, Society and Academy*, ed. Gunter Thomas, Rinse H. Reeling Brouswer and Bruce McCormack (Leipzig: CreateSpace, 2012), 134.
25. See Darrell Guder, ed, *Missional Church: A Vision for the Sending of the Church in North America* (Grand Rapids, MI: Eerdmans, 1998); and Darrell Guder, *The Continuing Conversion of the Church* (Grand Rapids, MI: Eerdmans, 2000).
26. John Flett has also sought to remedy this interpretative error in Barthian studies. See his *The Witness of God: The Trinity,* Missio Dei, *Karl Barth, and the Nature of Christian Community* (Grand Rapids, MI: Eerdmans, 2010).
27. Eberhard Jüngel, *God's Being Is in Becoming: The Trinitarian Being of God in the Theology of Karl Barth* (Grand Rapids, MI: Eerdmans, 2001).
28. Ibid., 1–7.
29. Ibid., 27. Quoting Barth from *CD* I/I, 304.

because "God's presence is always God's decision to be present" and God is "not *obliged* to reveal himself."[30] For revelation to be truly a revelation of God, "God reveals himself as the Lord."[31]

In his connection to history, and thus to particular contexts, this Lord becomes "God to specific men, eternity in a moment."[32] Barth's actualism or actualistic ontology refers to this event nature as "eternity in a moment." Bruce McCormack continues this line of thought and demonstrates that this actualism, genetically with the *Realdialektik,* runs through Barth's whole theological corpus.

Realdialektik as the Logic of Contextuality

McCormack presents a thesis that challenges the last forty years of Barth scholarship in America.[33] Rejecting von Balthasar's widely accepted premise that Barth turned from "dialectic" in his early works to "analogy" in his mature theology, McCormack identifies an "inner dialectic of the *Sache* (the matter)," a *Realdialektick* that is rooted in the nature of God's act, functioning from the beginning of Barth's break from liberalism.[34] This ontic dialectic is "the red thread which runs through the whole of the development, making it to be a unified whole in spite of the differing models of explication employed from one phase to the next."[35] This interpretive proposal is not only of interest for historical study, but has profound implications as well for understanding Barth's contextuality. The consequence of this correction is a Barth who seeks to be "orthodox *under the conditions of modernity,*" so as to be faithful to the gospel in his particular context.[36]

According to McCormack's argument, Barth was consciously engaging in contextual theology, a theology that interacted with the particular context in a reciprocal manner. However, it is at this juncture that we encounter a potential minefield of interpretative

30. Ibid., 31.
31. Ibid., 33.
32. Ibid.
33. McCormack, *Karl Barth's Critically Realistic Dialectical Theology*.
34. Ibid., 6.
35. Ibid., 464.
36. Ibid., 17.

distortions. McCormack concludes that Barth was seeking to be *orthodox*, faithful to the witness of Scripture, in the *modern* context. To speak of Barth's contextuality must not and cannot devolve into a cultural domestication of the gospel, a return to the fleshpots of Egypt.

Barth's dialectical theology began with his break from liberal theology; this took an early form in his *Romans.* While there were various forms of dialectics in Barth's early theology, such as the noetic dialectic of thought-form (*Denkform*) that guided his theological discourse, an ontic dialectic (*Realdialektik*) rooted in God was underlying all of these forms.[37] Because this ontic dialectic is based on the real relations between God and humanity, it is the functional logic of Barth's overall theology. McCormack describes this ontic *Realdialektik* as an actualistic, indirect identity within Barth's doctrine of revelation, which is critical to the whole of Barth's project.[38] The three key elements of this *Realdialektik* as an actualistic, indirect identity are as follows:

First, in revelation, God condescends to make the divine self identical with the creaturely medium. Otherwise, there would be no way for us to know God with our human faculties. It means that God is truly revealed, not just in part, but as a whole. This identity states that God really has revealed the divine self and we are not left to only our experience, mysticism, or atheism. This aspect is a corrective against liberal anthropocentricity.

Second, however, this identity is *indirect*, meaning that the creaturely medium is not divinized or altered into some form of *tertium quid* (a third thing). God is not simply unveiled for all to see. Rather, God's self-revelation is hidden behind the veil of the medium. The

37. Ibid., 5–14. McCormack integrates Michael Beintker's examination of various forms of dialectics in *Romans II* with Eberhard Jüngel's insight into a single turn from liberal theology, along with Ingrid Spieckermann's discovery of a form of analogy in early Barth. The final result is a single unifying thesis about the subterranean *Realdialektik*, which persisted all through Barth's theology after his break from liberalism.

38. McCormack, *Orthodox and Modern*, 109–13. This indirect identity is also what Hunsinger identifies as the Chalcedonian pattern. George Hunsinger, *How to Read Karl Barth: The Shape of His Theology* (Oxford: Oxford University Press, 1991), 185–88. Metzger makes use to this "pattern" as the logic between Word and the world. See Paul Louis Metzger, *The Word of Christ and the World of Culture: Sacred and Secular through the Theology of Karl Barth* (Grand Rapids, MI: Eerdmans, 2003), 54–55.

creaturely medium *in and of itself* cannot contain or mediate God's presence. God is the Subject of revelation. By God's gracious power in unveiling Godself, we receive God's revelation. This aspect critiques the conservative positivism of revelation and tradition.

Third, through this indirect identity, revelation occurs *actualistically* as an event that is wrought by God. God remains the Lord over revelation. At no point does revelation in the creaturely medium become our possession for us to handle under our control. Rather, it ever remains God's gracious gift, to be received again and again. As seen above in Jüngel's analysis, Barth critiques the ontology behind both liberal and conservative positions, both subjective-oriented and objective-oriented ones. It should be noted that Barth's concern with this actualism is not so much the issue of temporal continuity of divine presence, but of divine sovereignty and causality over this indirect identity.[39]

Positively, this actualism, which establishes the event nature of God's act, demands that God be engaged contemporaneously. While God's self-revelation in Christ is the basis of God's contemporary presence, God cannot simply be accessed through past divine actions. Negatively, the reason why God cannot simply be encountered through past divine actions is that God never becomes encapsulated in past events, because *in and of themselves,* they cannot reveal God: *finitum non capax infiniti* (the finite cannot bear the infinite). Every single time God is encountered, it is a fresh miracle of the living God, not some lingering residue in the divine wake. Again, we must not misunderstand this to mean that there cannot be temporal continuity of God's presence. There can be no question of Lessing's ugly ditch, because Christ is risen and not dead.

Realdialektik as actualistic, indirect identity shows us how God's self-revelation occurs, as God becomes an object while remaining the sovereign Subject. More generally, it gives us a way to understand how God is present in the world, working through creaturely media.

39. Joseph L. Mangina, *Karl Barth: Theologian of Christian Witness* (Louisville, KY: Westminster John Knox, 2004), 154.

However, by itself, *Realdialektik* functions like the ordering criterion for contextuality, but it does not provide the basis for affirming a positive engagement with the context. That basis is found in Barth's doctrines of election and reconciliation, which is the topic of the next chapter. For our purposes here, it is important to note that through Barth's innovation in the doctrine of election, there is a real *de jure* participation of all creation in Christ. Of course, this participation is hidden, but Christ is present in creation because of election, and he can summon and unveil any part of it to witness to himself.

Without the *Realdialektik,* Barth would become a contextual theologian without any diastasis, only affirming God's act in the world. Without the implication of election, Barth would be only a theologian of the Word, critiquing a totally lost world, utterly devoid of God's presence.[40]

In the next section, the way that Barth's actualistic insight plays out in his contextuality will be outlined, especially addressing concerns about text and context and about the universality and particularity of theology.

Contextuality as Ordered and Reciprocal Relationality

At its most basic level, contextuality means ordered, reciprocal relationality between the text and the context, working *from above* and *from below.* Barth's doctrine of election provides the basis of just such an interaction between the Word and the world that moves in both directions. Of course, we must immediately add that this basis is rooted in the one event of God's self-revelation in Jesus Christ, which stands at the center of all theological reflection. Moreover, the *Realdialektik,* with its actualistic, indirect identity, works in both directions to maintain

40. For example, in *Models of Contextual Theology,* Bevans misses crucial aspects of Barth's contextuality by presenting it as a modern representative of the praxis model, also known as situational theology, theology of the signs of times, or the liberation model (78). Christocentricism, which grounds the witness of alien "signs" upon God's self-revelation, is altogether missing in this model as well as the diastasis that the *Realdialektik* affirms between context and revelation. Thus, Bevans's description of Barth's work as a "highly contextual theology of the Word of God" lacks substantive content even as it possesses some forms of truth (9). See Stephen B. Bevans, *Models of Contextual Theology,* rev. ed. (Maryknoll, NY: Orbis, 2002).

that no creaturely medium is divinized and that God remains the Subject at all times.

Moving from the text to the context, Barth's dialectical actualism claims the event nature of Scripture and the church. *In and of themselves* as creaturely media, these entities do not and cannot be faithful witnesses to God. However, as they become the locus of God's living presence, God speaks and acts through these media to work in particular situations. Moving from the context to the text, the issues and questions of the context address theology only through the Word, and therefore, indirectly. The world's questions are first counter-questioned by God before they are answered.

This *from above–from below* dynamic, however, must be properly connected to the universality of the church so that it does not result in tribal or advocacy theologies. Therefore, this section will close by describing a way to correctly relate the universal and the particular. All these aspects of contextuality will be summed up using the Reformed motto of *reformata semper reformanda.*

From Above: Double Particularity

Within Barth's understanding, this movement from above can be roughly described as the movement from God revealed in Scripture, to dogmatics, and on to practical theology and ethics. The key point is that through his *Realdialektik*, God's presence, which is essential at every point of this movement, is actualistic. Human beings are at the mercy of the living God, who speaks and acts in the event of revelation. Like manna, God's living presence must be anticipated anew every time, not simply dealt with as a past artifact. In *CD* I/2, Barth poses the unity of biblical, dogmatic and practical theology:

> In biblical theology it is a question of the foundation, in practical theology a question of the form, but in dogmatic theology—in transition from the one to the other—a question of the content of Church preaching, its agreement with the revelation attested in Scripture. These three theological tasks are completely, or almost completely, implicated in each other, so that none can be even correctly seen or defined with the other.[41]

In all three tasks of theology, the *Realdialektik* plays a critical role in controlling their correspondence to God as an event: without God's gracious act, they would utterly fail. As an event, they cannot be made into abstract principles or universal concepts.

Dogmatic theology plays an ancillary task, helping the church to discern a true hearing of God in Scripture. It serves as a transition between "observation" (*explicatio*)" and "assimilation (*applicatio*)."[42] Here, we see that the origin is Scripture and the *telos* is ethics. The contextuality involved in exegesis and ethics is about an awareness of one's situation. In other words, dogmatics is a secondary reflection upon that primary particularity of hearing and obeying God in one's own situation. The contextuality of dogmatics has to do with the use of contemporary words, concepts, and thoughts to explicate the Word for one's own time.

The ground for the contextuality of Scripture is found in the being of Scripture in its becoming, an actualistic view of revelation. This event nature of Scripture brings about a *double particularity*. What this double particularity means can be explained in this way: on the one hand, Scripture is established upon *the particularity of that one event of God's Self-revelation*. This is the first particularity. The unity of Old and New Testament is found in that one event of Christ. In fact, Jesus Christ is the foundation of not only a formal unity, but a material one as well.[43] Scripture is a witness to Jesus Christ, and in that sense, is authoritative.

On the contrary, this Jesus Christ is the living God and does not remain in the past. The resurrected Christ is present with us. In Barth's sacramental view of Scripture, it is the living Christ's presence in the Scripture that makes it the Word of God. Christ's real presence occurs as a result of God's gracious act, and not through some mechanical manner like apostolic historic succession.[44] The point is that the living Christ is never a human possession; rather, his presence is a gracious gift that must be prayed for and received gratefully.[45] In this sense,

41. Barth, *CD* I/2, 766.
42. Ibid.
43. Ibid., 481–85.
44. Barth, *CD* I/1, 95–99.

Scripture is alive as Jesus is alive.[46] This *living Christ in Scripture speaks to our particular* situation. This is the second particularity. In sum, double particularity places contextuality between the *particularity* of revelation in Jesus Christ and the *particularity* of the present time and space.

Barth states "the *Deus dixit* [God has spoken] is present with the Church in its various times and situations".[47] This particularity means "wherever and whenever God speaks to man, its content is a *concretissimum* [most concrete thing]. God always has something specific to say to each man, something that applies to him and to him alone."[48] What is required of us is that we hear the Word of the prophets and apostles and "take it up into our own particular situation, seeing that in Holy Scripture it has, in fact, already entered into our situation".[49]

The *Realdialektik* of actualistic, indirect identity means that the human words of Scripture really do become united with God's presence in whole, not in part. However, this presence is indirectly identified with Christ. At no point is Scripture divinized. The living Word is veiled in human words and must be unveiled by the gracious act of God every single time. This *Realdialektik* is the rubric of the double particularity.

Barth also talks about "a twofold contingency" of Christ's contemporaneity, in which "a contingent *illic et tunc* [there and then]" and "a contingent *hic et nunc* [here and now]" come together as a divinely orchestrated event.[50] It should be noted that this event nature of Scripture does not imply the temporal presence of Christ or the lack thereof. Rather, the point is the miraculous agency of the divine Subject, rather than anything inherent in the text itself.

In terms of practical theology, Barth's view of ethics functions in the same manner of double particularity. The command of God is an event.[51] This just means that it cannot be reduced to a principle. Barth

45. Ibid., 98–99.
46. Ibid., 104.
47. Ibid., 120.
48. Ibid., 140.
49. Barth, *CD* I/2, 699.
50. Barth, *CD* I/1, 149.

argues that casuistry makes God's command into our possession, ignoring its actualism.[52] Just like revelation, theological ethics cannot be reduced to general principles, which lack particularity and definition. The point is to retain and protect God as the Subject; in that way, contextuality is also affirmed.

So, on the one hand, there is the particularity of God who commands and the particularity of the human being who receives his command, revealed in Jesus Christ, as attested in Scripture. In Jesus Christ, we know who the commanding God is and that this God is the God who has created, has reconciled, and will redeem humanity. This God is not "a general or a neutral god."[53] Therefore, the event of God's command is "determined and limited" by the identity of this God.[54] In Jesus Christ, we also know who the human being is who receives God's commands. He "is not a being whose existence has any hope apart from God," but "is the creature of God . . . justified before God, sanctified for him and called to his service."[55] This knowledge of true humanity also makes the encounter when God's command is received "fixed and limited."[56]

On the other hand, there is the particularity of the situation of the receiver. God's commands in Scripture cannot simply be extracted from their immediate context as universal rules.[57] Rather, we must hear God's command in our concrete situation:

> One who here commands is the living, eternally rich God, who is true to Himself even in the fact that He never simply repeats Himself . . . for God every encounter with every man at every historical moments is of sufficient individual importance for Him on His side to encounter man in His command in a unique way, for which there is neither precedence nor recurrence.[58]

Again, this double particularity is rooted in the dynamic of the

51. Barth, *CD* II/2, 548.
52. Barth, *CD* III/4, 10.
53. Karl Barth, *The Christian Life: Church Dogmatics IV, Part 4: Lecture Fragments* (Grand Rapids, MI: Eerdmans, 1981), 6.
54. Ibid., 6.
55. Ibid., 6–7.
56. Ibid., 7.
57. Barth, *CD* III/4, 12.
58. Ibid., 16.

Realdialektik in which God is the Subject, meaning the living God who is with us today.

The contextuality inherent in Barth's view of Scripture and ethics should now be clear. One must actually deal with the living God in a dynamic manner.[59] There can be no complacency when dealing with God. For that reason, Barth actually works grace and prayer into his theology.[60] Engaging with a real living Person means that we open ourselves to a real interaction in our concrete existence. However, this interaction is actually grounded in the concrete revelation of God in Jesus Christ, so there cannot be any questions of abstract subjectivity.

Given different situations, God can and does say different things and his commands require varying responses in different situations. This is Barth's contextuality as it relates to Scripture and ethics. Our concrete situation matters a great deal, but does not function independently, because this contextuality owes its "particularity and concreteness, not to any natural process, fate or chance, but to a particular purpose and disposition of God."[61] In other words, contextuality is a predicate of the living God. This is why Barth's contextuality is not simply about his methodology, but is, rather, at the core of his theology, his knowledge of God.

As God's Word is received in its double particularity, the role of theology is to critique and train us to more faithfully hear and obey God's Word. In this ancillary function, theology has an "essentially 'gymnastic' character."[62] The content of God's living Word

> must be found each time in the middle space between the particular text in the context of the whole Bible and the particular situation of the changing moment. Dogmatics can only be a guide to the right mastery and right adaptability, to right boldness and the right caution, for the given moment when this space has to be found.[63]

59. See Paul T. Nimmo, *Being in Action: The Theological Shape of Barth's Ethical Vision* (New York: T&T Clark, 2007).
60. See Karl Barth, *Evangelical Theology: An Introduction* (Grand Rapids, MI: Eerdmans, 1963), 159–70.
61. Barth, *CD* III/4, 17.
62. Barth, *CD* I/1, 78.
63. Ibid., 79.

Theology must be a commentary on the Word so that one can hear it in its double particularity. Thus, theology cannot replace God's Word, nor can it be mistaken for God's Word. It can only follow God's Word and must continually return to it. In this sense, because theology leaves the realm of the double particularity of divine encounters, by its very nature, it is open to temptation and could "all be in the process of fleeing from the living God."[64]

The significance of tradition must be understood in this regard. The relationship of theology in contextual particularity to the theological reflection of the wider Church, that is, the relationship between the particular and the universal, will be addressed below. Here, we are just commenting on the tradition's relationship to Scripture. While tradition is not binding upon us like Scripture is, the *sanctorum communion* (communion of saints) in the form of the church fathers, the creeds and the confessions, are our teachers when we read Scripture. As such, they have "no independent value and authority beside that of the Word of God."[65] If Scripture alone is the teacher, the church fathers are "the older and more experienced fellow-pupils."[66] Of course, we must not forgot the contextual limitation of these older pupils as well. Nevertheless, we reject their instruction only at our peril, for in learning from them, we avoid being in bondage to the present, and are led to a genuine hearing of the Word of God.[67] We must proceed with the recognition of this kind of ecclesial authority, which is based on Scripture.

To be faithful to God's self-revelation, dogmatics must be a *theologia viatorum* (theology of pilgrims), continually returning to the Word attested in Scripture. All of its conclusions must remain provisional, open to the criticism of the Word. It can only be faithful by God's grace. Pure doctrine is also an event determined by God as the Subject.[68] This

64. Karl Barth, *Evangelical Theology*, 141.
65. Barth, *CD* I/2, 828.
66. Ibid., 607. Walls argues that the transmission of Christianity is more serial through various contexts than it is one continual tradition in a single context. This idea limits how much the church fathers should be considered as "older and more experienced" since this older wisdom might not apply across the board in other contexts. See Andrew Walls, *The Cross-Cultural Process in Christian History: Studies in the Transmission and Appropriation of Faith* (Maryknoll, NY: Orbis, 2002).
67. Barth, *CD* I/2, 607.

actualism means that the task of dogmatics is not just a repetition of past articulations, but a creative and contemporary work.[69] Theology is the task of "the teaching Church of to-day" and cannot be timeless.[70] Just as God is a living God, theology is the task of the living church, not a dead one.[71]

Here, we once again encounter Barth's contextuality. Theology must speak in the contemporary vernacular. It cannot be content simply to rehash the historic confessions and creeds. In this light, the role of philosophy is granted and acknowledged to be necessary, as long as dogmatics understands that philosophy is only a servant and not the master.[72] "Full use of human words, phrases, sequences of thought and logical construction" are required for the integrity of doctrine.[73]

For Barth, a theologian "does not deny, nor is he ashamed of, his indebtedness to a particular philosophy or ontology, to ways of thought and speech."[74] The critical point is, first, that the theologian is "aware of his condition" with its philosophical presuppositions.[75] Second, a theologian must be "ready to submit the coherence of his concepts and formulations to the coherence of the divine revelation and not conversely."[76] Thus, a faithful theologian is "a philosopher 'as though he were not,' and he has his ontology 'as though he had it not.' . . . His ontology will be subject to criticism and control by his theology, and not conversely."[77] The point is that the subject matter remains constant as Jesus Christ and not philosophical systems, which are merely means or tools. Barth also notes that it is not necessary for the theologian to "feel obligated to the philosophical *kairos*, the latest prevailing philosophy."[78] So the emphasis is generally placed on

68. Ibid., 768.
69. Ibid., 779.
70. Ibid., 839.
71. Ibid., 850.
72. Ibid., 775–78.
73. Ibid., 778.
74. Karl Barth, "The Gift of Freedom," in *The Humanity of God*, 92.
75. Ibid.
76. Ibid.
77. Ibid.
78. Ibid.

speaking and thinking in the vernacular, not on following the latest philosophical fad.

The *Realdialektik*, as the inner logic of the *Sache* (the matter), serves as an example of what Barth had in mind. God's Word has a logic of its own that philosophy must submit to if it is to be a servant and not a lord of theology. This means that theology often moves in a paradoxical or dialectical manner that is counter-intuitive, rather than in a straightforward, logical one. The science of theology still retains the mystery of God. Again, we are back to the indirectness of the *Realdialektik* that cannot be penetrated without the actualism, the event of God's gracious act.

This particular use of philosophy under the coherence of theology is a significant aspect of Barth's contextuality. As a provisional and vernacular enterprise, theology is a contemporary work that is done in a particular situation using the intellectual tools of the times. This contextuality is why Barth can be described as both "orthodox and modern" or "orthodox *under the conditions of modernity*," as stated above.[79] With the use of "Kant's epistemology and (later) Hegelian ontology," Barth felt free to reconstruct a Christian orthodoxy that was true to the spirit of the confessional tradition but not to its letter.[80] Barth's theology was old orthodox content in new modern formulations.

At the most general and formal level, Barth was consciously both a theologian and a modern man, like Schleiermacher.[81] Of course, the crucial difference between these two theologians is the relationship of the two descriptions in their works. But the issue of contextuality, of being both orthodox and modern, might be the reason why Barth found Schleiermacher so fascinating. In 1968, the year of his death, Barth started a colloquium on the church fathers of the nineteenth century by means of Schleiermacher's *Speeches*.[82] Even to the very end

79. McCormack, *Orthodox and Modern*, 17.
80. Ibid.
81. Barth describes Schleiermacher as "a theologian" and "a modern man with all his heart, with all his feelings, and with all his strength" (Karl Barth, *Protestant Theology in the Nineteenth Century*, New ed. [London: SCM, 2001], 420).
82. Busch, *Karl Barth*, 493.

of his life, Schleiermacher was still with Barth. Like Barth, Schleiermacher understood theology to be "the science which systematizes the doctrine prevalent in a Christian Church at a given time."[83] McCormack argues that the continuity between these two church fathers is that they both were "able to combine academic rigor with ecclesial concern in the setting of [modernity]."[84]

Having outlined the contours of Barth's contextuality *from above* regarding God's Word in Scripture and doctrine, we now address the movement *from below*, arising out of the context.

From Below: God's Counter-Questions

Barth's contextuality shows that concerns *from below* are also a part of the theological task. In *CD* IV/2, Barth notes that in affirming the movement *from below*, he was addressing the concern of Roman Catholics and Pietists.[85] Here, Barth unpacks the doctrine of reconciliation, reasserting the moves that he first made in his doctrine of election. By including humanity within God, Barth finds a way to affirm the movement *from below*, from context to text, from situation to theology. Barth's ordering of Gospel-Law serves as a guide to how he can have a version of a "method of correlation" where the questions from the world are examined. The concerns of continuity, the point of contact, and natural theology will be clarified here as well.

McCormack claims that "Barth was not altogether lacking in what Tillich called a 'method of correlation,'" with the major difference being that Tillich's was founded upon "the Lutheran understanding of the relation of law and gospel, while Barth's was erected on the soil of a Reformed view of the priority of gospel over law."[86] The genesis of gospel-law ordering comes from Barth's 1935 lecture, "Gospel and Law," when he returned to visit Germany from Switzerland, a couple of

83. Friedrich Schleiermacher from *The Christian Life* as quoted by McCormack in his essay, "What has Basel to do with Berlin?," in *Orthodox and Modern*, 76 (Friedrich Schleiermacher, *The Christian Life*, 2nd ed. [Philadelphia, PA: Fortress Press, 1976]).
84. Ibid., 88.
85. Barth, *CD* IV/2, 392.
86. McCormack, *Karl Barth's Critically Realistic Dialectical Theology*, 27n57.

months after he had been dismissed from Bonn for refusing loyalty to the Führer.[87]

In his lecture, Barth laid "a radical criticism of the German Christians and their doctrine of 'the law of the people'" by reversing the traditional order of law-gospel in Luther and Lutheranism.[88] This new ordering has support in Calvin's view of the third use of the law as "the principle use"[89] and his view of the unity of covenants in "substance and reality."[90] However, its precise formulation is Barth's own; he uses Reformed logic to reframe a Lutheran category. The core concept is this:

> The Gospel is not Law, just as Law is not Gospel; but because the Law is in the Gospel, from the Gospel and points to the Gospel, we must first of all know about the Gospel in order to know about the Law, and not vice versa.[91]

A year earlier, in 1934, Barth had replied to Brunner, "*Nein!*" regarding natural theology. Both of these texts must be read as Barth's theological clarifications as they relate to the political context of his day, which was the German Church's struggle with the state.

Natural theology, the *analogia entis*, the point of contact, creation-reconciliation continuity, and law-gospel order all are different ways of posing the same issue—the movement *from below*. On one level, Barth's response is a simple No and his reasons are found in the *Realdialektik*, the heart of his theology. Thus, there cannot be a question of his negative response being contextual or politically driven.

All of the above concepts of natural theology assume that because of God's past action, that is, creation or lawgiving, God is now directly available to us, as our possession and at our disposal. Brunner states that "In creation the spirit of the creator is in some way

87. Busch, *Karl Barth*, 266.
88. Ibid.
89. John Calvin, *Institutes of the Christian Religion*, Library of Christian Classics 20–21 (Philadelphia, PA: Westminster, 1960), 2.7.12. Simply put, the third use of the law is as a guide to the grateful and joyous obedience of a Christian who has been saved through faith apart from works.
90. Calvin, *Institutes*, 2.10.2.
91. "Gospel and Law," in Karl Barth, *Community, State and Church* (Garden City: Anchor Books, 1960), 72.

recognizable."[92] Creaturely media *in and of themselves*, apart from God's act, provide us with divine presence. This givenness of God's presence in the creaturely medium is what Barth is protesting, because God is now made into a predicate of the medium. The decisive aspects of the dialectic are indirectness and actualism.

Barth's response begins with a technical definition of natural theology as a "*formulation of a system* . . . whose *subject* differs fundamentally from the revelation in Jesus Christ and whose *method* therefore differs equally from the exposition of Holy Scripture.[93] Barth precisely condemns such independence, according to which God is not the Subject of revelation. Such abstraction leads to a domestication of the gospel, whereby God must fit into our given categories, and thus, become our own projection rather than being the true God revealed in Jesus Christ. Barth would argue that because not only our will, but our minds are in bondage to sin and rebellion, humanity is totally lost, blind, and dead, apart from God's work in Christ.

However, Barth's rejection is nuanced and enables a movement *from below* within the bounds of revelation. Just how this movement is possible is clarified in his doctrine of election. Hidden in the Barth's No is the Yes of the priority of Jesus Christ and the inclusion of all creation in Christ. Although some have argued that Barth engages in natural theology while denying it, this is a misreading, because natural theology by Barth's definition is abstract and independent from revelation. If it is reemployed within revelation, it ceases to be "natural." Thus, God must be affirmed as the Subject of any movement *from below*. This point is fundamental to Barth's version of the "method of correlation."

Natural theology cannot exist independently as a given alongside revealed theology, but must be replaced by a theology of creation that exists as the external basis of the covenant.[94] The *analogia fidei* (analogy of faith) that presupposed faith in God's self-revelation replaces the *analogia entis* (analogy of being).[95] Only retrospectively through the

92. Karl Barth and Emil Brunner, *Natural Theology* (London: The Centenary, 1946), 24.
93. Ibid., 74–75.
94. Barth, *CD* III/1, 94.

eyes of faith is God's presence evident in the world. Thus, there is a point of contact, but it is the one that God creates miraculously *ex nihilo*.[96] This is the continuity that overcomes the radical discontinuity that exists between God and humanity as sin and rebellion. Also, the gospel-law ordering means that God's work must be presupposed in order for true knowledge of the law and of the world to be received.

Given these features, Barth's rendition of a "method of correlation" might look like this: First, the world poses its questions to God. These questions are taken seriously, regardless of how godless or disreputable the source is, because Christ has *de jure* united himself with the world. Christ can freely make these questions *de facto* witnesses to himself:

> For we must not forget that, while man may deny God, according to the Word of reconciliation God does not deny man. Man may be hostile to the Gospel of God, but this Gospel is not hostile to him. The fact that he is closed to it does not alter the further fact that it is open for him. Nor does the fact that he does not recognise the sovereignty of Jesus Christ, and if he did would perhaps rebel against it in his autonomy, result in its losing any of its validity even in relation to him.[97]

Second, God counter-questions the world's questions. This is an issue of preceding coherence. In order for a question to be properly theological, truly addressing the living God revealed in Christ, it must already presuppose divine revelation. The question must be delimited by God's answer:

> The Word of God cannot be the object of genuine questioning. On the contrary, it is the Subject which puts the only genuine question which can arise in this respect, namely, whether and to what extent its reception by those to whom it comes is true reception, a reception which corresponds to its declarations, and therefore the only reception which can be seriously called reasonable.[98]

95. Barth, *CD* I/1, 243–44.
96. Ibid., 239–40.
97. Barth, *CD* IV/3.1, 119.
98. Ibid., 161.

Third, God answers this question in Jesus Christ. Christ is the answer to the world's questions as they have been reframed by God. In Christ, the world sees the extent of its problems and the radical questions that underlie its inhabitants' stated questions. In Christ, the world finds the answer it did not know it was looking for, but which it truly needs for its very existence.

Since so much of Barth's dialogues and engagements are indirect or subterranean, it is hard to see this threefold movement occurring. Of course, this indirectness does not mean unawareness. For example, in *CD* IV/1, Barth notes that throughout it, he was involved in "an intensive, although for the most part quiet, debate with Rudolf Bultmann. His name is not mentioned often. But his subject is always present."[99] So, this kind of correlation could be happening indirectly, but nevertheless, very intentionally.

At this point, we offer as an example Barth's engagement with Feuerbach in *CD* IV/3. Barth takes up Ludwig Feuerbach's question of whether God is simply an outward projection of humanity's inward nature as it relates to Christ's prophetic work in us.[100] Barth takes Feuerbach's question seriously and seeks an answer for it. However, Barth is aware that in his attempt to answer this question, he can "deny the very thing which [he is] seeking to prove, falling victim to Feuerbach in [his] very attempt to resist him."[101]

The vaccine, which gives Barth immunity, is his recognition that Feuerbach, along with all humanity, is "quite unfitted to play the role of questioner."[102] Feuerbach's question cannot stand because he, along with all humanity, has no rights, authority, or basis upon which he can question God's Word. God does not answer Feuerbach's question, but rather, counter-questions him:

> But the point is that the question is put to us. It is not that we ourselves have the competence, or find ourselves in such a position in relation to Christ that we can and even must ask concerning the light of His life and

99. Barth, *CD* IV/1, ix.
100. Barth, *CD* IV/3.1, 72.
101. Ibid.
102. Ibid., 73.

> the Word of His act. But as His life is light and His act Word, as He is the truth, we are asked by Him whether we are aware of the fact, whether we realise what we are doing when we presuppose and assert that it is so, whether we know the basis and authority necessary to legitimate our action if it is not to be futile.[103]

But neither Feuerbach nor anyone can answer God's counter-questions. In questioning us, God shows that he is not like any other object within our control, but rather, is the acting Subject, who is Lord over us.[104]

Through this question/counter-question/answer interaction, Barth shows himself to be a biblical theologian who is also a contextual theologian. There is no question about the clear precedence of revelation over any contextual concerns. Just as in Barth's double particularity regarding Scripture, in which God's contemporaneous event is grounded in that one event of God's self-revelation, Barth's contextuality here lies in his version of a "method of correlation" which is framed and bound by the Word. However, within these limits, the contextual concerns do remain important. While the content of theology is not determined by these questions, in God's counter-questions, these questions are truly addressed. Theology responds to them, based upon the inner logic of its own Subject matter. In this response, the context impacts theology. That is why this movement is truly *from below*, because God as the sovereign Lord still condescends to engage with the question.[105]

Can the context ever become a source for theology? The answer is yes. Barth's contextuality affirms the possibility of content *from below* but never independently, apart from Jesus Christ as attested in Scripture. How the context is positively taken up in theology is addressed in depth in the next chapter. However, we will provide a short summary here for the sake of explicating the contextual logic.

103. Ibid., 76.
104. Ibid., 79.
105. Thinking along the similar lines, Torrance argues that a christological version of natural theology can be developed within a Barthian framework. For Torrance, Barth's theology is a part of the "interactionist" tradition in which God interacts closely with the world of nature and human history without being confused with it (Thomas F. Torrance, *Karl Barth, Biblical and Evangelical Theologian* [Edinburgh: T&T Clark, 1990], 136–49).

Positively, because of universal election, Christ can commandeer worldly witnesses to point to himself. These "true words" or "parables of the kingdom" are extraordinary and free communications beyond the normative witness of the Bible and the Church.[106] But, we must not mistake them for some outlying anomalies. In fact, the community of the Word "not only may but must accept the fact that there are such words and that it must hear them too, notwithstanding its life by this one Word and its commission to preach it."[107]

On the basis of the eternal election of God, all creation is now in Christ. This critical point is a corollary to Barth's innovation in the doctrine of election, as we will explore in depth in the next chapter. Therefore Christ can—and does—summon creation to witness to His truth for the sake of the church.[108] We can also hear "the voice of the Good Shepherd even there."[109]

This witnessing function has nothing at all to do with the inherent worth or power of these worldly elements. In fact, we should not be deceived by their appearances. Christ might use the publican as a true witness, whereas the Pharisee might only be promoting a culturally domesticated gospel, and therefore, be a false witness. These other words might come

> not only in so-called heathen territories not yet opened to missions, nor only—as we must say with qualification—in Eastern peoples now overrun by an avowedly atheistic culture, education, psychology and ethics, but also in the greatest proximity to the Christian Churches–a proximity which may contain within itself the greatest inward distance.[110]

We can see that this affirmation of other words concerns "the capacity of Jesus Christ" to create them; therefore, we "may thus expect, and count upon it."[111] Because of this christological basis, we "must be

106. Barth, *CD* IV/3.1, 114.
107. Ibid., 115.
108. Ibid.
109. Ibid., 117.
110. Ibid., 119.
111. Ibid., 118.

prepared to hear" and receive these other words as the true words of Christ.[112]

Yet, critically, the function of these other words must be clear. They must point to the Word as attested in Scripture. The purpose of these other words is to aid theology to be faithful in its particular context. The issue again is contextuality:

> Words of this kind cannot be such as overlook or even lead away from the Bible. They can only be those which, in material agreement with it, illumine, accentuate or explain the biblical witness in a particular time and situation, thus confirming it in the deepest sense by helping to make it sure and concretely evident and certain.[113]

Of course, these other words must be tested by Scripture, the confessions, their fruits, and their significance for the life of the church.[114] They will only speak to certain individuals within the church and can have no universal relevance.[115] They cannot be canonized to form another scripture.[116] Ultimately, it is possible that we can be deceived and "[confuse] the voice of a stranger with His voice."[117] However, that possibility of false witness exists within the church as well.[118] These other words function according to the logic of actualistic indirect identity, like all other creaturely media, such as Scripture and the church, that God uses for divine purposes.

We see that there is freedom for contextuality, for a movement *from below* if the movement *from above* is already presupposed. However, within this presupposition, there is real freedom for worldly witnesses.

Universal-Particular Dynamic

There is a danger in the idea of double particularity, the contextuality existing between the particularity of revelation and the particularity

112. Ibid., 124.
113. Ibid., 115.
114. Ibid., 125–30.
115. Ibid., 132.
116. Ibid., 133.
117. Ibid.
118. Ibid., 121.

of the situation. In order for any theology in its particularity not to degrade into a tribal theology, thereby merely advancing the selfish agendas of particular groups, it must be integrally related to the larger tradition that transcends a particular situation. What is the relationship between the theological reflection of a community in a concrete setting and the corporate theology of the church universal, especially if the Western tradition is recognized for what it actually is—one particular theological tradition among many?

Put another way, this universal-particular dynamic can be summarized in two phrases: *The universal must be mediated in the particular* and *the particular must be in service to the universal.*[119] On the one hand, *the universal must be mediated in the particular* means that God chooses to communicate his universal message through the mediation of a particular manifestation. There is no *a*cultural, pure, unadulterated gospel. All Christianity is mediated through cultures, and all theology is contextual.

As we explicated above, within Barth's theology, the idea of double particularity shows this mediation of the universal through the particular. In Barth's doctrine, the Trinity and election come together such that the eternal God of the universe takes up time into himself to become a particular man in history without losing the divine self.[120] Also, in terms of the task of theology, divine revelation is always mediated in a particular context.

Moreover, in his ecumenical involvement, Barth affirms the church's historical concreteness in specific localities and in the diversity of theological reflections that results from this concreteness.[121] This aspect of Barth's theology will be taken up again

119. In a similar fashion, Andrew Walls proposes two concepts that highlight how the gospel lives in tension with the host culture. The *indigenous principle* states the need for contextualization, for the gospel to feel at home in a particular context. The *pilgrim principle*, on the contrary, points to the constant Reformed (or reforming) dimension that counters the indigenous principle and connects each incarnation of the gospel with the universal faith community (Andrew F. Walls, *The Missionary Movement in Christian History: Studies in the Transmission of Faith* [Maryknoll, NY: Orbis, 1996], 7–8).

120. Of course, technically speaking, the issue is not simply mediation, but the fact that God becomes human. To be sure, there is no pure universal God behind the particular Jesus Christ. This was Jüngel's point in *God's Being is in Becoming*. Barth's essay, "Humanity of God," also stresses this insight (Karl Barth, *The Humanity of God*).

in chapter 4's discussion of contextual ecclesiology. Here, we simply note that Barth did not believe in some sort of unifying universality that can be achieved by rejecting particularities.

On the contrary, that *the particular must be in the service of the universal* implies that no contextual theology can become isolated unto itself or claim a privileged position over others. No theology can have a specific claim upon God. All expressions of the gospel in the end must be in service to the one, holy, Catholic, and apostolic church. Theology must not be a merely self-serving, tribal theology like the German Christianity of the Third Reich.

Referring back to his ecumenical work, Barth also warned that the particularities can become shameful divisions, which reflect "a plurality of lords, a plurality of spirits, a plurality of gods."[122] Rather, the same gospel must reside "in all places, in all ages, within all societies, and in relation to all its members."[123] Furthermore, Barth calls the churches to take their theological particularities seriously, but to continue to engage the Word of God, and thus, move toward true unity in Jesus Christ.[124]

We will continue to explore this dynamic between the universal and the particular in our discussion of the nature of the Reformed confessions below.

Theologia Reformata Semper Reformanda Secundum Verbum Dei

All the above dimensions of contextuality can be summarized within the nature of Reformed theology and Reformed creeds as Barth understood them.[125] After the success of *Romans II*, Barth was invited to be the honorary professor of Reformed theology at Göttingen, where he became "a confessional Reformed Christian" in reality, not just

121. Karl Barth, *The Church and the Churches* (Grand Rapids, MI: Eerdmans, 1936).
122. Barth, *CD* IV/1, 675.
123. Ibid., 707.
124. Ibid., 684.
125. Karl Barth, *The Theology of the Reformed Confessions* (Louisville, KY: Westminster John Knox, 2002); and Karl Barth, "The Desirability and Possibility of A Universal Reformed Creed," in *Theology and Church: Shorter Writings 1920-1928* (New York: Harper and Row, 1962), 112–35.

a nominally Reformed one.[126] Barth's Reformed stance in his overall theological outlook as well as in various doctrines is well known, such as the priority of gospel over law, the preeminence of the doctrine of election, and aspects of his Christology.

Barth, however, was not an orthodox Calvinist.[127] In fact, he sought to write his *Dogmatics* beyond the confines of any one tradition.[128] According to Barth's definition, Calvinists were not truly Reformed because the Reformed tradition is a tradition in perpetual transition. The Reformed motto of the church as *ecclesia reformata semper reformanda secundum verbum Dei* (The church reformed, always reforming according to the Word of God) correspondingly points to the nature of theology as being continually reformed by the Word of God.

Although Barth is describing the Reformed creeds, his insights regarding them summarize well his own understanding of contextuality.[129] The "sharp dialectic curve" in the components of the Reformed creeds

> concerns not conceptions of faith, but dogma; yet fundamentally variable, fluid dogma. Universal Christian truth; yet truth understood now and here in a specific way and expressed by *one* Christian community. A definite and specific Church, sure of its truth, "a Church of possessors" (*ecclesia possidentium*), but a Church which precisely as possessing is completely "a school of seekers" (*schola quaerentium*). It is the eternal revelation of God; but revelation and eternal only in the moment in which it is known as such through God himself.[130]

Here, we stress two elements that resonate with the ideas that we have presented above. First, Barth states that the Reformed creeds concern "fluid dogma." These confession are dogma, "insight for the time, given by God," a *tertium quid* other than the unchangeable Word of God or mere human opinions.[131] Put differently, these confessions

126. Ibid., viii.
127. Busch, *Karl Barth*, 211.
128. Ibid., 211. More specifically, Busch notes Barth's ecumenical intention to incorporate insights from Lutheranism, pietism, and Anglo-Saxon churches in his threefold doctrine of reconciliation with justification, sanctification, and vocation (Busch, *Karl Barth*, 338).
129. Barth's view here also serves as the framework for how he approached the Barmen Declaration (Barth, *Reformed Confessions*, ix).
130. Ibid., 119–20.

are about eternal revelation in the moment. Double particularity and counter-questions of contextuality are covered here. Because God is alive and speaking even now, we must return to Scripture and attend to God's voice where we are. Also, this voice is the voice of the sovereign Lord that answers our questions by radically questioning our presuppositions. In this sense, theology is "in flux" or in "recurring renewal."[132]

This continual reform stems from the acknowledgment of our sinful, human, and contextual limitations. Within the Reformed tradition, although ecumenical councils and synods of the past provided a wealth of wisdom, they were still human and capable of error.[133] There is only one authority, and that is the Bible. Tradition can, at best, only serve as a guide to this one authority. Thus, there has never been a one once-and-for-all Reformed confession that has been applied worldwide.[134] In a sense, the very writing of confessions admits that all theology is contextual for a particular time and place.

Within this understanding of the Reformed tradition, Calvinism could be a serious misnomer for the Reformed tradition. Having a set of theological material that must be accepted without critique is dangerous because this material can be distorted and domesticated. Moreover, such historic material would not be able to address the new challenges that the church faces. For example, holding Calvin's *Institutes* or *Westminster Standards* as one's sole confession, which many conservative Presbyterians do, is anomalous to the logic of the Reformed tradition, which eschews any single and timeless authority, apart from the Bible.

Barth argues that this continuously reforming aspect is what separates the Reformed tradition from the Lutheran one. For the Lutherans, the *Book of Concord* represents the "canon with the canon" of Scripture. This standard functions alongside the Bible to help interpret

131. Ibid., 114.
132. Ibid., 115.
133. Ibid., 19.
134. Barth, "Universal Reformed Creed," 121–23.

it and also to summarize it.[135] What Barth articulates on this matter leads us into the significance the Reformed view of Scripture:

> One has called the Reformed church the church of the *formal* principle of the Reformation, the principle of Scripture; in contrast, the Lutheran church has been called the church of the material principle, the doctrine of the justification. . . . The Reformed confession stresses that it is *only* form and vessel of this content and does *not* claim as its own the content itself.[136]

Scripture stands by itself, "neither to be repeated nor to be continued."[137] With this view of Scripture, there cannot be a theological statement that possesses any sort of perpetually binding authority. All theological reflection is relative and tentative and its function is that of a witness, confessing what it does not possess but only believes.[138] This strange paradox affirms, and at the same time, marginalizes theology as a task of the church.

Second, Barth describes the confessions as the "voice of the universal church, now and here" in a particular community. In a Reformed sense, each of these particular communities speaks as "the voice of the One Holy Church."[139] Yet, they do so at a particular place and time of "here, now"[140] This dialectic points right to the idea of how *the universal must be mediated in the particular* and *the particularity must be in service of the universal.* What we mean by theology that is contextual is not just that it advocates as the voice of a partisan community, but rather, that it is a particular reflection of the truth of the "One Holy Church."

Here, we pause to ask if Barth is naïve about the colonialist forces and systemic power dynamics in the global theological community. How are we to address the problems that arise from the hegemony of Western theology proclaimed as universal theology? What about the

135. Barth, *Reformed Confessions*, 3.
136. Ibid., 39.
137. Ibid.
138. Ibid., 38.
139. Barth, "Universal Reformed Creed," 114.
140. Ibid., 116.

corresponding problem of non-Western theologies being relegated to the status of merely perspectival theologies?

Given that contextual theology, especially in the form of liberation theologies that were acutely aware of their contexts, did not come on the scene until the 1970s, after his death, Barth simply does not confront those issues adequately.[141] Moreover, whatever contextual theologies Barth did see, he was very critical of, because they failed *to be in service of the universal.*[142] In other words, they became captive to their context, which became their lord, and violated the "first commandment as an axiom of theology."[143]

Perhaps to understand the struggle that non-Western theologies endured to actually speak as "the voice of the One Holy Church," we can look to Jürgen Moltmann's insights. Moltmann postulates the three processes of all non-Western contextual theology in this way: *Separation* from the dominant Western tradition, finding *identity* within its unique voice and concerns, and a future *integration* with the rest of the global tradition.[144] Due to the vestiges of colonialism, these theologies might very well have to take such a circuitous path to properly reflect the voice of the One Holy Church.

Moving forward, we note that Barth understood these Reformed confessions' practical significance "as a definition of the community for those outside, and as a directive for its own teaching and life for those within."[145] As we move to our last section of the levels of Asian American theological reflection, the practical import of theology's contextuality will be in the forefront of our discussion.

141. It should be noted that given his socialist stance, Barth did support his own version of "God's preferential option for the poor" (Barth, *CD* II/1, 386).

142. Busch, *Great Passion*, 71.

143. Karl Barth, "The First Commandment as the Axiom of Theology," in *The Way of Theology in Karl Barth: Essays and Comments*, ed. H. Martin Rumscheidt (Allison Park, PA: Pickwick, 1986), 63–78.

144. Jürgen Moltmann, *Experiences in Theology: Ways and Forms of Christian Theology* (Minneapolis, MN: Fortress Press, 2000), 269.

145. Barth, "Universal Reformed Creed," 117.

Three Levels of Asian American Theological Reflection

The last section summarized Barth's actualism in terms of *double particularity, divine counter-questions,* and the *universal-particular dynamic.* This section presents three levels of Asian American theological reflection—namely, the methodological, ecclesial, and personal levels of engaging the Asian American context.

From the side of revelation, the idea of actualism and the event nature of God's encounter with us serve as the basis of these different levels. From the contextual side, the dynamism and complexity of Asian American contexts requires these different levels as well. These three levels are related as concentric circles, with the outer methodological level encompassing the other two, and the ecclesial level nesting the personal level at the core.

Many Asian American theological works deal with all these levels without distinguishing between them, talking about the personal history of the author, the struggles of the community, and methodological assertions all together. The problem with this lack of distinction is the essentializing, stereotyping, and ethnic monopolizing that inevitably occurs. For example, the problem begins with calling a theological work "Asian American" in the first place. The many prominent so-called Asian American works are those by authors of East Asian heritages, and thus, the situations and struggles of Southeast and South Asians are ignored.[146] By distinguishing the place and the role of the proposed three levels of theological reflection, our goal is to clarify the ways these theologies will actually function in the life of the church, not merely in academic presentations. The questions that drive our agenda address the role of theology in the life of the community and in the lives of individual Christians. Thus, we delve into practical theology methods, incorporating those insights into the development of Asian American theologies.

146. See how Jung Young Lee and Sang Hyun Lee have no sense of Southeast or South Asian contexts. Jung Young Lee, *Marginality: The Key to Multicultural Theology* (Minneapolis, MN: Fortress Press, 1995); and Sang Hyun Lee, *From a Liminal Place: An Asian American Theology* (Minneapolis, MN: Fortress Press, 2010).

All that we have discussed in the last section about contextuality must be incorporated here, to avoid various captivities as well as an abstract universality. This means that at each of these three levels, we are engaged in three key tasks: knowing the context, critically engaging with the context, and remaining in communion with the one universal church.

The Methodological Level

In a technical sense, *Asian* American theology mostly resides at a general methodological level. *Asian* American cannot serve as a term for what actually is a *Korean* American or *Chinese* American theology; otherwise, we risk falling into crude and inaccurate stereotypes, such as "Eastern" versus "Western" values. As we have argued in the last chapter, the idea of "Asian America" is such a broad category that without the AAQ, we would not be able to even accept it as a single context.

As a methodological reflection, Asian American theology at this level stresses its "essentially 'gymnastic' character."[147] In that sense, we can describe its three key tasks: knowing the context, engaging with the context, and remaining in communion with the one universal church. First, we begin with knowing the context. We always encounter God in our particular situations, but we cannot assume that we are fully aware of just what that means. What exactly is this situation in which we find ourselves? Deciphering our context is in itself part of the theological task and cannot simply be assumed, especially in light of the dangers of cultural captivity.

This is where developments in the discipline of practical theology have been useful. In many ways, this discipline is another form of contextual theology, with its focus on praxis and on concrete situations. According to Don Browning, practical theology is a "critical reflection on the church's dialogue with Christian sources and other communities of experience and interpretation with the aim of guiding

147. Barth, *CD* I/1, 78.

its action toward social and individual transformation."[148] Browning proposes that "theology as a whole is fundamental practical theology and that it has within it four sub-movements of *descriptive theology, historical theology, systematic theology,* and *strategic practical theology.*"[149] This theological circle goes from praxis to theory, back to praxis. What Browning calls descriptive theology is vital for doing theology with contextuality in mind. In that sense, it is a critical part of any kind of theology.

Knowing the context, or descriptive theology, is a process of conscientization, that is, becoming critically conscious of the context. Paulo Freire stresses how important it is to name the world in order to change it.[150] At this methodological level, the goal is to present the AAQ, thus providing the categories and the language to become conscious of our world. These categories and concepts are given to Asian Americans as provisional, heuristic or investigative tools for the purpose of naming their lived experience.

As practical theologians point out, this step of knowing the context is only one step in a larger hermeneutical loop or spiral that involves other tasks. The loop or the spiral can be entered at any moment of the praxis–theory–praxis movement. Also, this conscientization process importantly complements Barth's idea of starting over and over again, beginning with God's Word, because this process makes one aware of the cultural and contextual captivities.

Second, knowing the context leads to critically and constructively engaging with the context. What are the questions that the context poses for the gospel, and what are God's counter-questions that bring about a paradigm shift in how we perceive and respond back to the context? The grammar of reconciliation in the next chapter will more

148. Don Browning, *Fundamental Practical Theology: Descriptive and Strategic Proposals* (Minneapolis, MN: Augsburg Fortress Press, 1991), 36.

149. Ibid., 8. Other practical theologians such as Heitink, Anderson and Groome, all in their own ways incorporate these sub-movements in their models. See Gerben Heitink, *Practical Theology: History, Theory, Action Domains* (Grand Rapids, MI: Eerdmans, 1999); Ray S. Anderson, *The Shape of Practical Theology: Empowering Ministry with Theological Praxis* (Downers Grove, IL: IVP Academic, 2001); Thomas H. Groome, *Sharing Faith: A Comprehensive Approach to Religious Education and Pastoral Ministry The Way of Shared Praxis* (San Francisco, CA: Harper San Francisco, 1991).

150. Paulo Freire, *Pedagogy of the Oppressed,* 30th anniversary ed. (New York: Continuum, 2002), 88.

specifically describe what this gospel paradigm looks like and how it works, but the important thing to note here is that engaging with the context means reading Scripture in light of what God is doing in that context. In this regard, Ray Anderson offers the idea of Christopraxis, "the continuation of Christ's own ministry of revelation and reconciliation" in the community of Christ through the power of the Spirit.[151] Contextual discernment comes not in isolated study of Scripture, but

> through participation in the work of God in such a way that accountability for the judgments made in ministry situations are congruent with Christ's own purpose as he stands within the situation and acts through and with us.[152]

Various constructive experiments and creative proposals for engaging with the context serve as a part of this hermeneutical process. Again, God is the living and sovereign Lord of the context as well as of revelation.

Third, all this must be done in communion with the one universal church in its historic, geographic, and cultural diversity. Communion in terms of biblical *koinonia* means fellowship and partnership. On the one hand, this means speaking in the voice of the One Holy Church, as Barth stated. The gospel, to which Asian American theology witnesses, must be the good news for all people, not just for Asian Americans. In other words, the one universal gospel encounters an Asian American context, not an Asian American gospel.

On the other hand, this gospel witness must be open to a critical engagement with the wider community of Christ, historically, geographically and culturally. If Asian American critical reflection diverges from what is considered as orthodoxy by this wider community of Christ, it must give an account according to God's revelation. Of course, the idea of actualism could justify the notion of God speaking something unique in the Asian American context, but that word still must witness to the God revealed in Scripture, the

151. Anderson, *The Shape of Practical Theology*, 54.
152. Ibid., 53.

God who is the Father of all. We should remember that there is a responsibility for Asian American theological reflection, along with the reflections of all other theologies, to stretch and contribute to global theology for its edification as well.

Asian American theological reflection at this methodological level, like this present work, exists to serve concrete theology at the ecclesial and personal levels.

The Ecclesial Level

The contextual complexity and diversity of double particularity is addressed by the particularities at the ecclesial and personal levels. Because chapter 4 discusses further Asian American ecclesiology, our discussion here will be brief.

At the ecclesial level, the AAQ finds a particular expression based on ethnicity, generation, and geographic location. For example, a Korean American second-generation community in Los Angeles would negotiate the AAQ quite differently from a Vietnamese American first-generation community in Louisiana. Furthermore, Asian American theological reflections are needed in pan-Asian and multiethnic communities as well.

Knowing the context does not involve only the concepts and language of the AAQ in general, but addresses them specifically as they are expressed in the life and being of a concrete community. As Robert Schreiter and Clemens Sedmak conceptualize it, what we are describing is doing Asian American theological reflection as local theology.[153] How the stories and conversations of the community intersect with the categories and language from AAQ is of the essence here. Branson and Martínez show how the praxis–theory–praxis process mentioned above can function at the local level in these five steps:

153. See Robert J. Schreiter, *Constructing Local Theologies* (Maryknoll, NY: Orbis, 1985) and Clemens Sedmak, *Doing Local Theology: A Guide for Artisans of a New Humanity* (Maryknoll, NY: Orbis, 2002).

- Step 1: Naming the Praxis
- Step 2: Thick Analysis of the Praxis
- Step 3: Theological Reflections
- Step 4: Stories and Conversations
- Step 5: Envisioning a New Praxis[154]

With the affirmation of the ecclesial level, we acknowledge that culture or context is a local reality even in our globalized world.[155]

Along with other issues discussed later in chapter 4, critically engaging with the context at this local level involves the community as theologians.[156] Groome's exposition of agent-subjectivity is insightful and helpful here. Groome, drawing on Freire, proposes that the community members be seen as "agent-subjects," which refers to the "dynamic capacities of people, by which they express their identity and realize their agency in the world."[157]

Communion with the greater body of Christ at this local level means actual concrete fellowship and partnership along the lines of ethnic heritage, geographic location, and cultural appropriation. The theological reflections of a local community must be in critical and constructive engagement with other Christians who share that same location/situation, especially because all of them are united in witnessing to the gospel together at that place.

Apart from this ecclesial reflection, there also must be theological reflections at the communal level about "the neighborhood" or the mission field as well.[158] In our post-Christendom situation, the culture within the church often diverges significantly from that of the local

154. Mark Lau Branson and Juan Martínez, *Churches, Cultures, and Leadership: A Practical Theology of Congregations and Ethnicities* (Downers Grove, IL: InterVarsity Academic, 2011), 33–58.
155. Sedmak, *Doing Local Theology*, 73–74.
156. Schreiter, *Constructing Local Theologies*, 16.
157. Groome, *Sharing Faith*, 86.
158. In a way, this is an appropriation of the wisdom of the Newbigin triad of Gospel-Church-Culture. For a succinct summary of this triad see George R. Hunsberger, "The Newbigin Gauntlet: Developing a Domestic Missiology for North America," in *The Church between Gospel and Culture: The Emerging Mission in North America*, ed. George R. Hunsberger and Craig Van Gelder (Grand Rapids, MI: Eerdmans, 1996), 3–25.

community. This means the appropriation of AAQ for a Korean American church in Los Angeles and for the wider Korean American community must be analyzed separately. For the local church to be missional, to engage with the world and the non-Christian Asian Americans, this interpretative task is crucial. While this theological reflection at the extra-ecclesial level must be distinguished from the ecclesial level reflection, it is nevertheless a part of the missionary task of the church. Moreover, to fully develop the ability to see the water in which Asian Americans swim, intensively personal reflections about one's identity and cultural heritage are necessary.

The Personal Level

Theological reflection at the personal level involves pastoral care, discipleship, and personal ethics. Asian American theological reflection at this level assumes the broader setting of the two previous levels. This personal level can only be legitimately situated within a particular community. The reason this level exists is because engaging the AAQ is ultimately a personal endeavor, not a communal one. In the individual lives of Asian Americans, we see the sheer diversity of negotiating the multiple elements of the AAQ, based on family histories and individual paths.[159] The particulars of the AAQ—namely, Asian heritage, migration experience, American culture, and racialization—are experienced personally at the individual level. Of course, we must not be myopic, believing that our limited personal experience represents the broader Asian American community.

Knowing the context at this personal level means knowing one's own ethnic and cultural history. Becoming critical conscious of the context in one's personal history inevitably involves psychological dimensions.[160] Insights from the discipline of family systems theory are

159. Without disparaging in any ways, their very significant contributions, many Asian American pastoral books are limited in the sense that they focus primarily on personal or ecclesial level reflections, while lacking a more developed methodological level. Thus, these works could fall into dangers of essentialism.

160. Barth was not particularly open to theological-psychological insights. However, Deborah Hunsinger proposes a Barthian approach of relating psychology and theology that draws from his

effective guides to organizing the larger narrative of one's family and to connecting one's family to one's faith community.[161] In particular, analyzing a genogram correlated to various dimensions of the AAQ would make explicit the implicit currents of cultural identity negotiation.[162]

In the newly developed interdisciplinary field of Interpersonal Neurobiology (IPNB), Daniel Siegel, drawing from the modern attachment theory of Allan Shore, points out that the ability to construct a coherent narrative of one's childhood has deep implications for the brain's bilateral integration, which is vitally linked to one's wellbeing and relationships.[163] Evelyn Reisacher makes a connection between this attachment theory and culture and identity.[164]

Critical engagement of the context at the personal level means bringing personal experiences together with theological insights and developing a coherent narrative of one's personal negotiation of AAQ elements. Contextuality at this personal level is at the core of Asian American theological reflection, which is ultimately about consciously integrating and being at peace with the AAQ elements within oneself. This is the point that the earlier generation of Asian American theologians asserted with their autobiographical theologies.[165]

Finally, communion with the wider church is expressed by being in living fellowship with members of a local community. Of course, this local community must be in communion with other communities. The

Chalcedonian pattern. See Deborah Van Deusen Hunsinger, *Theology and Pastoral Counseling: A New Interdisciplinary Approach* (Grand Rapids, MI: Eerdmans, 1995).

161. See Edwin Friedman, *Generation to Generation: Family Process in Church and Synagogue* (New York: Guilford, 1985).

162. Celia Falicov's multicultural ecosystemic comparative approach (MECA) is very similar to the AAQ, and her use in the Hispanic context can be instructive for how the AAQ could work within an Asian American family. See Celia Jaes Falicov, *Latino Families in Therapy*, 2nd ed. (New York: Guilford, 2013).

163. See Daniel J. Siegel, *The Developing Mind: How Relationships and the Brain Interact to Shape Who We Are*, 2nd ed. (New York: Guilford, 2012), 370–77. Kirkpatrick connects this attachment theory to one's relationship with God. See Lee A. Kirkpatrick, *Attachment, Evolution, and the Psychology of Religion* (New York: Guilford, 2004).

164. Evelyn A. Reisacher, "The Processes of Attachment between the Algerian and French within the Christian community in France" (PhD diss., Fuller Theological Seminary, 2001).

165. See Peter C. Phan and Jung Young Lee, eds., *Journeys at the Margin: Toward an Autobiographical Theology in American-Asian Perspective* (Collegeville, MN: The Liturgical, 1999).

personal level resides within the ecclesial level. The ecclesial level, in turn, is located within the methodological level.

This last section outlined the three levels of Asian American theological reflection and how they can function together, incorporating the contextual insights derived from Barth. When the different levels are not properly acknowledged, theological and contextual abstractions and confusions arise.

Conclusion

This chapter explored the contours of Barth's contextuality. Barth is either known as a theologian of the Word or as a highly contextual theologian, but the *Realdialektik* is the key to bringing these two descriptions together in an orderly fashion. His innovative moves regarding the doctrine of election guided Barth to move beyond his early one-sidedness of emphasizing God at the expense of humanity toward a theology that affirms contextual reciprocity, albeit without losing divine priority.

Seen *from above* and *from below*, his contextuality is clearly a basic intentional feature of his theology as a whole and not just a marginal unconscious one. Corresponding to his actualism, Barth's theological contextuality is ultimately a predicate to engaging the living God who is contemporaneously present with us. Because God is alive and working today through his Word, theology must be contextual.

The concrete implications of this actualism were summarized here in terms of *double particularity*, *God's counter-questions*, and the *universal-particular dialectic*. These themes were explored and analyzed within the *Church Dogmatics*. Double particularity described contextuality as existing between the particularity of revelation in Jesus Christ and the particularity of the present time and space. Moreover, God's counter-questioning was a way of describing Barth's version of the method of correlation, of interacting with the questions of the world. Since God is always Lord and revelation always authoritative, the gospel's answer to the world's questions includes God's counter-questions challenging the world's plausibility structures. Furthermore, the universal–particular dynamic was outlined in the phrases: *The universal must be mediated in the particular* and *the particularity must be in service to the universal.* Finally, this section closed with the presence of these three themes in Barth's understanding of the Reformed confessions.

Moving to specific applications in Asian American contexts, the above themes were translated into three tasks: knowing the context, critically engaging with the context, and remaining in communion with the one universal church. Also, the contours of these tasks had to be shown at the three levels of the Asian American theological reflection: the methodological, ecclesial, and personal levels.

This chapter provided a radically theological basis for contextuality drawing from Barth's actualism. In the next chapter, we will introduce a triadic reconciliation grammar as a new way of engaging with culture from Barth's doctrine of election and reconciliation.

3

Reconciliation: Dialectical Grammar for Cultural Engagement

In the last chapter, we presented the basis and the nature of theological contextuality drawing from Barth's actualism. Thus, what we have done so far is to address the *formal* questions about contextuality as double particularity, with Jesus Christ on the one hand and our situation on the other. However, the *material* questions about how Christ encounters our culture and context have yet to be discussed.

These questions are multiple and complicated and cannot be dealt with in a monolithic or static fashion. The task of shedding light onto these matters is the burden of this present chapter. Building upon Barth's thoughts on contextuality, we provide the structure—or more precisely, the grammar—for cultural engagement by exploring and extending Barth's doctrines of election and reconciliation. These two doctrines are the ways in which divine incarnation impacts and envelops humanity and creation.

The flow of the argument is summarized thusly. Barth's innovative doctrine of election with its christological, supralapsarian, and universal aspects allows a way for *de jure participatio Christi* (participation in Christ) of all humanity and entire creation. Of course, this does not lead to a static and abstract election of individuals disregarding faith, but its universalistic scope is evident and will be elaborated below.[1]

The content of this *participatio* is expanded in the doctrine of reconciliation. In its dialectical triadic modes of justification, sanctification, and vocation, Barth's doctrine of reconciliation unpacks the meaning of incarnation for humanity and creation, and it also further serves as the grammar for his dynamic and textured engagement with the context.

Especially, because of the specific complex nuances built into it, this doctrine of reconciliation includes various dimensions and facets of the ways Christ engages with culture or context. In Niebuhrian terms, Barth's doctrine of reconciliation makes it possible for *Christ against culture, Christ transformer of culture,* and *Christ of culture* to be brought together within this grammar in an orderly, but a unity-in-distinction kind of way. This grammar can then guide our complex and nuanced contextual engagements.

Also, the ordered relationality between reconciliation and creation within Barth's thought allows for this triadic rubric to be extended to Barth's doctrine of creation. The point here is that using this rubric creates possibilities of creation to be freely and fully creaturely. The present chapter continues the presentation pattern of previous chapters: Moving from Barth to contextuality in general, and finally, to the Asian American situation.

First, we will begin our analysis by reviewing proposals of Robert Palma, Paul Metzger, and Jessica DeCou, which all seek to explain or extend Barth's ideas of culture. Moving on to our proposal, we will build a foundation for engaging with culture based on Barth's doctrine of election and the notion of *participatio Christi*, drawing significantly upon Bruce McCormack's work. This idea of participation in Christ is

1. Barth's concern is precisely to affirm human agency along with and on the basis of divine agency. In God's freedom there is room for human freedom. See *CD* II/2, 295. Barth also rejects the simplistic or fatalistic *apokatastasis* as an abstraction.

connected to Barth's doctrine of reconciliation with its dynamic and complex features. Lastly, using the triadic doctrine of reconciliation as the grammar for cultural engagement furthers the discussion and better accounts for Barth's own dialectical dealings with culture.

Second, we connect and apply the dialectical and hermeneutical grammar that this doctrine provides to culture and context. In terms of contextuality, this approach helps to explain what God appears to be doing in his divine commandeering of culture. The result is that reconciliation as the inner structure of universal participation gives us a very dynamic and nimble approach to the interaction between theology and culture.

Last, the practical implication of this triadic grammar is demonstrated in the four dimensions of the Asian American Quadrilateral (AAQ)—namely, Asian heritage, migration experience, American culture, and racialization. A case study will demonstrate how the three modes of reconciliation guide the cultural engagement in each dimension.

Barth, Election, and Reconciliation

With his "*Nein!*" against Brunner, Karl Barth became infamous for his rejection of natural theology and point of contact, both considered crucial by others for the missionary and evangelistic calling of the church.[2] Furthermore, with his rejection of Tillich's theology of culture, Barth sealed his reputation as a cultural philistine among theologians in the eyes of many.[3] However, there have been some

2. See Karl Barth and Emil Brunner, *Natural Theology*. Barth's argument is that the Reformers' assertion about the bondage of the will must be applied to the mind as well. We cannot know God through our own power. To claim such is to entertain "the possibility of an intellectual work-righteousness" (102). This issue was not clarified during the Reformation, so claiming Calvin as support for natural theology as Brunner does is not helpful.

3. DeCou states that Barth's critique of Tillich centers on Tillich's confused eschatology. Tillich mistakenly believes that the biblical message and proclamation are merely symbols of the transcendent that can be experienced elsewhere; however, for Barth, such a direct experience of God is reserved for the eschaton (Barth, *CD* I/1, 64). Jessica DeCou, "'Serious' Questions about 'True Words' in *Culture: Against Dogmatics* IV.3 as the Source for Barth's Theology of Culture," KBSNA Panel, AAR/SBL Annual Meeting, San Francisco, 2011. Tillich retorts that in Barth's view of proclamation the message is "thrown like a stone" with no regard for any contextual sensitivities (Paul Tillich, *Systematic Theology*, vol. 1 [Chicago: University of Chicago Press, 1951], 7).

perceptive readers of Barth, who recognized that his view of culture was more nuanced than what these well-known, but limited reviews told.[4]

Brief Review of the Significant Literature

Before we proceed, it is helpful to see how the significant works of Palma, Metzger, and DeCou have tackled Barth's dealings with culture.[5] These three works represent the significant monograph treatments of this particular aspect of Barth's theology.[6] Our proposal of using Barth's doctrine of reconciliation seeks to incorporate and extend the insights of these works.

All these authors believe that Barth's view of culture cannot be reduced to simple "No," an undifferentiated diastasis. They also acknowledge Barth's multifaceted interaction with culture—that while sin and judgment are recognized, the goodness of the creation and even its witness toward God are present as well. In a sense, they are investigating how this complexity is internally coherent. What they all seek to do is to organize the inner rubric of Barth's complex dealings with culture.

Robert Palma, along with the other two, makes explicit Barth's implicit methodology regarding cultural engagement, as Barth did not have a theology of culture per se.[7] Palma's thesis is that "Barth not only

4. Tracy observes that Barth's dialectical method included a form of analogical language. "Karl Barth . . . released himself from a purely negative dialectics and articulated, in his *Church Dogmatics*, ever-new reformulations of a new theological language of analogy—his 'analogy of grace' language. . . . In the *Dogmatics* of Karl Barth, negative dialectics endures but does not prevail" (David Tracy, *The Analogical Imagination: Christian Theology and the Culture of Pluralism* [New York: Crossroad, 1989], 417). Tillich also recognizes that Barth "corrects himself again and again in the light of the 'situation' and that he strenuously tries not be become his own follower" and accuses him of "not realiz[ing] that in doing so he ceases to be a merely kerygmatic theologian" (Paul Tillich, *Systematic Theology*, vol. 1, 5).

5. Robert J. Palma, *Karl Barth's Theology of Culture* (Allison Park, PA: Pickwick, 1983); Paul Louis Metzger, *The Word of Christ and the World of Culture: Sacred and Secular through the Theology of Karl Barth* (Grand Rapids, MI: Eerdmans, 2003); Jessica DeCou, *Playful, Glad, and Free: Karl Barth and a Theology of Popular Culture* (Minneapolis, MN: Fortress Press, 2013).

6. Of course, there are various articles and chapters that have sought to discuss this rather sidelined area in Barthian studies. See, for example, Gabriel Vahanian, "Karl Barth as Theologian of Culture," *Union Seminary Quarterly Review* 28, no. 1 (1972): 37–49; Ralph C. Wood, "Karl Barth as a Theologian of Divine Comedy" and "Barth's Evangelical Theology of Culture," in *The Comedy of Redemption: Christian Faith and Comic Vision in Four American Novelists*, 34–79 (Notre Dame, IN: University of Notre Dame Press, 1988).

dealt with culture in a multiplex fashion but that he also conceived of free culture as having a multiplex character."[8] Accordingly, Palma argues that Barth deals with culture on three different levels: a *descriptive* or *dogmatic* theology of culture, which sets for a theological understanding of culture as such, a *critical* or *analytical* theology of culture, which states the diastasis between God and culture, and a *constructive* or *normative* theology of culture, which is reflective of the mature Barth, who finds human freedom along with divine freedom in Jesus Christ.

Palma notes that for Barth, Jesus Christ in his humanity serves as not only the "paradigm of truly free culture," he is also "the very source and basis of all free culture."[9] However, Palma does not unpack this christological claim. Rather, after stating "the major facets of his Christology will not be set forth but assumed, as they are by Barth himself," Palma moves on to the various ways in which the disparate cultural elements reflect this christological paradigm.[10] The crucial organizing core is simply "assumed," leaving us in the dark as to how Barth is able to have such a multifaceted engagement with culture *in Christ*.

Precisely this "assumed" christological lacuna is what Metzger seeks to address with his incarnational proposal. Metzger believes that "an analogical connection" exists between Barth's Chalcedonian Christology and "his pattern of engaging culture in view of Christ."[11] Drawing from the works of Hunsinger and McCormack, Metzger applies "'correspondence and extension' of Chalcedonian categories by Barth" to the Word of Christ and world of the culture.[12] These categories, which organize the relationship between the human and

7. Palma, *Karl Barth's Theology of Culture*, 1. Sze Chi Chan avers that Palma is "acting as a theologian of culture on Barth's behalf" (Metzger, *The Word of Christ and the World of Culture*, xv). Indeed, this way of organizing Barth's ideas about culture is what Palma, Metzger, and DeCou all do.
8. Ibid., ix.
9. Ibid., 31.
10. Ibid.
11. Metzger, *The Word of Christ and the World of Culture*, xx.
12. Ibid., 54. Also, Hunsinger's idea of double agency further elaborates how Barth creates room for human freedom. George Hunsinger, *How to Read Karl Barth: The Shape of His Theology* (New York: Oxford University Press, 1991), 185–88.

the divine in Christ, are "without confusion or change," "without separation or division," and are "the asymmetrical ordering of the relation," in which God retains precedence for the divine over the human.[13]

The resulting practical implications for cultural engagement are "contra deification and secularization." On the one hand, culture is given a clear limit, within which there is freedom to flourish. If it fails to live within this boundary, culture receives God's No. On the other hand, God never abandons culture. It is, first and foremost, a recipient of a deeper Yes before any inbreaking of nothingness or sin.

What Metzger has done is to flesh out in a comprehensive fashion the christological foundation that Palma only names. Metzger's incarnational thesis is a significant contribution; however, there are at least two issues that arise in relation to his work that call for further consideration.

First, Barth's mature and fully developed Christology is found in the doctrine of reconciliation. Here, Barth begins his whole *Dogmatics* anew, in a sense, and he reorganizes the material from Volumes I–III from a more expansive christological framework. The Chalcedonian pattern that Metzger employs, while correctly reflecting Barth's thought pattern, might be extended and enhanced by using the triadic and dialectics aspects of reconciliation, thus stressing the dynamic nature of how God encounters culture.[14] Barth's oft-discussed section on secular parables of the kingdom appears within one particular aspect—namely, vocation—in the larger context of the doctrine of reconciliation.[15] One must consider the significance it has by having been placed within that particular theological locus.

Second, this secular parables section echoes the section on active

13. Metzger, *The Word of Christ and the World of Culture*, 55.
14. Ziegler argues that it may be "that Metzger's preferred categories inadvertently conspire to encourage an overly *static* view of the relation of the Word of Christ to human culture" (Philip G Ziegler, Review of *The Word of Christ and the World of Culture: Sacred and Secular through the Theology of Karl Barth*, by Paul Metzger, *Scottish Journal of Theology* 59, no. 1 [2006]: 115). To his credit, Metzger clearly explores this actualistic *event* nature of divine commandeering of culture for revelation; however the issue appears to be developed within the Chalcedonian categories that serve as his interpretative rubric (Metzger, *The Word of Christ and the World of Culture*, 125–31).
15. Barth, *CD* IV/3.1, 38–165.

life in the doctrine of creation that includes both Christian witness and creaturely work in ordered relationality.[16] Given the close ordered relationship between creation and reconciliation in Barth's theology, is it possible that Barth's dialectical exposition of the doctrine of reconciliation can serve as a hermeneutical rubric for his later work in cultural engagement, in a way that extends and furthers Metzger's research?

In Palma's and Metzger's studies, the christological core of Barth's theology, and particularly, his engagement with culture is quite clear. Our thesis develops similarly along the incarnational lines via election and reconciliation. Before we present our arguments, we must discuss DeCou's recent work on using Barth to develop a theology of popular culture because she challenges this christological approach.

DeCou has a different perspective from Palma's and Metzger's in her development of a Barthian theology of popular culture. She argues "that Barth has two distinct approaches to culture," which are disconnected from each other: a "true words approach" that Barth only acknowledges theoretically, and a pneumatically eschatological approach that better reflects his practice.[17] This latter approach is what she seeks to promote. DeCou raises three main concerns with the true word approach.

First, the true words approach, rooted in *CD* IV/3 §69, is merely an extension of Barth's doctrine of revelation and not a real theology of culture. Here, Barth is "confusing the tasks of theology and culture."[18] The task of the former is to witness to divine revelation, whereas the task of the latter is to draw attention to the goodness of creation as an end in itself. The problem with this true words approach is that too much is made of culture, and its needed *secularity* is threatened.[19] Simply put, there is no need for culture to carry the burden of revelation.

16. Barth, *CD* III/4. 522–64.
17. DeCou, *Playful, Glad, and Free*, 55.
18. Ibid., 74.
19. Secularity does not mean autonomy or independence from God. As Metzger notes, God grants humanity "distinct existence" *from* God, but it is still *with* and *for* God; this idea of secularity should be understood along the same lines (Metzger, *The Word of Christ and the World of Culture*, 90).

Second, DeCou points out the lack of concrete examples in section §69 compared to Barth's expressed admiration for Mozart, raising questions about how seriously or practically his thoughts in this section should be taken. DeCou's own proposal is to build upon the fragments of eschatology that Barth left behind to stress the themes of free play and of God as the limit to human culture.

Third, DeCou raises important issues about affirming the goodness and calling of culture in its *secularity*. Culture should not have to bear the burden of being revelatory. Also, creaturely freedom within its rightful limits should be protected from the encroachment of revelation. While DeCou's concerns are well taken, there are a number of reasons why her rejection of the true word approach for her pneumatically eschatological approach should be limited in scope.

First, what Palma and Metzger do is develop a christological framework that accounts for §69 along with the rest of Barth's theology and is explicitly and unapologetically christocentric. For example, Metzger's incarnational thesis that uses Hunsinger's Chalcedonian pattern is not built upon the true words paragraph §69, but rather, establishes a rubric with which to understand it. They do not narrowly build upon the concept of "true words," so that categorization itself as a foundational motif appears to be a false one.

Second, DeCou's approach fails to account for Barth's core themes and mature movements. As a result, it reveals the weakness of her interpretative framework such as her inattention to Christocentrism to understand what Barth is doing with culture. By developing a Barthian method from his unfinished doctrine of redemption, while ignoring what Barth has made clear, is a precarious path to follow. Is the question of culture actually that marginal to Barth's overall theological project? It will become apparent in the course of our argument that Barth's concern about culture is a part of his larger concerns about revelation.

Third, much of DeCou's pneumatically eschatological approach to culture is found in Barth's doctrine of creation, in which he poses culture as a calling and a task of humanity, so her approach might aptly be relabeled a *creational* approach.[20] Furthermore, Barth's pneumatology is famously (or infamously) christocentric.[21] Also, his doctrine of reconciliation is thoroughly eschatological, so again, the categorizations are superficial.

Last, Barth's lack of examples is, in a sense, an argument from silence and could be explained by Barth's discomfort with the topic, as DeCou notes. However, do discomfort and the lack of examples necessarily mean that this approach is impractical? Not according to Barth at least, since he has argued otherwise.

As noted above, Barth does not have an explicit and thorough theology of culture, although he does address it in various places and times. So all these monographs as well as other essays are attempting to construct one with the ideas and discussions about culture that Barth has left behind. While DeCou raises important questions about the possible weaknesses of a true words approach, a theology of culture that is faithful to Barth's thought would have to incorporate this significant passage.

In this regard, Metzger's work is still the more comprehensive and feasible theology of culture from a Barthian basis. Metzger uses the doctrine of incarnation as the key rubric for the relationship between God and culture. For Barth, incarnation is a singular event in history where "the divine Word takes a concrete human nature to himself, not humanity in general."[22] Metzger shows Barth here is using analogical extension to connect incarnation to culture.

Building upon Metzger's insights, we seek to flesh out this analogical extension by focusing on Barth's idea of participation in the doctrine of election and reconciliation. Barth's interpretation of election as christological and universal is how the incarnation becomes universal. Moreover, the impact of the participation for humanity, world, and

20. DeCou's core blocks for constructing a theology of popular culture are mainly drawn from Barth's doctrine of creation in *CD* III/4, §56.

21. George Hunsinger, "The Mediator of Communion: Karl Barth's Doctrine of the Holy Spirit," in *The Cambridge Companion to Karl Barth*, ed. John Webster (New York: Cambridge University Press, 2000), 181–82.

22. Metzger, *The Word of Christ and the World of Culture*, 57.

culture is found in the doctrine of reconciliation. To these two doctrines, we now turn.

Election as the Basis of *Participatio Christi*

Barth's theological development after his break from liberalism to the end of his career can be represented as "a more-or-less continuous unfolding of a single theme: God is God."[23] Barth tries various proposals to bridge the diastasis between God and the world without losing the radical discontinuity. Therefore, the development of Barth's theology as a whole with its key breakthroughs is intrinsic to the concerns of theology and context.[24] In fact, the four stages that McCormack presents in his intellectual biography of Barth's early theology, *Karl Barth's Critically Realistic Dialectical Theology*, offer us a way to see Barth's advances and missteps in his efforts to connect God to the world while retaining the diastasis. We will trace the stages here with cultural engagement in mind.

During the first stage of "dialectical theology in the shadow of process eschatology," in *Romans I*, Barth uses an organological conceptuality to describe how the Kingdom of God grows progressive within our world. While the kingdom is present in history, it enters "as the irruption of powers of God from above, cutting through history 'longitudinally.'"[25] Kingdom is like an organism that is "set in motion by the reconciliation achieved in Christ," and is growing toward the redemption of the whole world, indeed the cosmos.[26] Although Barth "clearly maintains *no* direct continuity between God and the world,"

23. McCormack, *Karl Barth's Critically Realistic Dialectical Theology*, 134.
24. Tracy argues that "where analogical theologies lose that sense for the negative, that dialectic sense within analogy itself, they produce not a believable harmony among various likenesses in all reality but the theological equivalent of 'cheap grace': boredom, sterility and an a theological vision of a deadening univocity" (Tracy, *The Analogical Imagination*, 413). Whereas Tracy talks about retaining the dialectic within the framework of analogy, Barth begins with the dialectic to seek a way for the analogy that does not threaten it. Tracy notes this in Barth. Tracy, *The Analogical Imagination*, 417. Of course, the two different approaches are simply a matter of preference. Since for Barth, the analogy or the connection is purely an act of grace, a miracle and never a given.
25. Ibid., 144.
26. Ibid., 152.

the reviews of *Romans I* made it clear that he was misunderstood and that the diastasis was threatened.[27]

The Tambach lecture of this period shows Barth arguing for a "complete and total antithesis" between Christ and society.[28] Yet, "synthesis lies in God alone" and it is found in God alone.[29] As in *Romans I*, Barth could talk of our souls and our society having their origin in God and say that there is "an immediacy of all things, relationships, orders, and arrangements to God" that has been lost but must be regained.[30] Barth posits that "if God were not the Creator of this world, he would not be its Redeemer."[31] We will see that Barth has not clearly sorted out the relationship between creation, reconciliation, and redemption.

With the confused reception of *Romans I* that missed perceiving the diastasis between God and world Barth so sought to retain, Barth was compelled to move toward the next stage of "dialectical theology in the shadow of consistent eschatology." Looking back, Barth believed that in *Romans II*, there was "almost catastrophic opposition of God and the world, God and humanity, God and the Church."[32] The diastasis between God and the world was stated in such a radical form that there was really no connection between the two. This one-sidedness was required at the time to make sure that there was no confusion about this infinite qualitative distinction during those years of rampant anthropocentricism. Unfortunately, this Barth of *Romans II* continues to serve as his caricature to the undiscerning readers who perpetuate the old stereotype of him as a cultural philistine. However, Barth continued on toward developing a continuity that is totally from God's side and is thoroughly miraculous in its nature.

In the next stage, during his Göttingen days, Barth's discovery of

27. Ibid., 155, quoting Michael Beintker. Michael Beintker, "Der Römerbrief von 1919," in Gerhard Sauter, ed., *Verkündigung und Forschung: Beihefte zu "Evangelische Theologie,"* 2 (1985), 24.
28. Ibid., 197.
29. Karl Barth, "The Christian in Society, 1919," in *The Word of God and Theology*, trans. Amy Marga (London: T&T Clark, 2011), 65–66.
30. Ibid., 46.
31. Ibid., 52.
32. McCormack, *Karl Barth's Critically Realistic Dialectical Theology*, 244. Quoting Barth from *Die Menschlichkeit Gottes* (Zurich: EVZ, 1956), 8.

the anhypostatic-enhypostatic Christology, albeit pneumatocentric in expression, helped to bring the doctrine of incarnation to the center of his theology. Through this new Christology, Barth now found the whole existence of Christ to be the site of revelation, not just the crucifixion.[33] Moreover, extending this incarnational logic, Barth "can speak both critically and positively about God's Word's engagement of the world and human culture."[34]

In his "Church and Culture" lecture, this analogical extension from the doctrine of incarnation leads Barth to state that "the divine logos . . . while he is wholly man in Jesus of Nazareth none the less fills *heaven and earth*" via *Extra Calvinisticum*.[35] Barth even makes claims about human activity carrying "within itself a spark of the seminal logos."[36] Barth still has not arrived at the kind of connection between God and the world that he thought would properly retain its gracious and miraculous nature because this extension would not survive the crucible of the *Kirchenkampf.* The necessity of the *Nein!* toward natural theology proved that the kind of extension that Barth sought through the incarnation was insufficient. Barth's final and crucial breakthrough regarding the relationship between God and the world came through Pierre Maury and his christological revision of the doctrine of election.[37]

In the final state of anhypostatic-enhypostatic Christology with Christocentricism, Barth's radical revision of election addresses his concerns about abstractions, such as *decretum absolutum* (absolute decree). Election is "the whole of the Gospel, the Gospel *in nuce* [in a nutshell]."[38] However, how is it to be the heart of the gospel if the electing God is an abstract God apart from revelation, and the elected humanity is equally abstract? An unrevealed God who exercises unlimited power in an abstract manner can too easily become demonic.

33. Ibid., 366.
34. Metzger, *The Word of Christ and the World of Culture*, 59.
35. Karl Barth, "Church and Culture," in *Theology and Church: Shorter Writings, 1920-1928* (New York: Harper and Row, 1962), 342.
36. Ibid., 351.
37. Ibid., 461.
38. Barth, *CD* II/2, 13–14.

Also, while this eternal decision of God safeguards against synergism, it also makes no room for true human freedom alongside God's freedom. Thus, Barth's solution was to assert Jesus Christ, the God-man, as the electing Subject as well as the elected One, the electing God and the elected man.[39] The electing God is Jesus Christ, who had reconciled the world to himself. The elected man is Jesus Christ, who obediently exercised human freedom that corresponded to divine freedom.

The consequences of this radical move are far-reaching and profound. In Barth's doctrine of God, the being of God became established in the act of revelation. Also, the christocentric move of election became the source of "the humanity of God," where there is no isolation of God from man in Jesus Christ.[40] The continuity in the relations between creation and God was now established as the pure act of God's grace from all eternity to all eternity, while firmly retaining the fundamental diastasis.[41]

For Barth's anthropology, this move in election meant that all humanity is now *de jure* participating in Christ's election and reprobation. Just as there is no God apart from the divine self-determination of election, "there is no such thing as human being apart from its being 'in Jesus Christ.'"[42] Passively all human beings are *de jure* in Christ, participating in Christ's election, whether they are aware of it or not. Actively, now human freedom is fully affirmed in humanity's *de facto* participation in Christ even as it is delimited by divine freedom. However, because this *de facto* participation is an eschatological reality, it retains its event character. On the basis of God's freedom, human freedom and obedience truly matter.

For Barth's theological methodology, the doctrine of election becomes for Barth "a 'regulative principle' which 'stands at the beginning of and behind all Christian thinking.'"[43] Barth's

39. Ibid., 115–16.
40. An outline of the implications of his doctrine of election is found in Karl Barth, *The Humanity of God* (Richmond, VA: John Knox, 1960), 37–65.
41. For Barth, God's revelation in Jesus Christ and God's eternity is pre-temporal, supra-temporal, and post-temporal.
42. Adam Neder, *Participation in Christ: An Entry into Karl Barth's* Church Dogmatics (Louisville, KY: Westminster John Knox, 2009), 17.

Christocentricism becomes "a rule which is learned through encounter with the God who reveals Himself in Christ," in which we seek "to understand every doctrine from a centre in God's Self-revelation in Jesus Christ."[44] At this juncture, Barth finally finds the material content of his Christocentricism, which he already shared formally with Herrmann and even Schleiermacher.

The implication for engaging with culture is that Jesus Christ becomes "the origin of all things" and even "their most fundamental presupposition," as Palma states.[45] More concretely, the doctrine of election serves as the underpinning of Barth's doctrine of creation, in which Jesus Christ, very God and very man, is stated as the basis of creation:

> In respect of His Son who was to become man and the Bearer of human sin, God loved man and man's whole world from all eternity, even before it was created and in spite of its absolute lowliness and non-godliness, indeed its anti-godliness. . . . The fact that God has regard to His Son–the Son of Man, the Word made flesh is the true and genuine basis of creation.[46]

This means that all creation is in Christ. There is a real *de jure* participation of creation in Christ.

To understand the material structure of this *participatio Christi*, however, we must turn to the doctrine of reconciliation. Without this content, the nuances and the diverse ways God works in and through humanity, creation, and culture will be overlooked, making for a simplistic engagement.

Reconciliation as the Structure of *Participatio Christi*

Barth identifies three forms of the conversion of humanity to God. Like Calvin's *duplex gratia*, these three graces are what we experience through our union with Christ through faith. This reconciliation is,

43. McCormack, *Karl Barth's Critically Realistic Dialectical Theology*, 460. Quoting Barth in *Gottes Gnadenwahl*, Theologische Existenz heute, 47 (Munich: Chr. Kaiser Verlag, 1936), 35.
44. McCormack, *Karl Barth's Critically Realistic Dialectical Theology*, 454.
45. Neder, *Participation in Christ*, 17.
46. Barth, *CD* II/1, 50–51.

first and foremost, an event that occurs in Jesus Christ. Thus, *munus Triplex* (threefold office) of Jesus is the basis of the three forms:

> In all three developments we must ensure that Jesus Christ is constantly known and revealed as the One and All that is expounded. He is the One who justifies, sanctifies and calls. He is the High-Priest, King and Prophet.[47]

The first aspect, justification, has two sides, a negative one and a positive one. The negative pardon means the forgiveness of sin. The positive pardon is the declaration of righteousness. To put it in another way, sin is revealed and condemned and "the sentence executed and revealed in Jesus Christ."[48] In Jesus Christ's death and resurrection, God's No and Yes is declared upon him, and through participation with him, humanity shares in this No and Yes. As Metzger has rightly articulated, justification means becoming de-divinized, and also humanized within proper limits.[49] It is also the rejection of a simple direct continuity between God and the world, affirming an indirect continuity that incorporates within it a radical discontinuity. Justification means the condemnation of natural theology and the affirmation of a christological supralapsarian election.

The second aspect, sanctification, is the "necessary consequence" of justification and it is the "subjection of [humanity] to the divine direction"[50] Whereas justification is to decide and declare that "every person is his child, at peace with him in his kingdom," sanctification means God's command "to occupy this space, to live in this kingdom."[51] Barth clarifies that this aspect "does not mean our self-sanctifying as the filling out of the justification which comes to man by God," but rather, that sanctification is still a blessing that comes from our participation in Christ.[52] In both aspects, we are still taking hold of "Jesus Christ, who, according to 1 Cor. 1:30, is made unto us both

47. Barth, *CD* IV/1, 147.
48. Ibid., 96.
49. Metzger, *The Word of Christ and the World of Culture*, 63–64.
50. Ibid., 101.
51. Neder, *Participation in Christ*, 54. Quoting Barth from *CD* IV/1, 98–99.
52. Ibid., 101.

justification and sanctification."[53] In the relationship between justification and sanctification, "there can be no question of a temporal order, the only order can be that of substance."[54] Furthermore, "justification is first as basis and second as presupposition, sanctification first as aim and second as consequence; and therefore both are superior and both subordinate."[55] Therefore, there is no priority of either in terms of importance or worth.

Finally, the third aspect, vocation, means that humanity in Christ is "not merely in passion and action but also in expectation" of participation.[56] Although Barth does not articulate it in this particular way, we can decipher two aspects to vocation. On the one hand, Barth notes that vocation is the "the source of the two first, and it comprehends them both."[57] That is, the prophetic work of Jesus reveals to people their justification and sanctification, and therefore, vocation is the source of both. For Barth, revelation is reconciliation, or they are two sides of God's one salvific work. Through the aspect of vocation, the connection between revelation and reconciliation is established. Charges of universalism in Barth's theology arise from an insufficient grasp of this linkage. On the other hand, vocation is "the telos of justification and sanctification."[58] The ultimate and eternal calling of human beings is to serve God in praise of God's glory. They are to reflect this divine glory and be God's witnesses forever. For Barth, the eternal life is an active life, life corresponding to divine activity.[59]

These three forms are in dialectical union and cannot be divided just as Christ cannot be divided.[60] One cannot exist without the others. Interestingly, Busch describes Barth's ecumenical intention:

> Barth no longer wanted the decisive orientation of the knowledge of salvation to be merely on justification (as in Lutheranism) or on sanctification (as in pietism) or on vocation (as in Anglo-Saxon churches);

53. Ibid.
54. Barth, *CDIV/2*, 507.
55. Ibid., 508.
56. Barth, *CD* IV/1, 100.
57. Ibid., 135.
58. Ibid., 113.
59. See Barth, *CD* III/4, 470–86.
60. Neder, *Participation in Christ*, 51.

> he wanted to do ecumenical theology by stressing these three perspectives equally in the light of the knowledge of Christ.[61]

Keeping this intention in mind, the importance of affirming all three equally is clearly evident. However, vocation plays a particular function from the perspective of our present experience because of its connection to revelation. Johnson stresses that vocation be the mode of our present experience with justification as its ground and sanctification, its goal.[62] Johnson is developing what Hunsinger pointed out as the "existential moment" placed upon the doctrine of vocation. Hunsinger elaborates that "justification and sanctification, as Barth presents them, can be interpreted as the external basis of vocation, and vocation as the internal basis or the *telos* of justification as sanctification."[63] Again, while this existential moment should not lead to emphasizing vocation over the other forms, it helps to note the connection to the present task of culture, for example.[64]

This unity means that there is relative freedom as to what comes first in order. Barth cites Calvin as an example of freedom in practice because all three forms are just different ways to see the whole, all being benefits of *participatio Christi*.[65] This lack of a temporal order does not mean that there is no grammar in their organization at all. As stated above, justification serves as the basis of sanctification, and vocation serves as the basis and the *telos* of the other two. But temporally, there is relative freedom. Also, there is no ordering on the basis of importance: all three aspects are eternal because they are aspects of Jesus Christ himself.[66]

61. Eberhard Busch, *Karl Barth: His Life from Letters and Autobiographical Texts* (Minneapolis, MN: Fortress Press, 1977), 338.
62. William Stacy Johnson, *The Mystery of God: Karl Barth and the Postmodern Foundations of Theology* (Louisville, KY: Westminister John Knox Press, 1997), 139.
63. Hunsinger, *How to Read Karl Barth*, 154.
64. With his desire to develop this role of vocation, Johnson appears to actually put undue emphasis upon vocation, which Hunsinger does not do, perhaps precisely because he comes from an Anglo-Saxon perspective. This way of emphasizing one over the other, even if in terms of only our experience, seems to be contrary to Barth's ecumenical, and more importantly, christological logic of emphasizing the whole Christ.
65. Barth, *CD* IV/2, 510–11.
66. While some interpreters of Barth have posited the logical precedence of justification and sanctification over vocation, no such precedence of significance exists. See John G. Flett, *The*

Along with this complex ordering, it is essential to note the *simul* that runs throughout the doctrine of reconciliation.[67] Although Barth rejects the idea of justification being the *articulus stantis et cadentis ecclesiae* (doctrine by which the church stands or falls), he nevertheless retains Luther's concern by affirming the precedence of the objective union that occurs *de jure* over the subjective *de facto* participation.[68] *Triplex gratia* (triple grace) is, from the beginning to the end, thoroughly *extra nos* in Jesus Christ. Jesus is not only the entrance point, but also life itself. Apart from Christ, there is no righteousness, holiness, or calling. Moreover, the *simul* means that sin and salvation, God and humanity, are related in a *totus/totus* (total/total) manner, not *partim/partim* (partly/partly).

Proposed Hermeneutical Key for Creation

This christological *triplex gratia* serves as a template of sorts or a hermeneutical key for Barth. Obviously, in *CD* IV/1–3, his views of sin, salvation, the Holy Spirit, the church, and Christian life are organized around his threefold Christology. But this threefold form could also be delineated within his doctrine of creation and providence. When Barth talks about the center and circumference in regard to creation and providence, the center is Christ in this threefold way.

For example, Barth breaks down the work of God the Creator as Creator, Sustainer, and Ruler. This threefold work overlaps the work of providence, where God preserves, accompanies and rules the world. While the *triplex gratia* pattern is implicit and not tightly organized in these early volumes of the *Church Dogmatics*, there are enough signs to deduce its presence.

First, Barth explicitly makes a connection between the divine act

Witness of God: The Trinity, Missio Dei, *Karl Barth and the Nature of Christian Community* (Grand Rapids, MI: Eerdmans, 2010), 224.

67. The Lutheran shorthand, *simul*, comes from the phrase *simul iustus et peccator* (simultaneously just and sinner) and explains the *extra nos* and eschatological character of justification, and salvation in general. This salvation is an already/not yet eschatological reality that we experience in the present. In Barth's work and in ours as well, this little *simul* serves as a way to infuse a theological idea with the dialectical and eschatological reality of justification.

68. Neder, *Participation in Christ*, 57.

of creation and justification in *CD* III/1.[69] Because justification is the hidden center of creation, God declares that all creation is good, very good. This declaration of goodness cannot be lost even after the Fall because God's No to sin "can only be uttered and valid as it is enclosed and concealed in the greater Yes."[70]

Second, the first two aspects of providence—namely, preservation and accompaniment—summarize God's sustaining work. Preservation as the first aspect of providence reflects justification as well, albeit not fully developed. God continues to keep sin, chaos, and destructive forces at bay so that Christ may become human.[71] This echoes the downward movement of justification. However, in the second aspect of providence, divine accompaniment, Barth's language sounds very much like sanctification. Divine accompaniment is about how God is active in a way that leaves room for the creature to be free.[72] Tanner summarizes that "God's initiative and the creature's response assume the form of direction and obedient acknowledgement or the call and response of love."[73] While accompaniment is God's work, it is also an affirmation of creaturely freedom within that divine work. This affirmation of the human response resonates with the doctrine of sanctification. In fact, Barth incorporates divine accompaniment at the beginning of his discussion of sanctification in *CD* IV/2.[74]

Lastly, divine ruling, in which the doctrines of creation and providence clearly overlap, is where Barth discusses the task that God gives to human beings, their vocation. Barth's discussion of witness and work in *CD* III/4 under the Creator's command is taken up again in *CD* IV/3 under the doctrine of vocation.[75]

What we have tried to do here is to flesh out what Barth means when he states that creation is the circumference and the covenant is the center.[76] To put it in another way, creation is the external basis

69. Barth, *CD* III/1, 366–414.
70. Ibid., 386.
71. Kathryn Tanner, "Creation and Providence," in *The Cambridge Companion to Karl Barth*, ed. John Webster (New York: Cambridge University Press, 2000), 122.
72. Barth, *CD* III/3, 92.
73. Tanner, "Creation and Providence," 123.
74. Barth, *CD* IV/2, 52–53.
75. Barth, *CD* III/4, 470–564.

of the covenant, and the covenant is the internal basis of creation.[77] However, election is the inner basis of the covenant, and thus, the ultimate internal basis of creation:

> The inner basis of the covenant is simply the free love of God, or more precisely the eternal covenant which God has decreed in Himself as the covenant of the Father with His Son as the Lord and Bearer of human nature, and to that extent the Representative of all creation.[78]

Furthermore, what election and covenant means in terms of God's salvific works is reconciliation:

> If what He does as the Founder and Lord of this covenant is not the same as what He does as Creator, He does not do either without the other, but does both simultaneously and in co-ordination. The work of His creative grace has in view His reconciling grace. But the converse is also true, so that He is always the Guarantor, Sustainer and Protector of His creaturely world, of the cosmos or nature, thus giving it constancy in the being with which He endowed it at creation.[79]

In sum, to say that Christology is the basis and foundation of all Barth's theology concretely means that he grounds his theology in Christ's *munus triplex* found in the doctrine of reconciliation. This is the christological foundation that Palma assumes. When Metzger takes hold of Christology *in nuce* in the Chalcedonian pattern, surely he is not mistaken. However, we must continue on to arrive at Barth's fully developed Christology that appears in the doctrine of reconciliation.

Culture and Reconciliation

So what does this mean for culture? We begin by summarizing the two ways that Barth discusses culture in the *Church Dogmatics*: as work and as witness.

76. Ibid., 516–17.
77. Barth, *CD* III/1, 94–97.
78. Ibid., 97.
79. Barth, *CD* IV/3.1, 138.

Culture as Work

In his discussion of culture as work, Barth gives culture its proper creaturely freedom while setting it within a teleological trajectory of eternal praise. This is the source of DeCou's theology of culture in its secularity. Culture as work falls under the command of God in the doctrine of creation. For Barth, the command of God assumes the dialectical union of dogmatics and ethics. There exists an "inseparability of indicative and imperative," meaning that in encountering God, we are summoned under divine lordship.[80] This command means "permission, 'the granting of a very definite freedom,'" through which we are free to be who we really are.[81] Because our true identity is found in Christ, God's command, "in effect, says not only: This is what you must do! But also: This is who you are!"[82] Culture as work is a human response to the command of God, a call to an "active life."

Basically, the source of cultural context is humanity. For Barth, culture is defined as an expression of human work. As a response to God's command, humanity is given a task. While ultimately and in a Christian sense, this task is to witness to the kingdom, penultimately and in a creaturely sense, there is a legitimate place for this task as work. Barth again limits the scope of culture so that it does not become somehow beyond human agency.

This is akin to what Kathryn Tanner notes as the postmodern rejection of culture as "a principle of social order."[83] What Tanner is pointing out is that culture does not impose order, apart from all the different ways of appropriating it. What postmodern anthropologists reject, Barth also rejects for theological reasons. Culture is not somehow beyond creation, as though God willed culture to be:

> *Culture stands or falls with the man who actually expresses himself in it. . . .* It

80. John Webster, *Karl Barth*, 2nd ed. (New York: Continuum, 2004), 154.
81. Ibid., 155. Quoting from Barth, *CD* II/2, 585.
82. Ibid., 156.
83. Kathryn Tanner, *Theories of Culture: A New Agenda for Theology* (Minneapolis, MN: Fortress Press, 1997), 47–51.

> does not have the intrinsic values and existence of a hypostasis superior to him. Thus it cannot have more than an earthly character, and only by way of illusion can it conceal or replace heaven. Above all, it can have only a creaturely and not a divine character.[84]

This critical limitation is simply a boundary of culture's freedom. Within this proper creaturely boundary, the work of culture, along with every other kind of work, can be affirmed as obedience to God's command.

In this creaturely sense, Barth offers some criteria for consideration regarding this human task. This set of criteria evaluates if and in what sense an expression of work is "specifically human in character."[85]

The first criterion has to do with *objectivity*. Because work is a response to God's command, an act of obedience, how well the job is done matters: "Right work is righteous work, i.e., work which to the best of its ability does justice to each specific task and end."[86]

The second criterion is about the *worth* of human work. The question here is "whether human existence is served, or not served, or perhaps even ignored by it."[87] Instead of seeking or applying some universal categories of good or bad work, Barth recommends that Christian communities take up this issue for their own times and situations.

Third, the criterion of *humanity* is about people's relationships with their fellow human beings. For Barth, the *imago dei* in humanity is found in our relationality.[88] Does work promote human coexistence and cooperation? Affirming our relationality is what makes us fully human.

The fourth criterion of proper human work is the criterion of *reflectivity*. Right work involves all of ourselves, not just external actions, but inward work as well, such as "application, industry, attention and devotion."[89]

The final criterion of right and true human work is *limitation*. This

84. Barth, *CD* III/4, 522. Emphasis added.
85. Ibid., 527.
86. Ibid., 529.
87. Ibid., 530.
88. Barth, *CD* III/2, 226–32.
89. Barth, *CD* III/4, 546.

criterion mirrors the Sabbath commandment, but in a form that applies to all humanity. There must be rest from work and rest in work. Rest in work means that work does not become an oppressive taskmaster or an idol. Work must be done with joy—in some sense, like play.

In this sense, there is still right and true work that is within its creaturely limits. Along this line of thought, various cultural expressions that take the form of human work can be evaluated with these five criteria. In talking of right or true expressions of culture, Barth is strictly referring to the ways these expressions reflect their true humanity, in their *secularity*, as DeCou has stressed.[90]

Culture as Witness

Barth relates culture as work and witness as an ordered relationship between the circumference and the center, respectively.[91] In *CD* III/4, right before he discusses creaturely work, Barth claims that the calling and task of the Christian community is to witness to the gospel, to praise God's glory. This is the true calling of all humanity, yet it is a task that only Christians, at the moment, are privy to in Christ. By asserting that there is "no human existence for its own sake nor work for work's sake," Barth is simply stating that creation is made for God's love and delight.[92]

However, whether privy to its true purpose or not, secular culture can and does witness to God and offer praise. Already in *CD* I/1, Barth had averred, "God may speak to us through Russian Communism, a flute concerto, a blossoming shrub, or a dead dog."[93] However, here, the possibility of such a witness was not grounded in the doctrine of

90. See DeCou, *Playful, Glad, and Free*, 75.

91. This metaphor of a circle with a center and circumference is a rejection of Ritschl's ellipse with two foci, God and humanity. Barth believed that this way of synergistic thinking was one of the fatal flaws of Schleiermacher and nineteenth century theology in general. See Flett, *The Witness of God*, 203n12.

92. Barth, *CD* III/4, 524. Jonathan Edwards argues that same point, that the world was created for God's glory, love and delight. See Jonathan Edwards, "Concerning the End for Which God Created the World," in *Works of Jonathan Edwards*, vol. 8, *Ethical Writings*, ed. Paul Ramsey (New Haven, CT: Yale University Press, 1970), 405–63.

93. Barth, *CD* I/1, 55.

election as argued above. Rather, Barth was more generally noting the freedom of God over his Word, even as God has committed himself to Scripture and the sacraments.

However, in *CD* II/2, along with his new understanding of election, in discussing ethics, Barth can now affirm the existence of secular witnesses of "'Christian' ethics in the loose sense" that has "a place alongside theological ethics."[94] "Indirectly, [the secular witness] too could easily be a proclamation and glorification of the grace of Jesus Christ, and could therefore give the glory to God alone" even when "[its] Christian presuppositions are wholly concealed, or where a closer investigation would reveal all kinds of suppositions that are only a small extent Christian."[95]

This is an embryonic form of what Barth explores in full in *CD* IV/3.1 in his doctrine of lights. In stating that Jesus Christ is *the* one and only light of life, Barth declares emphatically that there are other lights that witness to the Word, besides those of the Bible and the church. In fact, the community of the Word "not only may but *must* accept the fact that there are such words and that it *must* hear them too, notwithstanding its life by this one Word and its commission to preach it."[96] The existence of these alien witnesses to the truth is grounded in Christ's reconciling work:

> We can count it as and because we come . . . from the revelation of the reconciliation of the world with God effected in Jesus Christ. . . . In Him there has taken place the co-ordination of the whole world with God in disclosure, condemnation, yet also remission of the sin of man. He has taken over the rulership of the world. . . . [*D*]*e jure* all men and all creation derive from His cross, from reconciliation accomplished in Him, and are ordained to be the theatre of His glory and therefore recipients and bearers of His Word.[97]

94. Barth, *CD* II/1, 542.
95. Ibid., 542.
96. Barth, *CD* IV/3.1, 115, Emphasis added.
97. Ibid., 116–17. While there are significant divergences regarding the idea of order of creation or sovereignty spheres, we cannot but notice the convergence of thought between Abraham Kuyper and Barth at this junction, where Christ, and not just God, is the sovereign over creation. Kuyper famously stated that "no single piece of our mental world is to be hermetically sealed off from the rest, and there is not a square inch in the whole domain of our human existence over which Christ, who is Sovereign over all, does not cry: 'Mine!'" (Abraham Kuyper, "Sphere Sovereignty," in James D. Bratt, ed., *Abraham Kuyper: A Centennial Reader* [Grand Rapids, MI: Eerdmans, 1998],

Even outside of the church, we can and must "hear the voice of the Good Shepherd."[98]

Moreover, culture can also simply function as witness to creaturely truth and not necessarily to revelatory knowledge. Again, culture is here speaking truth in its *secularity*, not as revelation but as "luminosity of the creaturely world."[99]

Culture as work and witness are the ways that Barth discusses this topic. However, we are after not only his discussion, but the inner christological reasoning that is found in his doctrine of reconciliation. Given these categories of work and witness that Barth uses to discuss culture, the three aspects of reconciliation function as a hermeneutical grammar, formally and materially.

Reconciliation as a Grammar for Cultural Engagement

Under creation, culture as work, the form and content of *triplex gratia* means the goodness of creation, freedom of humanity, and joyful affirmation of work. This means that culture retains its goodness despite sin and corruption. What upholds this goodness is the deep hidden Yes that is revealed in Christ. The basis of this Yes is that christological supralapsarian election is finally revealed as justification. Culture is also freely and truly human work even as God is working through it. However, God's work does not violate human freedom, but rather, is the basis of it.[100] The humanity of God revealed in Christ, especially in the doctrine of sanctification, concretizes this freedom. Finally, there is a joyful affirmation of work as a task given to human beings. Their end is not in themselves, but in God and the glory of God, which is revealed in their calling of witness in the doctrine of vocation.

488). In comparison to Kuyper's general revelation, the strength of Barth's doctrine of election is evident in that he thinks through the deeper meaning of Jesus Christ as the Subject of this claim.

98. Barth, *CD* IV/3.1, 117.

99. Ibid., 39.

100. On this very important issue of human freedom, see Hunsinger, who argues that the Chalcedonian pattern allows for the double agency of the human and the divine, protecting the distinct character of each side, and yet, allowing God to remain as Lord (Hunsinger, *How to Read Karl Barth*, 185–224).

Moreover, the very content of good, right culture should reflect the goodness of creation, the freedom of humanity, and the joyful affirmation of human work. This material content of creation is the basis of Barth's criteria for right and true work, as discussed above. The hidden purpose of creation is to be a witness of the God revealed in Christ. All of creation is to be a witness of Christ, as articulated in the doctrine of reconciliation.

Barth makes it clear that nothingness that has appeared to bring "menace, corruption and death" impacts not only humanity, but all creation.[101] God confronts this nothingness or sin "in us and all creation, what is alien and opposed to His gracious will."[102] Of course, correspondingly, salvation involves not only humanity, but is "a work which embraces all creation, heaven and earth and all that therein is."[103] Finally, throughout *CD* IV/3, Barth notes that God's reconciling work is not only for humanity, but for "humanity and all creation."[104]

In culture as witness, the dynamics of reconciliation are more explicit. When secular cultural material witnesses to the gospel, that means that Christ is commandeering it, unveiling its *de jure* participation in Christ. Within the doctrine of reconciliation, its participation means *triplex gratia,* so this cultural material's justification and sanctification must be assumed while it is serving as God's witness. When a Christian creates cultural material to witness to the gospel, the situation is only different in that this hidden reconciliation dynamic is already known and accepted. Of course, in both cases, God remains the Subject of revelation as we have stated in the discussion regarding Barth's actualistic indirect identity in the previous chapter.[105]

Because this use of the culture for God's self-revelation is a matter of divine freedom, Barth does not give concrete examples when he discusses "secular parables" of the kingdom in *CD* IV/3. Not even

101. Barth, *CD* III/3, 297.
102. Ibid., 331.
103. Barth, *CD* IV/2, 520.
104. Barth, *CD* IV/3.1, 43, 117, 137, etc.
105. McCormack's research about Barth's actualism and *Realdialetik* affirms this crucial point. See McCormack, *Karl Barth's Critically Realistic Dialectical Theology.*

Mozart is offered here. However, the reason for this supposed omission is not that Barth does not believe these secular witnesses actually exist.[106] Rather, giving a concrete example would be a denial of the very freedom that Barth is arguing for.

In fact, this lack of examples could be attributed to Barth's distrust of casuistry in ethics or his rejection of the idea of a Christian worldview. Anderson reveals that during his Safenwil pastorate, Barth had already rejected the idea of a Christian worldview because like the idea of religion, "it covers over an underlying rebellion against Jesus Christ with a self-righteousness ideology about Jesus Christ."[107] Contra Abraham Kuyper's theological outlook, for Barth, "there can be no definite Christian worldview because God continues to speak the same Word to us today in different forms."[108] Barth proposed that an establishment of such a thing "would necessarily mean that in taking to-day the insight given him to-day man hardens himself against receiving a new and better one to-morrow."[109]

Barth expresses this wariness of a Christian worldview and the need for respecting human limits in his ethics of reconciliation:

> Hence Christians, looking always to the only problem that seriously and finally interests them, must allow themselves the liberty in certain circumstances of saying only a partial Yes or No where a total one is expected, or a total Yes or No where a partial one is expected, or of saying Yes today where they said No yesterday, and vice versa. . . . Their Yes and No in this sphere can always be only a relative Yes and No, supremely because if it were more they would be affirming and acknowledging the existence of those absolute or lordless powers, canonizing their deification, and instead of resisting the true and most dangerous enemies of man and his right, life, and worth, offering them the most hazardous and fateful help.[110]

106. DeCou decries the absence of concrete examples and argues "that the material in paragraph §69 was never intended to serve as a basis for the everyday, practical engagement of the theologian with cultural forms" (DeCou, *Playful, Glad, and Free*, 64).
107. Clifford Blake Anderson, "Jesus and the "Christian Worldview": A Comparative Analysis of Abraham Kuyper and Karl Barth," *Cultural Encounters* 2, no. 2 (2006): 76.
108. Anderson, "Jesus and the "Christian Worldview," 77.
109. Barth, *CD* III/3, 56, alt, as quoted by Anderson, "Jesus and the 'Christian Worldview,'" 77.
110. Karl Barth, *The Christian Life: Church Dogmatics IV, Part 4: Lecture Fragments* (Grand Rapids, MI: Eerdmans, 1981), 268.

Whereas here Barth is talking about political discernment, the same could apply to cultural engagement as well. Unless our cultural engagement or discernment "remains dialectical and *aporetic* . . . it can easily degenerate into hegemonic personal or communal commitments"[111]

God is the one who unveils the reconciliation that is hidden in this very creaturely medium. Since all creation and all humanity are *de jure* in Christ, there is really no limit to what can be commandeered as a witness. Also, even if Mozart functioned as a witness for him, Barth cannot claim such a witness for the church, because this witness, unlike Scripture and preaching, is an extraordinarily free action of God. These secular witnesses might speak to certain individuals within the Church, with limited relevance for others.[112] More importantly, they cannot be canonized to form another scripture or something that stands beside Scripture.[113] Thus, no examples are offered.

Barth makes an interesting point that these secular witnesses "may be recognised as true words by what they signify for the life of the community itself, for its activity under the special command and promise of its Lord."[114] It is not that we are to sit around and discern, but in life of the community, in action, the witness of God may already be functioning to reveal God, clarifying what was confused or missed in our reading of Scripture.

While Barth exhorts us to truly listen for God in secular witnesses, his discussion about them, and also, his grammar of reconciliation are actually helpful in terms of understanding how God uses them as a way of thinking *fides quaerens intellectum* (faith seeking understanding). After we experience God through a secular witness, Barth helps us to see how that can occur theologically. For example, after Barth experiences God through Mozart, his categories help to interpret how that can be so.

111. David Haddorff, "Introduction: Karl Barth's Theological Politics," in *Community, State, and Church* by Karl Barth (Eugene, OR: Wipf and Stock, 2013), 46.
112. Barth, *CD* IV/3.1, 132.
113. Ibid., 133.
114. Ibid., 127–28.

In fact, not only formally, but materially, reconciliation controls the witness of culture. Barth notes that these witnesses

> may, e.g., speak of *the goodness of the original creation*, a second of *its jeopardising*, a third of *its liberation*, a fourth of the *future revelation of its glory*. Each does this authentically if and as and to the extent that what it says individually and specifically is only apparently and at a first hearing an abstraction, but really declares the *goodness*, *peril*, *triumph* and *future glory* of the divine work of creation which is enclosed in Jesus Christ, executed in Him and directed towards Him, so that, even though it may seem to be concerned with only individual aspects, it really declares the totality of this work and the whole context of the particular statements.[115]

Again, the cultural materials

> may speak of the *psycho-physical or social determination* of man, or of his *defects*, *rights* or *dignity*, or perhaps of the *forgiveness of his sins*, or *the marching orders* which he is given, or the shadow of *death* under which he lives, or the *joy* in which he may live even under this shadow.[116]

So practically speaking, what is the point of using reconciliation as a hermeneutical grammar? The first benefit is in interpreting Barth's theology in its dealings with culture. Using Barth's reconciliation grammar to decipher his approach to culture provides clarity and detail to go beyond the previous works on Barth's cultural engagement discussed above. For example, Palma notes that Barth has a "multiplex" manner of engaging culture, but what this means is not explained in any rigorous fashion.[117] In comparison, the proposed *triplex gratia* approach explains what this multiplex interaction with culture is by teasing out how Barth can affirm the justification, sanctification, and vocation of culture. Also, this reconciliation grammar continues and enriches Metzger's christological shape of engagement of culture that rejects the deification and secularization of culture by locating it within broader movements of Barth's theology.[118]

Second, and more significantly for the mission of the church today,

115. Ibid., 123. Emphasis added.
116. Ibid. Emphasis added.
117. Palma, *Karl Barth's Theology of Culture*, 33–35.
118. Ibid., 55

beyond this interpretative task regarding Barth's theology, his reconciliation grammar can guide our complex and nuanced engagement with culture. Tanner notes the need for such a complexity in our contemporary dealings with culture, in that "some of these materials seem almost to be left alone, others are directly contradicted, and in the vast gray middle are varying degrees of resistance, contestation, and compromise"[119] However, Tanner and many others who believe that there are some good, some bad, and some neutral aspects are missing the deeper dialectical dimension of culture.

In his insightful critique of Niebuhr's *Christ and Culture*, John Howard Yoder points out that "[e]verything we call 'culture' is in some way creative and positive, and in other ways rebellious and oppressive. This is not a fifty/fifty mix, but a far more complex dialectical challenge, whereby we are called to exercise discernment."[120] Although Yoder seems to say basically the same thing as Tanner, he further argues that Satan can represent "both order and disorder" and that only "paradoxical and dialectical discourse can do justice to the evil within human goods and the room for redemption with human sin."[121] It is clear here that what Yoder wants to address through his dialectical and paradoxical approach is the shadow side of the good and the hidden Yes to redeem the evil.

Along with giving an ordered account of how this can occur, Barth's *triplex gratia* as a cultural hermeneutic is precisely able to function in such a dialectical and paradoxical way because the categories of reconciliation work with sin and salvation in a *totus/totus* manner, instead of *partim/partim*. As we noted above, this *totus/totus* aspect is the meaning of the *simul* that runs through the whole doctrine of reconciliation; outside of Christ we are wholly lost, but in Christ, we find his *triplex gratia*.

Concretely, this *totus/totus* manner, or the *simul*, here, means that

119. Tanner, *Theories of Culture*, 144.

120. John Howard Yoder, "How H. Richard Niebuhr Reasoned: A Critique of Christ and Culture," in *Authentic Transformation: A New Vision of Christ and Culture*, ed. Glen H. Stassen, D. M. Yeager, and John Howard Yoder (Nashville, TN: Abingdon, 1996), 85.

121. Yoder, "How H. Richard Niebuhr Reasoned," 88. Referring to René Girard's lecture, "The Satan of the Gospels," AAR Presentation, 1992.

no cultural material can be *a priori* rejected as something that God cannot use to be God's witness. Of course, nothing can be affirmed *a priori* either. As we have stated above, that does not mean that there is no such thing as right and true cultural work in terms of creation. However, in the secular cultural witness, God is revealing the hidden *participatio Christi* that all creation shares *de jure*. Of course, even in the Christian cultural witness, the same divine freedom and prerogative exists as well.

Also, since the cultural material can witness to any aspect of justification, sanctification, or vocation, the content of witness does not necessarily have to be good, beautiful, or true. The witnesses do not have to be positive per se. The key is that God actually uses it to reveal the gospel and draw people closer to the divine life.

Within Tanner's description of the postmodern notion of culture with its cross trajectories, fluid boundaries, and hybrid identities, the true impact of Barth's dialectical and paradoxical engagement with culture might be realized.

In a sense, if we were to use Niebuhr's typological categories, justification would embody *Christ against culture*, sanctification, *Christ the Transformer of culture*, and vocation, *Christ of culture*.[122] The beauty and the power of employing Barth's movements of reconciliation become immediately clear in their ability to incorporate and organize all three categories in dialectical union.

Using Niebuhrian language, Newbigin provides a missiological illustration of how these movements work together.[123] Newbigin points out that in the missionary context, the gospel-culture interaction involves at least two cultures, that of the missionary and that of the mission field. Also, this interaction is not static but dynamic, changing through the generations.

Members of the first generation to receive the gospel usually react

122. Harper and Metzger argue for an approach to culture that accounts for the multiple types found in Niebuhr's work, though in a critical and dialectical manner (Brad Harper and Paul Louis Metzger, *Exploring Ecclesiology: An Evangelical and Ecumenical Introduction* [Grand Rapids, MI: Brazos, 2009], 208–26).

123. Lesslie Newbigin, *The Open Secret: An Introduction to the Theology of Mission* (Grand Rapids, MI: Eerdmans, 1995), 148.

strongly against their own culture by believing in a total discontinuity between their former religious and spiritual worldview and that of the Bible. This rejection is analogous to the judgment of justification. The elements in their old cultures are perceived "even if not evil in themselves (such as music, drama, and visual arts) . . . [as] evil because of their association with the rejected worldview."[124]

The second or third generation, however, seeks to recover its cultural heritage that had been rejected wholesale. This recovery process mirrors the sanctification and vocation processes blended together. Since these cultural elements no longer possess a direct relationship with their pagan roots, the church begins to reflect upon the Christ of the traditional culture. What often results in these heritage projects is a new cultural domestication of the gospel and what is just a different form of a functional Christendom. The need then occurs for a reform movement, which begins the process all over again in recovering the radical discontinuity of gospel and culture.

What Newbigin describes as a multigenerational dynamic occurs now all commixed and overlapping because of the various currents of globalism. Different people in various demographics can experience the same cultural element in widely divergent ways. Or put another way, God could be commandeering these cultural elements particularly tailored for different people or communities. The key is that there is a unified inner logic, a grammar that makes sense of these divergent convictions and expressions. As described in chapter 1, the complexities of the Asian American contexts require a theology of culture that is as multifaceted, dynamic, and nuanced as Barth's reconciliation grammar.

Engaging the Asian American Quadrilateral

So what might Barth's concepts of engaging culture look like in Asian American contexts? In this section, we offer various possibilities of God's work of reconciliation in the four spheres of the AAQ discussed

124. Ibid.

in chapter 1. These spheres are the very building blocks of the Asian American experience. Therefore, theological engagements with these spheres serve as the formative elements of any Asian American theology. We have noted in chapter 1 that unfortunately not all Asian American theological works deal with the full breadth of the Asian American experience reflected in these four spheres. While various Asian American theologies are referred to below, a full review of their approach to these spheres is beyond the scope of this work. As we have done before, our focus is envisioning and proposing what a Barthian approach to engaging these four spheres would look like.

Recalling Barth's reticence toward examples, we understand the dangers of misunderstandings at this precise juncture. As Barth stressed, whatever judgments we make must remain provisional even while decisive and confident. Within each of the four contextual spheres, examples are given more to show the grammar of reconciliation discussed above, than to show how various aspects of culture should be addressed. Moreover, regarding the three levels of theological reflection proposed in chapter 2, the grammar would guide this process at both the communal and personal levels. The point here is to discern God's work and presence in a community or an individual, and also, to guide the life of discipleship and the task of mission. As Barth reminds us, our Yes and No to a cultural element is *partial* and *relative*. With that in mind, we begin with Confucian filial piety as an example of the Asian heritage.

Asian Heritage: Confucianism

The particular cultural-religious-philosophical heritages of Asian Americans vary widely, depending on one's ethnicity and family history. Many with East Asian roots must deal with Confucianism as a part of their identity and experience. Out of the "Three Teachings" (Confucianism, Daoism, and Buddhism), Confucianism is arguably the most foundational and influential, causing some to suggest that Confucianism is to East Asia what Christianity is to the West.[125] A key aspect of Confucianism is a kind of agnostic moralism that focuses on ethical discipline and training as a central element of being human. It is significant that although Confucius refers to Heaven (*tian*) and the Mandate of Heaven (*tian ming*), he does not believe that we can gain any concrete knowledge of the divine.[126] Rather, Heaven represents the moral principle (*li*) that governs the cosmos and that all people should cultivate within themselves. Any concrete knowledge of Heaven is moot. This reticence toward theological discourse leads Confucianism to an almost exclusive emphasis on ethics within the bounds of human relationships.

The fact that Confucianism is agnostic and humanistic does not mean that it can simply function in a complementary fashion with Christianity, the latter dealing with spiritual matters and Confucian wisdom addressing relational and societal aspects. In this way, Buddhism found a niche within East Asian culture as a spiritual domain in relation to Confucianism. On the one hand, God's work of reconciliation is all-encompassing in our lives and even in the cosmos, and on the other hand, Confucianism's reach cannot simply be limited to a certain layer of reality.

Justification

Engaging Confucianism with the reconciliation rubric presented above means, first, the justification of Confucianism hearing God's No to its autonomy and integrity apart from God. We shall see a little later that this No could serve as a Yes as it so often does in Barth's theological imagination.[127] There is no neutral position to evaluate as good or evil various aspects of this tradition, such as its communalism, concept of harmony, emphasis upon education, and respect of elders.[128] This divine No is *totus*, not *partim*. Any *a priori* concept of good and evil

125. Xinzhong Yao, *An Introduction to Confucianism* (New York: Cambridge University Press, 2000), 2.
126. Yao, *An Introduction to Confucianism*, 46.
127. In his introduction to Barth's *On Religion*, Garrett Green corrects the caricature of Barth's response of religion as totally negative. By correctly translating *Aufhebung* as sublimation and not abolition, Green recovers Barth's dialectical outlook on religion, an outlook that says a resounding No, but that could say a qualified Yes as well (Karl Barth, *On Religion: The Revelation of God as the Sublimation of Religion*, trans. and intro Garrett Green [New York: T&T Clark, 2006], 6–14).
128. This kind of *a priori* judgment is the weakness of some Asian American pastoral books.

that we might use to evaluate the different aspects of Confucianism misunderstands the comprehensive nature of sin, and moreover, the integrative inner connections among elements within this tradition.

Also, this divine No means that Confucianism cannot be a Procrustean bed for the gospel if it is to be authentically "Asian." The message of Jesus Christ is a stumbling block and an offense in every culture, Eastern or Western, Northern or Southern. There are Babylonian captivities of every kind in every context.[129] Moreover, since culture is continually in flux, more than ever before, contextualizing toward a particular system is practically impossible and pastorally problematic.[130]

Xiaofeng Liu, a modern Sino-Christian theologian, captures precisely these themes. Influenced by Barth, Liu believes that there is a clear distinction between revelation in Christ and all other human religions. The Christ-event at the center of Christianity "is, in Karl Barth's words, a critique of all religions. The Christ-event demonstrates the crises of all religions."[131] The attempts at Chinese theology that expressed "Christian confession through a syncretism of the Confucian, Taoist and Chinese Buddhist systems of thought with Christian theology" were faulty because they failed to acknowledge this qualitative distinction.[132] Of course, this rejection goes for Western systems of thought as well, such as Neo-Platonism or Aristotelianism, so this statement is not a bias against Chinese religions. Liu does not believe that being a Christian makes him Western or erodes his identity as a Chinese.[133]

129. Rah's argument about the reality of the white captivity of evangelicalism, while pertinent, downplays the reality of the black, brown, and yellow captivities. The problem is not simply white captivity, but the power of that captivity in its hiddenness. Even as other minority or immigrant churches enrich and teach mainstream evangelicalism, the dangers of their own cultural captivities are real (Soong-Chan Rah, *The Next Evangelicalism: Freeing the Church from Western Cultural Captivity* [Downers Grove, IL: InterVarsity, 2009]).

130. Along these lines, Jung Young Lee's objection to a nonhierarchical view of the Trinity based on his Confucian heritage is theologically and contextually questionable (Jung Young Lee, *The Trinity in Asian Perspective* [Nashville, TN: Abingdon, 1996], 88).

131. Liu Xiaofeng, "Sino-Christian Theology in the Modern Context," in *Sino-Christian Studies in China*, ed. Yang Huilin and Daniel H. N. Yeung (Newcastle: Cambridge Scholars Press, 2006), 74.

132. Ibid., 77.

133. Fredrik Fällman, *Salvation and Modernity: Intellectuals and Faith in Contemporary China*, rev. ed. (Lanham, MD: University Press of America, 2009), 57.

Again, Liu states that while no theology should be fused to a particular ontological system, it always exists "through the life and linguistic experiences of ethno-geographical history."[134] This means that for the task of Sino-Christian theology, the focus should be "the original life experiences of individuals rather than the ethnic world-and-life views."[135] Labeling misguided syncretistic theologies as *ontological* and his perspective as *ontic*, Liu establishes his foundation for the development of a faithful Sino-Christian theology.

Sanctification

Confucianism sanctified is Confucianism under the lordship of Christ, where the logic of grace overrides its internal reasoning, and where the old plausibility structure is demolished and the new paradigm of the upside-down Kingdom is embraced.

Continuing the rejection of Confucianism as a system that tries to limit God's revelation, sanctification means that various Confucian components must be reordered or even completely transformed by the gospel. In the same way that Bonhoeffer defines cheap grace as grace separated from God's sovereignty, legalism is abstract law, separated and autonomous from God.[136] Confucian *li* and even filial piety must become reordered or even totally transformed under Christ's lordship.

Vocation

We must remember that the divine No is in the service of a Yes. Because this judgment is not a moral evaluation just as sin is a not moral category, but a theological one regarding relationship to Jesus Christ, it does not imply that Confucianism is not without its wisdom, truths, and knowledge into human relationships and development,

134. Liu, "Sino-Christian Theology in the Modern Context," 77.
135. Ibid., 78.
136. Bonhoeffer argues that "idolizing the law and legalizing God were Israel's sins. Inverted, removing divinity from the law and separating God from God's law would be the sinful misunderstanding of the disciples. In both cases, God and the law would be separated from each other, or identified with each other, which is basically the same thing" (Dietrich Bonhoeffer, *Dietrich Bonhoeffer Works*, vol.4, *Discipleship* [Minneapolis, MN: Fortress Press, 2001], 117).

especially after it has been de-divinized and humanized within proper limits.

Of course, beyond this kind of creaturely truth, God can also use elements of Confucianism for self-revelation. In fact, God's commandeering of Confucian elements goes beyond what appears to be good or evil, useful or worthless. The existence of a shadow side makes ambiguous what superficially appears to be good. Also, God's redemptive power might make an apparently useless element significant. Hence, our judgments, however decisive and resolute, are partial and relative. The truth of justification is that there is no direct path, no direct continuity, between Confucianism and Christianity. For example, Confucian filial piety does not directly connect to the fifth commandment. Confucianism's justification means the existence of this radical discontinuity that is only crossed by God's gracious act.

In the interreligious works of Julia Ching, Xinzhong Yao, John Berthrong, and Robert Neville, we find respectful and sympathetic studies seeking common themes and resonances for mutual understanding and dialogue.[137] While this approach is problematic for theology because it fails to take seriously the justification aspect of cultural engagement, its contribution toward global cooperation and peaceful coexistence might be valuable and must be recognized at the level of creaturely, humanistic truth. However, in that very creaturely way, their insights into Confucianism can provide new language, concepts, or interpretative lenses to understand God's revelation in ways that can deepen Asian American theological reflections and even enrich global Christianity.

Also, if the justification and sanctification elements are sufficiently acknowledged, then Matteo Ricci's appeal to Original Confucianism could be an example of vocation of culture. In his *The True Meaning of the Lord of Heaven*, Ricci argues that the Original Confucianism of the

137. See Julia Ching, *Confucianism and Christianity: A Comparative Study* (New York: Kodansha International, 1977); Xinzhong Yao, *Confucianism and Christianity: A Comparative Study of Jen and Agape* (Brighton: Sussex Academic, 1997); John H. Berthrong, *All Under Heaven: Transforming Paradigms in Confucian-Christian Dialogue* (Albany, NY: State University of New York Press, 1994); and Robert Cummings Neville, *Boston Confucianism: Portable Tradition in the Late-Modern World* (Albany, NY: State University of New York Press, 2000).

classical age held a belief in the almighty deity *Ti* or *Shang-ti*, the Lord-on-High.[138] Of course, Ricci's Confucian–Christian engagement results in a truncated Christianity, overemphasizing as it does the ethical dimension and leaving out much of the work of Christ. However, Legge's thoughts along similar lines hold more promise as they retain the other dimensions of reconciliation.[139]

As we can see, because there is no temporal order to the *triplex gratia*, any one of the reconciliation aspects can be an entrance point for the other two aspects or be engaged when assuming the other two. Recognizing the unity of the reconciliation aspects is crucial.

Migration Experiences: Identity

There are various themes that arise out of the migration and postmigration experiences for Asian Americans, but here, we will simply focus on one aspect of this very complex global sociological phenomenon—the issue of identity formation. How does God reconcile our identities?

Justification

The aspect of justification as applied to identity means that any identity that is posed in an absolutist sense is condemned as an expression of idolatrous divinization. As we covered in chapter 1, Barth argues extensively in his discussion of "Near and Distant Neighbors" that the boundaries of definition are reversible, fluid, and removable.[140] We also noted that Tanner's articulation of a postmodern notion of culture affirms these convictions of Barth. In a sense, justification validates postcolonial attacks upon essentialism as absolutizing a particular view of identity. The hybridity posed against orientalism protects humanity from idolatrous ideology encroaching upon the

138. John D. Young, *Confucianism and Christianity: The First Encounter* (Hong Kong: Hong Kong University Press, 1983), 34.
139. See James Legge, *Confucianism in Relation to Christianity: A Paper read before the Missionary Conference in Shanghai, on May 11th 1877* (London: Trubner, 1877).
140. Barth, *CD*, III/4, 287–303.

freedom of humanity. Asian American sociologists propose a fluid ethnic/racial identity development for Asian Americans, in which the self shifts to reflect the situation and purpose.[141] This shifting can be understood in terms of affirming inner hybridity.

Another form of idolatrous divinization can be the collapse of theological and ethnic identities. Trying to frame theologically their identities amid migration, many Asian Americans seek to establish their experience in the migration stories or bicultural identities in Scripture. On the one hand, as immigrants, Asian Americans can be viewed as God's people living in exile in the American empire, like Daniel, Esther, or Jeremiah.[142] On the other hand, some tell Asian Americans that they are like Ruth, blessed to live among God's people in America.[143] While not denying that theological and hermeneutic insights can come about through these ways of encountering the text, if the ethnic/cultural identity and covenant identity of God's Israel are conflated, then an idolatrous form of election or exceptionalism can arise, whether the subject be American or a particular ethnicity. This kind of ebionitic identity formation overemphasizes the particular at the expense of the universal and spiritual identity.

In a different light, justification of identity also means God's Yes to creation and to humanity, and thus, to the particularities of our creaturely identity. Some Asian American evangelicals stress their spiritual identity at the expense of, or even at the denial of, their bodily one.[144] This docetic identity, while seemingly spiritual, is a denial of God's good creation that has been justified in Christ, and also a

141. Deborah Hearn Gin, "Asian American Ethnic/Radical Identity Development," in *Asian American Christianity: Reader*, ed. Viji Nakka-Cammauf and Timothy Tseng (Castro Valley, CA: Institute for the Study of Asian American Christianity, 2009), 189.

142. See for example, Rachel A. R. Bundang, "Home as Memory, Metaphor, and Promise in Asian/Pacific American Religious Experience," *Semeia* 90/91 (2002): 87–104, or Eleazar S. Fernandez, "From Babel to Pentecost: Finding a Home in the Belly of the Empire," *Semeia* 90/91 (2002): 29–50.

143. See Roy I. Sano, "Shifts in Reading the Bible: Hermeneutical Moves among Asian Americans," *Semeia* 90/91 (2002): 105–18.

144. See Russell Jeung, *Faithful Generations: Race and New Asian American Churches* (New Brunswick: Rutgers University Press, 2004) or Rudy V. Busto, "The Gospel According to the Model Minority? Hazarding an Interpretation of Asian American Evangelical College Students," in *New Spiritual Homes: Religion and Asian Americans*, ed. David Yoo and Russell Leong (Honolulu: University of Hawaii Press, 1999), 169–87.

rejection of the resurrection whereby our bodies remain a part of us for all eternity.

Sanctification

Sanctification of Asian American identity begins with fully owning and bringing the multiple facets of our identity to the way of discipleship. This ownership and integration does not necessarily mean uncritical affirmation because every part must be reconciled to Christ and no doubt each must fall under the judgment of God's Word, as we discussed above in relation to Confucianism. However, the judgment must be God's and not ours. Thus, there cannot be escapism of any kind, either to the ebionitic or to the docetic identity distortions, to "an escapist nationalism" and assertion of Asian superiority or to the "extreme assimilationist perspective" under the forces of orientalism and "self-hatred."[145]

The way of discipleship, through which the multiple facets are brought under the sovereign rule of God, must respect the particularities of individual experiences but take place within the larger faith community. The great diversity of contexts, experiences, backgrounds, trajectories, and interpretations of Asian Americans must not be homogenized.

The dialectical and dynamic approach to engaging culture and context in this chapter, of course, respects this individual particularity. The triadic mode of reconciliation reveals the logic of the way various elements of culture *can* be experienced differently by different people and still be the work of God. Precisely this kind of nuance is what is needed to avoid various expressions of essentialism. The nondialectical approach of seeking to identify the good and the bad elements of the culture, in Confucian social relationality, for example, cannot but essentialize the Asian American experience and violate the particularity of individual experiences.

However, theological reflection and discernment, while personal,

145. Sang Hyun Lee, *From A Liminal Place: An Asian American Theology* (Minneapolis, MN: Fortress Press, 2010), 16, 105, 128.

is not simply an individualistic affair. Jung Young Lee begins his *Marginality* with the statement that "theology is autobiographical, but it is not an autobiography"[146] If theology is to be contextual, the primary context for theology is one's life. Lee believes that this is the reason "why one cannot do theology for another."[147] This sentiment echoes C.S. Song's rejection of the universality of Western theology for him and for Asia. Lee's particular life story that situates his theology is his immigration and subsequent marginalization within American society. However, this autobiographical approach courts danger in its lack of a larger communal discernment as well as a global and historically ecclesial one. In his *Biography as Theology*, McClendon warns that while other people's lives might be engaged for theological reflection, autobiography and autobiographical data risk "the very important moral phenomena of self-deception."[148] Again, this biographic thinking can devolve to an ebionitic view of Asian American identity.

Vocation

In a creational sense, the work of fully embracing the racial and ethnic identity of Asian Americans in freedom is a crucial calling to be followed and honored. This affirmation is not about a reference to God's creation of an Asian race or particular ethnicity. The Table of the Nations in Genesis 10 cannot be extrapolated to refer to the particular race and ethnicity of Asian Americans, nor can it be about how every nation and tribe will be represented in the eschaton in Revelation. Given that the boundaries of definition are reversible, fluid, and removable, such extrapolation would be vulnerable to ideological subversions. Rather, the theological basis of embracing racial and ethnic identity is found in the doctrine of providence, in the divine accompaniment of creation. There are no ultimate claims about this

146. Jung Young Lee, *Marginality: The Key to Multicultural Theology* (Minneapolis, MN: Fortress Press, 1995), 7.
147. Lee, *Marginality*, 7.
148. James William. McClendon, Jr., *Biography as Theology: How Life Stories Can Remake Today's Theology* (Philadelphia, PA: Trinity Press International, 1990), 165.

creational identity; the claim is rather that the body matters in its present particularity.

In the sense of God's reconciling work, the concept of liminality as it relates to Asian American identity presents many possibilities. This concept of liminality that allows openness to the new and creates *communitas* cannot be *a given*, a form of *theologia naturalis*, unique to Asian Americans and other marginalized people. Sang Hyun Lee's proposal is that Asian American place of liminality, only when converted by God's grace, can lead to new openness toward others of different cultural or ethnic backgrounds and can be instrumental in reconciling different peoples.[149]

As before, the *triplex gratia* are united in Christ and always come together, although their temporal or noetic ordering might vary. Moreover, it is possible that one of the modes might be hidden to our awareness or experience, given the *simul*—meaning dialectical and eschatological—nature of reconciliation. For example, even while we lack the signs of sanctification, God can use people as his witnesses. As Paul says, in our weakness, we are strong (2 Cor 12:10).

American Culture: Western Tradition

American culture, of course, is a continuing, ever kaleidoscopic reality, which includes Asian American contributions and experiences. While American culture is as complex as the Asian heritage, here, we focus on the idea of Christendom, which will be defined as a prolonged engagement with Christianity that encompasses the Western theological tradition as well.[150]

The Western theological tradition with its Christendom context is often problematized in its relevance for Asian Americans. Kwok Pui-

149. Lee, *From a Liminal Place*, 161–71.

150. I am using the term "Christendom" in a much broader way than just territorial Christianity or the conflation of state and church. Andrew Walls argues that the Western tradition is not a single continuous entity, but rather, a number of different gospel-culture encounters connected to each other in a serial fashion. However, regardless of this serial nature, there is a strong sense of continuity because of steady historical resourcing through which the past wisdom was appropriated and expanded (Andrew Walls, *Cross-Cultural Process in Christian History: Studies in the Transmission and Appropriation of Faith* [Maryknoll, NY: Orbis, 2002], 27–48).

lan avers that there is nothing within Western Christianity that has escaped the influence of Western imperialism: Scripture, tradition, church, and even the idea of God.[151] However, the hybridic and bicultural identity of Asian Americans means that Western tradition and culture, this Christendom, cannot be merely cast off as something external, but must be considered a vital part of identity.

Justification

Declaring the culpability of Western Christendom and its theological tradition in imperialism, racism, and wholesale violence around the world is commonplace in our postcolonial context. This guilt of the Western church/state fusion—in other words, Christendom—does not only refer to its egregious sins, like anti-Semitism, inquisition, and the slave trade. The *simul* of reconciliation makes the fallenness of even Christianity as a whole true. The question is never if our Christianity is sinful through and through, but in what sense it is, and how we might look to God's grace for redemption.

Moreover, while this historic reality of the so-called West cannot and must not be denied or glossed over, we are mistaken if this cultural captivity of Christendom points to some essential characteristic of the Western world. Barth notes that

> since the dawn of the post-apostolic period, and then more clearly in the Middle Ages, and in the earlier as well as the later modern period, there has always been this as it were non-Christian Christendom, and it no doubt exists also even in the sphere of the so-called younger churches of Asia and Africa.[152]

Because many contextual theologians, including many Asian American theologians, are at this stage still focused on resisting the hegemonic and universalizing influence of Western tradition, the possibility and the reality of cultural captivity in their own Christian tradition and even their theological works are not readily affirmed. However, the

151. See Kwok Pui-lan, *Postcolonial Imagination and Feminist Theology* (Louisville, KY: Westminster John Knox, 2005).
152. Barth, *CD* IV/3.2, 872.

possibility and the reality of such a captivity is a theological fact. While rightfully challenging the universalist claims of Western tradition, contextual theology can make the context into an idol if it interprets revelation in terms of and within the bounds of this context.[153] Revelation itself comes to us via a thoroughly creaturely medium that is open to distortive interpretations. Therefore, any expression of Christianity in history is utterly subject to God's mercy and grace. There is no hope of self-justification for Western Christendom or tradition or for any other expression of Christianity. Only the grace in the name of Jesus Christ is their justification for being true religion.[154]

Sanctification

Cultural captivity is unavoidable and even continually reoccurring. Newbigin realized this reality when he returned to a post-Christian England after years of missionary work in India.[155] The church is "always in a state of crisis" as it is continually struggling with the temptation to domesticate the gospel within its institutional structure.[156] Its sanctification means that no expressions of Christianity can stop being converted to the gospel, but they must rather be continually converting.[157] The Reformed self-critical dictum of *reformata, semper reformanda secundum verbum Dei*, mentioned in chapter 2, points to the path that Western Christianity and every other cultural expression of Christianity must follow to be faithful witnesses.

In this manner, the Protestant Reformation represents one expression of breaking out of a cultural captivity. In his "Disputation against Scholastic Theology (1517)," Luther locates his chief target by stating that "[virtually] the entire Ethics of Aristotle is the worst enemy of grace."[158] Realizing the integrating logic of Aristotelian ethics

153. Eberhard Busch, *The Great Passion: An Introduction to Karl Barth's Theology* (Grand Rapids, MI: Eerdmans, 2004), 72.
154. Barth, *CD* I/2, 358–59.
155. Lesslie Newbigin, *Foolishness to the Greeks: The Gospel and Western Culture* (Grand Rapids, MI: Eerdmans, 1986), 1.
156. Hendrik Kraemer, *The Christian Message in a Non-Christian World* (New York: IMC 1947), 24.
157. Darrell L. Guder, *The Continuing Conversion of the Church* (Grand Rapids, MI: Eerdmans, 2000), 144.
158. Martin Luther, "Disputation against Scholastic Theology (1517)," in *Luther's Works*, vol. 31, *Career of the Reformer I* (Minneapolis, MN: Fortress Press, 1957), 12.

to be *ratio* (reason), Luther reestablishes his gospel understanding upon foolishness and paradox. In fact, he calls the theses of the "Heidelberg Disputation" "theological paradoxes" which are the building blocks of *theologia crucis.*[159] This paradoxical nature of the revelation is why Luther believes that true theologians must become foolish in Christ before using Aristotelian concepts, the particular captivity of Luther's time.

This reforming approach did not begin with Luther's theological revolution, as he was only appropriating Augustine's understanding of Paul in *The Spirit and the Letter*, and Paul was simply struggling with the mystery of the cross. After Luther, Søren Kierkegaard took up the concept of the paradox and applied it to his "attacks upon Christendom," where every single person was infant-baptized, and therefore, no one really needed to confess his or her faith as a Christian.[160] Kierkegaard's criticism of cultural Christianity resonated with Barth as he searched for a new foundation for Christianity after World War I. Barth discovered that Christianity is about God in Christ and not about a "Christian" culture or a worldview. Later on, Dietrich Bonhoeffer drew from Kierkegaard and Barth to describe how even grace, as articulated in the doctrine of justification, can become meaningless and cheap if it ever became separated from the living God and domesticated for the purposes of self-justification.[161] Notably, Bonhoeffer would later give a devastating assessment of American Christianity as a Christianity that had missed the Reformation, and therefore was missing the self-critical dimension.[162] This kind of continual conversion represents the best of the Western tradition and points to the vocational aspect.

159. Martin Luther, "Heidelberg Disputation," in *Luther's Works*, vol. 31: *Career of the Reformer 1* (Minneapolis, MN: Fortress Press, 1957), 39.
160. Søren Kierkegaard, *Attack upon "Christendom"* (Princeton, NJ: Princeton University Press, 1944), 103.
161. Bonhoeffer, *Discipleship*, 44.
162. Dietrich Bonhoeffer, *Dietrich Bonhoeffer Works*, vol. 15, *Theological Education Underground, 1937-1940* (Minneapolis, MN: Augsburg Fortress Press, 2011), 438–39.

Vocation

In the previous chapter, we proposed the dialectical nature as summarized in these two ideas: *Universality must be mediated by Particularity* and *Particularity must be in service of Universality*. When the Western tradition is stripped of its universalist and normative delusions and treated only as a particular expression of Christianity, then it can begin to function in service of the Universal, God's revelation. Here, Barth's view of tradition points the way.

Barth's use of tradition in his theological method is nuanced and critical. He believed that the theological task included reconsideration of the tradition, "testing and rethinking it in the light of [God's Word,] its enduring foundation, object, and content."[163] More specifically, Barth explained that the authority of tradition "can only be indirect, formal and relative,

> i.e., it can only be what the concept prescribes: the authority of a human doctor of Holy Scripture whose task it is to acquaint his pupils not so much with himself as with the object which is his and their concern, to point and bind them not so much to himself as to this object.[164]

Barth is arguing that the authority of tradition is valid only as it witnesses to the authority of Scripture. In the sense of appropriating the authority of Scripture, tradition's own authority can only be indirect. Only as a commentary on Scripture can tradition serve as the wisdom of our elders, or maybe even of our siblings.[165] Also, tradition cannot be a material authority, but only a formal one. Tradition is the wisdom of *how* the Scriptures should be read; therefore, this wisdom and not always its particular expression of knowledge is its authority. Finally, the relative aspect of tradition's authority points to the freedom that we have as we relate to it. Tradition is limited and criticized by the scriptural witness and cannot be set alongside it. As

163. Karl Barth, *Evangelical Theology: An Introduction* (Grand Rapids, MI: Eerdmans, 1963), 42.
164. Barth, *CD* I/2, 617.
165. Ibid., 621.

we become a part of the historical church as the recent vanguard of tradition, we also contribute to it.[166]

Now from a wider perspective and without overstating things, Christianity with its Scripture is the root of Western culture, along with Greek and Roman antiquities. Christianity's spiritual influences, theological connections, and scriptural imagination in Western culture are undeniable, however marred or hidden. The *simul* should remind us of the dialectical nature of this witness, but to disregard this heritage because of its historic abuse of power and hegemonic hubris is unwarranted.

Racialization: Race and Racism

Asian Americans have been a part of American history since the early nineteenth century, but even then, they were entering into a world that had already framed race in terms of a black and white binary. This means that Asian Americans' physical features override their ethnicity as they become racialized. What does reconciliation mean for racism?

Justification

Divine judgment of racism takes at least two forms. First, racism is condemned as an offense to God's good creation that occurs when anyone is mistreated or oppressed for his or her physical features. Of course, racism takes myriad forms and expressions from microaggressions to systemic racism, and from subtle to blatant forms of discrimination.[167]

For example, the systemic nature of American racism toward Asian Americans is historically well established. The Chinese Exclusion Act of 1882 stands out as a particularly egregious policy when "for the first time in its history as a nation . . . the United States had enacted legislation barring a specific ethnic group from immigrating to the

166. Ibid., 711.
167. Lee explores "subtle discrimination" of Asian Americans through microaggressive acts and provides a list of various themes that these acts can take (Sang Hyun Lee, *From a Liminal Place*, 18–20).

United States solely on the basis of their country of origin."[168] Like the Chinese earlier, Japanese immigrants were also singled out in the Executive Order 9066 of 1942, becoming the "only racial-ethnic group in the United States who suffered the ignominy of mass imprisonment without trial in concentration camps merely on the basis of their ethnicity."[169] For the Koreans, the Los Angeles riots of 1992 became their baptism into the realities of American racial politics, stuck as they were between black and whites as the "middle minority."[170]

Second, racism is condemned as a totalizing narrative. Victor Anderson critiques James Cone's idea of ontological blackness, and others build upon this idea, calling it a form of "cultural idolatry."[171] White racism cannot be overcome by turning the tables on the oppressors. Of course, the label of reverse racism fails to see the extent and power of the historical and structural oppressor. Nevertheless, Cone's ontological blackness fails to become free from the totalizing narrative because it still stays within its own power structure. J. Kameron Carter rightly analyzes this ontological blackness as a theological abstraction, but his own "mulatto" language still appears to remain in this race framework, even as he identifies Jesus's flesh is covenantal.[172] This American race fixation is largely in terms of a black–white binary that marginalizes ethnic and cultural distinctions, which could arguably be just as, or more, significant for Asian Americans and Hispanic Americans, as well as for others in the global context.

Interestingly, in keeping with Barth's rejection of apologetics, Brunner's eritics and Tillich's method of correlation take the context, the world, or even sins like racism too seriously. According to Hunsinger, Barth saw these kinds of methodological moves as a denial of revelation, where "its necessity and sufficiency to impart itself are

168. Jonathan Y. Tan, *Introducing Asian American Theologies* (Maryknoll, NY: Orbis, 2008), 26.
169. Ibid., 31.
170. Ibid., 40.
171. See Victor Anderson, *Beyond Ontological Blackness: An Essay on African American Religious and Cultural Criticism* (New York: Continuum, 1995).
172. Carter, *Race*, 192. Carter, Jennings, and Bantum, all critique racism, but still fail to free themselves from its totalizing narrative, projecting the American race fixation universally. See Jennings, *The Christian Imagination*, and Bantum, *Redeeming Mulatto*.

circumscribed or whenever its content is subjected to alien standards."[173]

Sanctification

The direction of its transformation begins with the decentering of race as a theological category. Even in its more demonic manifestations, racism is still only one form of sin. Jung Young Lee notes that the call for justice and liberation must go hand in hand with the embodiment of reconciliation, which presupposes our common humanity and shared brokenness.[174] For Asian Americans, various dimensions of Asian American culpability must complement the rhetoric of white racist oppression. Here are some nuances to the racism talk.

First, even as a "middle minority" instrumentalized by the majority culture, Asian Americans are still culpable for the part they have played in the racist structures that have oppressed African Americans. Some have argued that "the primary source of Korean American racism towards African Americans is American racial ideology" as it was propagated through the US presence in Korea since the Korean War.[175] However, although locating the source might explain the reason, it does not exonerate the Asian American from the act of racism itself. In addition, this shift of blame to American racial ideology is, in itself, oppressive to Asian Americans because it denies their agency as subjects, and instead, relegates them to being mere puppets of Western influence. Furthermore, there is a limit to this blame-shifting because more recently, Korean storeowners have discriminated against Mexican immigrant workers.[176] Where can the blame for this injustice be located? Accepting the blame is the first step toward peace, healing, and justification.

Second, "Asian Americans as a whole (especially among the native

173. Hunsinger, *How to Read Karl Barth*, 52.
174. Lee, *Marginality*, 73. Also, see J. Deotis Roberts, *Liberation and Reconciliation: A Black Theology*, 2nd ed. (Louisville, KY: Westminster John Knox, 2005).
175. Nancy Abelmann and John Lie, *Blue Dreams: Korean Americans and the Los Angeles Riots* (Cambridge: Harvard University Press, 1997), 150.
176. Pyong Gap Min, "Korean Americans," in *Asian Americans: Contemporary Trends and Issues*, ed. Pyong Gap Min (Thousand Oaks, CA: Pine Forge, 2005), 243.

born) tend to have higher average levels of educational attainment" than everyone else in America, including whites.[177] If the focus is narrowed to just East Asian Americans, their average becomes even higher. The average earnings of Asian Americans are comparable to those of whites, and as expected, East Asian Americans as a group earn even more.[178] However, we must note that this educational attainment and average earning vary widely among Asian Americans of divergent ethnic heritages and the model minority myth is erroneous and hurts the needy and the poor among this community. Even with this very significant point, we must acknowledge that even while facing racism as perpetual foreigners, many well-educated and employed Asian Americans are part of the oppressor class, a part of the system of structural racism that oppresses other minorities.

Third, although Jung Young Lee states that "most Asian never experienced racism" before coming to America, racism does exist in Asia.[179] In Japan, based upon Japanese aesthetics apart from any Western influence, "white" skin has always been considered beautiful and "black" skin ugly.[180] When the Japanese saw the African slaves of the first Westerner visitors, they projected their aesthetics upon the Africans. Also, under the threat of Western imperialism in the eighteenth and nineteenth centuries, China employed social Darwinism to establish its place in the world, as one influential thinker and essayist writes: "Only yellows and whites are not far removed from one another. . . . The brown and black races are stupid and lazy."[181] This

177. Arthur Sakamoto and Yu Xie, "The Socioeconomic Attainments of Asian Americans," in *Asian Americans*, 59.

178. Ibid., 61.

179. Lee, *Marginality*, 38. Along with racism, Japan and China both have their own sets of historically oppressed minority ethnic groups within their borders. Whether toward the Muslim ethnic people in western China or the native people of northern Japan, sin abounds. Of course, Japan and China have both at different periods oppressed Korea, seeing it as a nation of lesser people. See Dru C. Gladney, *Muslim Chinese: Ethnic Nationalism in the People's Republic* (Cambridge: Harvard University Asia Center, 1996); and Michael Weiner, *Japan's Minorities: The Illusion of Homogeneity* (New York: Routledge, 1997).

180. Hiroshi Wagatsuma, "The Social Perception of Skin Color in Japan," in *Racism: A Global Reader*. ed. Kevin Reilly, Stephen Kaufman, Angela Bodino (Armonk, NY: M.E. Sharpe, 2003), 28.

181. Richard Lufrano, "The 1988 Nanjing Incident: Notes on Race and Politics in Contemporary China," in *Race and Ethnicity: Critical Concepts in Sociology*,ed. Harry Goulbourne (New York: Routledge, 2001), 8.

sentiment is not some distant historical fact. Some years ago, in China, the public racist vitriol against a mixed heritage reality TV contestant drew international attention.[182] Furthermore, Social Darwinism took root in the Korean mind in the early nineteen century and sowed the seeds of nation-building using ethnocentricity, which solidified under Japanese colonialism.[183] Korean ethnocentricity has also strongly discriminated against bicultural individuals, a growing group from mixed marriages in Korea.[184]

Black–white racism as we know it in the USA might not have fully developed in Asian countries, but various forms of it existed and were used for these countries' own self-preservation as well as self-promotion. Therefore, broadly speaking, Asian Americans through their American experience and Asian roots are victims as well as perpetrators of racism. Engaging racism with this grammar means confessing the various layers and trajectories of victimhood and oppression, even while fighting racial injustices with conviction and humility.

Vocation

As Barth states, culture can witness to not only the goodness and glory of creation, but to its peril as well. The witness of racism is the ugliness and the reach of sin and its destructive and dehumanizing forces, pointing to human depravity and our need for redemption. Also, racism as a backdrop witnesses to the fierce display of God's amazing grace to deliver the oppressed and overcome evil, through the lives of John Newton, William Wilberforce, Frederick Douglass, and Martin Luther King, Jr., just to name a few. In these cases, God paradoxically created and brought forth good out of great wickedness. As stated above, God can commandeer all creation for his revelatory

182. Stephen Vines, "China's Black Pop Idol Exposes Her Nation's Racism,"*The Observer*, November 1, 2009. http://www.guardian.co.uk/world/2009/nov/01/lou-jing-chinese-talent-show.

183. See Gi-Wook Shin, *Ethnic Nationalism in Korea: Genealogy, Politics, and Legacy* (Stanford, CA: Stanford University Press, 2006).

184. Tae Yang Kwak, "The Republic of Korea in the Southeast Asia: Expanding influences and relationships," in *Korea's Changing Roles in Southeast Asia: Expanding Influence and Relations*, ed. David I. Steinberg (Singapore: Institute of Southeast Asian Studies, 2010), 317.

pleasure. No *a priori* judgment of what God can use or how God will use them is ultimately helpful.

What we have done in this section is to engage themes from the Asian American context with the triadic grammar of reconciliation. Aspects such as the unity-in-distinction of justification, sanctification, and vocation, their atemporal ordering, and the eschatolgical *simul* all contribute to a cultural engagement that is dynamic, nimble, and nuanced. These features are the true strength and contribution of this reconciliation grammar. With it, we are able to practice concrete *fides quaerens intellectum*, discerning God's movement and work in the particular lived realities of people.

Conclusion

In this chapter, we proposed a triadic reconciliation grammar as a new way of engaging culture. To arrive at this grammar, which is derived out of Barth's doctrine of reconciliation, we began with a review of other approaches to understanding Barth's theology of culture—from Palma's and Metzger's to DeCou's. Our approach sought to further Metzger's incarnational rubric by looking to Barth's mature Christology in his doctrine of reconciliation. However, to arrive at the doctrine of reconciliation, which provided the content of *participatio Christi*, Barth's doctrine of election had to be addressed, because it is here that Barth offers the universal, *de jure participatio Christi* of all creation.

Arriving at reconciliation via election, we identified its triadic content of justification, sanctification, and vocation, as well as its distinctive features, like its thorough *simul* nature, the unity-in-distinction of the *triplex gratia*, its atemporal ordering, and finally, its *totus/totus* dynamic. Superimposing reconciliation over Barth's doctrine of creation, we argued that this *triplex gratia* rubric served well as a hermeneutical key to understanding his views of creation and of culture.

Starting with Niebuhr's typology and drawing from the critique and insights of Tanner, Yoder, and Newbigin, we sought to show how

Barth's doctrine of reconciliation can serve as a grammar for cultural engagement that is dynamic, dialectical, and nuanced. This grammatical approach stresses the divine freedom to judge, transform, and call any aspect of culture for divine purposes.

Finally, using this triadic grammar, we engaged a theme from each of the four aspects of the Asian American context, displaying its strength and flexibility to cover diverse topics and areas. The goal here was simply to demonstrate how this grammar would work rather than to give a conclusive assessment beyond the grammar's inner logic.

In the next chapter, we will present an Asian American ecclesiology. Asian American theological reflection with its cultural engagement must occur within a faith community, not just in individual lives. If theology is to be genuinely ecclesial and missional, it must go beyond the autobiographical to the communal.

4

Missionality: Asian American Ecclesiologies

In the previous chapter, we proposed a triadic reconciliation grammar as a new way of engaging with culture, showing how this grammar can be used to critically and constructively engage with the Asian American Quadrilateral (AAQ), that is, the four key aspects of the Asian American experience: Asian heritage, the experience of migration, American culture, and racialization. In this chapter, we will address Asian American ecclesiology using concepts and resources from Barth. More particularly, Barth's christological logic and explication of the dual nature of the church provide a set of analytical tools with which to creatively engage an Asian American constructive ecclesiology. Moreover, his missional outlook provides the crucial ecclesial trajectory for our postmodern, post-Christendom context.

We could take up Asian American ecclesiology more narrowly in terms of pan-Asian churches, where people of diverse Asian ethnicities form worshipping communities. However, this narrow focus would not reflect the diversity and dynamics of the present Asian American experience. Throughout this work, we have underscored and integrated the dynamic hybridity of current Asian American contexts as well as the deep differences among those of various ethnic backgrounds, generations, and geographic locations within the USA. Therefore, we discuss here the multiple Asian American ecclesiologies present in the form of ethnic churches, pan-Asian churches, and multiracial churches.[1] All these forms and many more transitional ones between them exist and require theological reflection regarding their ecclesial being and practices.

Barth understood the task of theology as "the scientific self-examination of the Christian Church with respect to the content of its distinctive talk about God."[2] and in respect to God, about humanity as well. Asian American theology exists and is needed because these Asian American churches do indeed exist, and for the sake of its faithfulness, this kind of "self-examination" must occur.

While the promise of Barth's christological and missional ecclesiology is rich, some concerns and questions must be acknowledged. What does contextual ecclesiology, especially dealing with churches "segregated" by ethnicity or race, have to do with Barth's theology? Referencing the situation of apartheid in South Africa and segregation in the USA in the 1950s, Barth questioned the "[ratification of] the social distinctions between whites and blacks by a corresponding division in the Church, instead of calling it in question in the social sphere by the contrary practice of the Church."[3] Carys Moseley even proposes that nationalism served as a key catalyst for Barth's break with the anthropocentric legacy of liberalism.[4]

In a particularly poignant section, Barth asserts that divisions according to nations, race, culture, and class (*Völker, Rassen, Bildung,* and *Klassen*) must not be in the Christian community if it is to be a faithful witness to

1. Given the myriad diversity of ethnic churches and the absence of any centralized structure, keeping track of their numbers is a challenge. According to Chuang, over seven thousand Asian ethnic churches exist currently, compared to around two hundred and fifty pan-Asian churches. D.J. Chuang, "9 Things about Asian American Christianity," *The Exchange: A Blog by Ed Stetzer,* November 7, 2013. http://www.christianitytoday.com/edstetzer/2013/november/9-things-about-asian-american-christianity.html.
2. Barth, *CD* I/1, 4.
3. Barth, *CD* IV.1, 703.
4. Carys Moseley, *Nations and Nationalism in the Theology of Karl Barth* (Oxford: Oxford University Press, 2013), 1.

> the supreme fellowship, namely, that of the Father with the Son and the Son with the Father in the Holy Spirit, and on this basis the particular fellowship of Jesus Christ as the Head with the community as His body and each of its members, and on this basis the more general fellowship which God has newly and definitely established between Himself and the whole world as created by Him.[5]

Barth's leadership during the *Kirchenkampf* against German Christianity is well known, and as John Flett points out, Barth's rejection of natural theology has clear implications for ethnic ecclesiology, or at least for missiology that emphasizes a contextual ecclesiology.[6]

Barth's critique of divisions within the Christian community will be discussed in detail below. However, as was noted in the introduction to this study, Barth knew the limitations of his own context and was not a theological imperialist who confused his particular work for a universal theology. This is clearly seen in his letter in *The South East Asia Journal of Theology*.[7] Of course, Barth makes it clear in the letter and also throughout his *corpus* that the context must not become a "Babylonian captivity" of sorts. On the contrary, we have argued in the previous chapters that there is no such a thing as an acontextual theology either. Because God is a living God, people must attend to God's Word in their own particularities.

Moreover, this present work is not a Barthian work in the sense of simply "repeating [his] words as our own or making his views ours," as Barth discussed in the introduction to a work that discussed how Calvin ought not to be studied.[8] Barth avers that being taught by Calvin and Herrmann is not simply to follow them, but to enter into dialogue

5. Barth, *CD* IV/3.2, 898.
6. German missiologists such as Christian Keysser advocated for a *völkisch* Christianity based on their fieldwork, eventually supporting Nazi German Christianity. The fact that Keysser is enthusiastically supported by Donald McGavran of the Church Growth Movement with its homogenous unit principle only complicates any theological justification for "segregated" churches (John G. Flett, *The Witness of God: The Trinity,* Missio Dei, *Karl Barth and the Nature of Christian Community* [Grand Rapids, MI: Eerdmans, 2010]: 78–122).
7. Karl Barth, "No Boring Theology! A Letter from Karl Barth," *The South East Asian Journal of Theology* 11 (Autumn 1969): 3–5.
8. Karl Barth, *The Theology of John Calvin*, trans. Geoffrey W. Bromiley (Grand Rapids, MI: Eerdmans, 1995), 4.

with them and allow the dialogue to kindle in the readers their own ideas and convictions.[9]

This present study is not written from the context of the church in Western Europe in the middle of the last century. Rather, it is written in the concrete situation of Asian American Christian communities facing contemporary challenges from cultural change and globalization.

Given this bit of ground-clearing for the task before us, the rest of this chapter will be presented as follows. First, the contours of Barth's ecclesiology will be outlined, with special attention given to issues of unity, diversity, and particularity. The development of Barth's theology with its critical turning point at the doctrine of election will be discussed. Then, the triadic formula of the gathering, upbuilding, and sending of the community within the doctrine of reconciliation will give the overall structure for Barth's ecclesiological insights. In terms of the community's gathering, special focus will be given to Barth's exposition of the marks of the church, especially its unity in relation to ecumenical diversity. The section on the upbuilding of the community will explore the relationship between the human body and the divine head of Christ, discussing distortions and deviations of this relationship expressed in docetic and ebionitic ecclesiologies. Finally, the doctrine of vocation and the sending of the church to participate in Christ's mission will be highlighted. The church does not exist for itself, but for its mission to the world.

Second, contextual ecclesiology will be engaged using Barth's theological apparatus. The Church Growth Movement with its homogeneous unit principle will be analyzed since it still represents one of the more prominent, albeit outdated, contextual ecclesiological reflections. Moreover, the view that multiracial churches are the answer to the issue of race will be critiqued as well. Along with covering Barth's idea about various divisions, we will argue that both homogeneity and multiracial diversity can become theological abstractions, and therefore, be cultural captivities for the church.

9. Ibid.

Last, guided by the Asian American Quadrilateral, we will propose Asian American ecclesiologies within various ecclesial expressions. Corresponding to the four aspects of the AAQ,[10] the church will be described as a contextual community, a transitional community, a missional community, and a liberational community. Echoing Barth's triadic doctrine of reconciliation, the theological basis, formational dialectic, and missional calling of each of these community conceptions will be offered. Throughout the discussion, ethnic, pan-Asian and multiracial churches will be kept in mind.

Barth's Christological and Missional Ecclesiology

In this section, we will provide an overall outline of Barth's ecclesiology. Given the expansive nature of his theology, special attention will be paid to those areas that resonate with contextual matters. After explaining the development of Barth's ecclesiological thought with the doctrine of election as a turning point, the rest of the section will be organized into three topics: the gathering, upbuilding, and sending of the community. This section will show Barth's nuanced understanding of unity and plurality, his contextual awareness via the community's concrete existence, and the missional innovation in his ecclesiology.

Barth's Early Ecclesiology

As discussed in the previous chapter, one of the results of Barth's break from liberalism was a recovery of the radical diastasis between God and creation. However, as he matured as a theologian, he sought a way to recover the connection while retaining this gulf. We saw how this developed along four main stages, which McCormick described so well, guided Barth's engagement of culture.[11] In his *Karl Barth's Christological Ecclesiology*, Kimlyn Bender builds upon McCormack's analysis and unpacks Barth's ecclesiological trajectory.[12]

10. Asian heritage, the migration experience, American culture, and racialization.
11. McCormack, *Karl Barth's Critically Realistic Dialectical Theology*.
12. Kimlyn J. Bender, *Karl Barth's Christological Ecclesiology* (Burlington, VA: Ashgate, 2005).

Bender notes that between the first two developmental stages, which are marked by process eschatology and consistent eschatology, Barth's understanding of church does not change significantly.[13] Of course, Barth's views on revelation are modified quite a bit. In the first and second versions of *Römerbrief*, which represent these first two stages, Barth places the church with religion and unbelief, with the church "situated on this side of the abyss which separates men from God."[14] In the second version, he merely intensified the critique. Since Barth was frustrated with the reception of the first version, in which his readers generally missed the diastasis that he had sought, this intensified critique is understandable.[15]

Barth's concern is mainly the "the ultimate and final distinction between God and humanity," so he stresses that the church, along with every individual human being, is sinful.[16] Barth points out that the "problem of 'Religion or Irreligion'—not to speak of the problem 'Church or World'—is no longer a fundamental problem."[17] Even a couple of years earlier in his 1919 Tambach lecture on "The Christian in Society," Barth stresses that what we mean by "Christian" is really "*the Christ*" which dwells within us.[18]

The critique did not mean that the church was godless, but its positive element was limited to the moment of revelation. Using the dialectic between the invisible church of Isaac and the visible church of Esau, Barth explains this moment:

> The Church is divided into the Church of Esau–where no miracle occurs, and where, consequently, men are exposed as liars, precisely when they hear and speak about God; and the Church of Jacob–where miracle is, and where, consequently, the Truth appears above the deceit of men. The two Churches do not, of course, stand over against one another as two things. The Church of Esau alone is observable, knowable and possible.[19]

13. Ibid., 25n28.
14. Karl Barth, *The Epistles to the Romans* (London: Oxford University Press, 1968), 332.
15. McCormack, *Karl Barth's Critically Realistic Dialectical Theology*, 155.
16. Bender, *Karl Barth's Christological Ecclesiology*, 29.
17. Barth, *The Epistle to the Romans*, 40.
18. Karl Barth, "The Christian in Society, 1919," in *The Word of God and Theology*, 36.
19. Barth, *The Epistles to the Romans*, 341.

Mirroring the nature of revelation at this stage, "the invisible church touched the visible church only as a tangent touching a circle."[20] Correspondingly, the church as human community is simply passive with no particular constructive vocation toward the world. As McCormack summarizes, "Barth's positive valuation of the Church in this phase remains strictly in the vertical dimension. It does not extend to the horizontal."[21] Defined strictly formally, the church was the only place where revelation occurred. The material dimension of the church is still amorphous here.

In the third developmental stage, during his Göttingen days, Barth's discovery of the anhypostatic-enhypostatic Christology from the patristic and Reformed traditions began the material development of his ecclesiology.[22] With the doctrine of the incarnation at the center of Barth's theology, Chalcedonian logic became "a paradigm for understanding all divine and human relations" by ordering these relations in differentiated asymmetric unity.[23] In ecclesiological terms, this means that Barth can now state that the "doctrine of the invisible and visible Church in ecclesiology is, as it were, the analogy to the doctrine of justification in soteriology and the doctrine of the person of Christ in Christology."[24]

In a markedly different tone, even while still referring to the invisible church of Isaac and the visible church of Esau, Barth began to affirm the positive dimension of the historical form:

> One can and must believe in the visibility of the church precisely because it has pleased and still pleases God to give to the mystical Body of Christ a visible, historical body. The true church does not remain invisible in a Platonic or docetic sense, but rather the true church has assumed and assumes a form in history just as God in Christ took on flesh.[25]

20. Bender, *Karl Barth's Christological Ecclesiology*, 35.
21. Ibid., 36. Quoting Bruce McCormack from "A Scholastic of a Higher Order: The Development of Karl Barth's Theology, 1921–31" (PhD diss., University of Michigan, 1989), 190.
22. Ibid., 62.
23. Ibid., 65.
24. Karl Barth, *Unterricht in der christlichen Religion, III: Die Lehre von der Versöhnung / Die Lehre von der Erlösung*, ed. Hinrich Stoevesandt (Zürich: Theologischer Verlag Zürich, 2003), 366. (My translation.)
25. Bender, *Karl Barth's Christological Ecclesiology*, 72. A paraphrase of Barth in *Unterricht in der christlichen Religion*, 3:363.

Finally, Barth's revision of the doctrine of election marks McCormack's fourth developmental stage, which is characterized by a Christocentric anhypostatic-enhypostatic Christology. In Barth's doctrine of election, Jesus Christ, the God-man, is the electing subject as well as the elected one, the electing God and the elected man.[26] The electing God is Jesus Christ, who has reconciled the world to himself. The elected man is Jesus Christ, who obediently exercised a human freedom that corresponded to divine freedom. Barth retains the Chalcedonian patterns of the previous stage, but the significant difference is his idea of God's humanity; more specifically, he gives Christ's humanity a fuller articulation and affirmation. This allowed for "a more positive place to human freedom and agency" in Jesus Christ, in the human community, as well as in creation in general.[27]

The asymmetric relationship between God and the human community as well as the actualistic ontology still protected God's subjectivity, of course. As it participates in Christ through election, the community exists as the provisional reality and witness for the sake of the world, which is already *de jure* in Christ.[28] Compared to Barth's early ecclesiology in *Römerbrief*, the contrast is clear. No longer is the church indiscriminately grouped together with religion and the world. Rather, in a provisional sense, the church now actually participates in Christ's mission for the sake of the world.

Just as in the previous chapter, the pivotal moment of Barth's positive turn toward the world and humanity is found in his doctrine of election. However, the context for the full exposition of this turn is his doctrine of reconciliation in three modes. The triadic soteriological division of justification, sanctification, and vocation orders the gathering, upbuilding and sending of the church. Of course, the entire doctrine of reconciliation is thoroughly christological.

26. Barth, *CD* II/2, 115–17.
27. Bender, *Karl Barth's Christological Ecclesiology*, 119.
28. Barth, *CD* II/2, 197–201.

Gathering of the Community: Unity and Plurality

Barth begins his ecclesiological discussion by acknowledging the gathering of the community as the work of the Holy Spirit. Staying clear of anthropological reductions, the Holy Spirit is named as "the power in which Jesus Christ attests Himself, attests Himself effectively, creating in man response and obedience."[29] Identifying the spiritual origins of the community, Barth continues to stress this divine subjectivity by employing his actualism with the church as an *event*.

This *event* language with its connection to being-in-becoming should not be understood as denying "the church's existence as a continuous, visible intuition," but rather, as "the divine mystery of the church's existence at every moment of its life."[30] In other words, there is "no direct identity" between the invisible and the visible church.[31] Rather, the identity is indirect, a work of the Holy Spirit and therefore a gracious and sovereign work.[32]

Barth unpacks the marks of the church in this christological identity. Although the Chalcedonian dialectic is not always explicit, it is still always present to guide against errors in the articulation of the dual nature of the church.[33] For the unity of the church, the dialectical unity of Jesus Christ becomes the pattern for the unity between visible and invisible community, between the *ecclesia militans* and the *ecclesia triumphans*, and between Israel and Church.[34]

Later, echoing the lectures he presented at the 1937 Edinburgh World Conference on Faith and Order, Barth addressed the issues of plurality as related to the church's geographic separation.[35] Displaying

29. Barth, *CD* IV/1, 648.
30. Joseph L. Mangina, *Karl Barth: Theologian of Christian Witness* (Louisville, KY: Westminster John Knox, 2004), 154.
31. Barth, *CD* IV/1, 657.
32. This indirect identity is, of course, that *Realdialektik* that was discussed in relation to Barth's contextuality in chapter 2. It is "the motor which drives Barth's doctrine of analogy and makes it possible" (see McCormack, *Karl Barth's Critically Realistic Dialectical Theology*, 18).
33. In his discussion of this section, Bender helpfully makes explicit the various docetic and ebionitic expressions that Barth avoids. Because of the limitations of this study and the primary goal of Asian American ecclesiology, we will be not discussing these matters (Bender, *Karl Barth's Christological Ecclesiology*, 181–88).
34. Barth, *CD* IV/1, 668–85.
35. Karl Barth, *The Church and the Churches* (Grand Rapids, MI: Eerdmans, 1936).

his nuanced understanding of unity in diversity, Barth states that in the church's historical concreteness in many localities,

> it is essential to it that in its unity it should exist in this geographical separation and difference which corresponds to its environment and history and language and customs and ways of life and thoughts as conditioned by the different localities, and also to its personal composition. In this respect the same thing does not suit every Church or every place and time. This has never been taken seriously enough in our missionary thinking. But it can, of course, be taken too seriously, as has often happened.[36]

As we have noted throughout this present work, Barth continues to take seriously the particularity of human diversity and cultural contexts without deifying or essentializing them. While Barth considers this geographic, essentially contextual, diversity to be legitimate, he rejects any other plurality, such as denominational and confessional ones, considering them scandalous divisions that signify "a plurality of lords, a plurality of spirits, a plurality of gods."[37]

Barth's response to this scandalous disunity is precise and realistic. He rejects pseudo-unities that are brought about by "externally satisfying co-existence and co-operation of different religious societies," and which are often caused by toleration or indifference to theological differences.[38] Rather, Barth calls divided churches to take their theological particularities seriously, seriously enough to seek critique and revision by the Word of God, and thus, move toward true unity in Jesus Christ. The decisive step is the openness of all the churches to the "voice of the Lord by them and for them," and then, to the voices of others.[39] The unity of the church, even in history, is never an abstraction, because true unity is rooted in Jesus Christ.

In terms of holiness, here again, the "community is holy because and as Jesus Christ is holy."[40] In union with Christ and in fellowship with him by the power of the Spirit, the church also lives as *ecclesia semper*

36. Barth, *CD* IV/1, 671–72.
37. Ibid., 675.
38. Ibid., 678.
39. Ibid., 684.
40. Ibid., 689.

reformanda. Moreover, this holiness is hidden, not external.[41] Thus, the community's holiness is in its faith, but a faith that leads to obedience.

Barth defines the church's ecumenicity as "an identity, a continuity and a universality, which is maintained in all the differences.[42] The same essence must be maintained "in all places, in all ages, within all societies, and in relation to all its members."[43] In connection to our concerns, even though there will be contextual plurality,

> in essence the Church is the same in all races, languages, cultures and classes, in all forms of state and society. If it is to remain a true church, it cannot be essentially determined by any of these societies. It cannot allow its concepts of itself to be dictated by them. It cannot adjust itself to them. . . . Christians will always be Christians first, and only then members of a specific culture or state or class or the like.[44]

This essential sameness is the other end of the dialectic with the plurality that was stressed above. No Babylonian captivities are allowed in the name of legitimate plurality.

Finally, apostolicity refers to the apostolic witness in Scripture that is "the concrete spiritual criterion" of the first three marks, and thus, is the climax point.[45] Barth stresses that this mark is "not sociological or juridical or psychological, but spiritual."[46] Rather than a historical or judicial interpretation of apostolic succession, for instance, Barth avers that this criterion ultimately refers to the living Christ who is the Lord of his church and who rules through the witness of his Word. Moreover, Barth briefly points to what he will develop later in *CD* IV/3 about the sending of the community, noting the church's missional existence as a witness to the world. Christ's body does not exists for itself, but "points beyond itself."[47]

In the discussions that follow, Barth's articulation of this unity and

41. Ibid., 694–701.
42. Ibid., 701.
43. Ibid., 707.
44. Ibid., 703.
45. Ibid., 712.
46. Ibid.
47. Ibid., 723.

plurality, and specifically, of unity and ecumenicity, will be put in conversation with the Asian American situation.

Upbuilding of the Community: Christological Order

Barth states that the "community is the earthly-historical form of existence of Jesus Christ himself."[48] Using the Chalcedonian pattern, the human community and Jesus Christ are brought together without mixture, confusion, separation, or division. Here, Barth notes that both the docetic and ebionitic ecclesiologies must be rejected.

Following the logic of the dialectical identity, Barth affirms the Augustinian doctrine of *totus Christus*, where the full reality of Christ is: Christ the head, with the body, his church. This unity is asymmetric in that Christ takes precedence and is the source of the body, which has no existence apart from Christ. "Jesus Christ is the community" but the "community is not Jesus Christ."[49] Furthermore, Barth extends this identity to the kingdom of God: as Jesus Christ "is the kingdom of God," so "the kingdom of God is the community."[50]

Concretizing this identity means that the mere existence of the church is not its end. Rather, the community has a direction and a trajectory toward serving the Lord, for which purpose it was formed. Even in this direction, the christological logic of two natures is vital, because as the community's "upbuilding is wholly and utterly the work of God or Christ, so it is wholly and utterly its own."[51] Within the second mode of the doctrine of reconciliation, Barth examines how Christ by the power of the Spirit grows, sustains, and orders the community.

Regarding the growth of the church, Barth points out that true growth is not extensive numerical growth, but intensive spiritual growth. However, if the community is really engaged in this intensive growth, then at "some point and in some way . . . it will always experience" extensive growth, albeit possibly in different forms than

48. Ibid., 661.
49. Barth, *CD* IV/2, 655.
50. Ibid., 656.
51. Ibid., 634.

expected.[52] The two kinds of growth are not separated or confused, but it is very clear that the intensive growth takes determinative precedence.[53] If numerical growth takes precedence, then the community's witness becomes "propaganda on behalf of its own spatial expansion," and churches will become tempted to win converts by diluting the message.[54]

Regarding the sustaining or upholding of the community, the dangers that the church faces are from without and within. External threats include menacing questioning and sheer indifference from the world. More than persecution, these subtler threats endanger the community. Also, internal threats in the form of secularization, becoming molded by the world, and sacralization, not remaining in the world, can lead to the end of the community. While Scripture does uphold the community, it is Jesus Christ who "primarily and properly upholds the Church" as the Scripture's content.[55]

Ultimately, the upbuilding of the community means the process of becoming like Christ and being ordered by its Lord. Barth's presentation of church law should not simply be reduced to bureaucratic or administrative polity. Rather, it should be understood, first and foremost, christologically. The community is ordered so as to correspond to the life of Jesus Christ, who is the living law.[56] Following Christ as the living law means being ordered for service and worship. Of course, this ordering also means that the church law is living, following the activity of the living Christ in the church and the world. The community's order might change to be "best adapted to its edification and the discharging of its mission."[57] Also, as a community following the Lord of all creation, its law is a model of how the world should operate.

This christological ordering and the doctrine of *totus Christus* will function as the criteria for discerning how the ecclesial form can be

52. Ibid., 648.
53. Bender, *Karl Barth's Christological Ecclesiology*, 180.
54. Barth, *CD* IV/2, 646.
55. Ibid., 675.
56. Bender, *Karl Barth's Christological Ecclesiology*, 209–10.
57. Barth, *CD* IV/2, 660.

fully divine and fully human without leading to docetic or ebionitic distortions.

Sending of the Community: For Sake of the World

Barth understands the identity of the community with Christ, resulting in the community's distinction from general humanity, to be a result of an election that is "relative, provisional and teleological."[58] As the relatively or temporarily chosen community, the church exists "eschatologically" and "looks back to Easter Day and forward to the Last Day," when there will be a universal and direct revelation of Christ.[59] The provisional and teleological election points to its function and mission of existing as a witness of God's reconciliation to the world.

As we articulated in the previous chapter, justification, sanctification, and vocation exist in a differentiated unity. Also, Barth rejects any ordering of them in temporality, logic, or value. This means that Barth's ecclesiology must be understood as missional in its entirety:[60] "Jesus Christ would not be who He is if He lacked His community and if this community did not have or need not have a missionary character."[61]

Barth's missional breakthrough was his rejection of the "reception and enjoyment of the *beneficia Christi*" as the point of vocation, of Christian existence.[62] Moreover, "the community of Jesus Christ is for

58. Barth, *CD* IV/1, 666. Barth's view about election of the community resonates closely with Lesslie Newbigin's. Newbigin also understood "the logic of election" in this provisional and teleological manner. The community's election does not mean exclusive salvation, but rather "to be incorporated into [Christ's] mission to the world, to be the bearer of God's saving purpose for his whole world, to be a sign and the agent and the first fruit of his blessed kingdom which is for all" (Lesslie Newbigin, *The Gospel in a Pluralist Society* [Grand Rapids, MI: Eerdmans, 1989], 87). Guder notes this exact convergence, see Darrell L. Guder, "Mining Barth's Dogmatics for a Missional Ecclesiology," in *Dogmatics after Barth: Facing Challenges in Church, Society and the Academy*, ed. Günter Thomas, Rinse H. Reeling Brouwer and Bruce McCormack (Leipzig: CreateSpace, 2012), 137.

59. Barth, *CD* IV/1, 662.

60. Guder remarks, "Bosch argued that Barth developed his entire ecclesiology in volume IV of the Church Dogmatics as an expression of the conviction that the church by its very nature is missionary" (Guder, "Mining Barth's Dogmatics for a Missional Ecclesiology," 133, referring to David Bosch, *Transforming Mission: Paradigm Shift in Theology of Mission* [Maryknoll, NY: Orbis, 1991], 372–73).

61. Barth, *CD* IV/2, 275.

the world," and because it is part of the world, "as it exists for men and the world, it also exists for itself."[63] As it participates in Jesus Christ, who is "not for Himself but for the world," that church must be for the world as well.[64] Basing his innovation on the overwhelming witness of Scripture, Barth seeks to recover the church's thoroughly missional nature, which was missing in much of history and is so needed in the post-Christendom context:

> The work of the Holy Spirit in the gathering and upbuilding of the community (*C.D.*, IV, 1 § 62 and IV, 2 § 67) cannot merely lead to the blind alley of a new qualification, enhancement, deepening and enrichment of this being of the community as such. Wonderful and glorious as this is, it is not an end in itself even in what it includes for its individual members. . . . In the patristic and scholastic, and then again in the Reformation and post-Reformation doctrine of the Church, there is a gap at this point which in spite of the many correct insights makes it seem theoretically unconvincing from the standpoint both of Holy Scripture and of the matter itself, and which makes it veritably suspect in its practical outworking.[65]

Being for the world involves deep solidarity with the world as well as a clear and faithful witness to the truth of the world's condition and the hope found in Christ. This witness is presupposed to be fully in the world, but not of it. Concretely, Barth lists twelve forms of service of the missional church: praising God, gospel proclamation, instruction of its members, evangelization, missions, theology, prayer, cure of souls, personal examples of Christian life and action, the diaconate, prophetic action, and fellowship.[66] Here, we highlight three insights relevant to our contextual concerns.

First, in the service of missions, we again see Barth's awareness of and concern for the integrity of the local context:

> Neither the aim to strengthen confessional positions, nor to extend European or American culture and civilization, nor to propagate one of

62. Barth, *CD* IV/3.2, 573.
63. Ibid., 762.
64. Ibid., 763.
65. Ibid., 764.
66. Ibid., 865–901.

> the modes of thought and life familiar and dear to the older Christian world by reason of its antiquity, can be the motivating force behind true Christian missions, and certainly not the desire to support colonial or general political interests and aspiration.[67]

This concern covers world religions as well, and reflects Barth's dialectical perspective:

> Missions presupposes both that [world religions] will be valued and taken seriously, with a complete absence of the crass arrogance of the white man, and yet also that they not be allowed to exercise any pressure on the Gospel. . . . Missions are valueless and futile if they are not pursued . . . with sincere respect and yet also an equally sincere lack of respect for the so-called religions.[68]

Since in Asian American contexts, the pressure toward assimilation into the white dominant culture and the struggles of recovering and engaging Asian religious heritages are prominent, Barth's comments are welcome.

Second, in different ways, services of diaconate and prophecy both cover systemic injustices that the church is called to confront. Even if the state engages in similar service, the church is still called to seek "its own particular possibilities and to look for new ones" along with assisting the state, if possible.[69] This confrontation and prophetic service might lead to division in the church because this kind of kingdom work is "no more acceptable to many Christians than to semi-Christians and non-Christians."[70] Barth is pointing out how Christian political engagement is often seen by Christians and non-Christians as a task beyond ecclesiological bounds. However, this is a truncated version of the gospel as private piety that has been domesticated by modernity.

Last, the service of fellowship means that these worldly divisions are broken down, thus witnessing to the reconciling work of Christ. We have already noted above that Barth rejects ecclesial divisions

67. Ibid., 875.
68. Ibid.
69. Ibid., 893.
70. Ibid., 897.

according to nations, race, culture, and class.[71] Interestingly, Barth states in passing that "obviously, both in the sphere of the community and outside it, racially different people are to be seen and understood and taken seriously as such and therefore in their particularity."[72] Barth is not colorblind and clearly accepts as a given the concrete particularities of human diversity as long as they are not absolutized.

The richness of Barth's christological and missional concepts provides much fodder for the construction of an Asian American ecclesiology. Before we move on to that constructive task, we will analyze two contextual ecclesiological proposals in light of Barth's incarnational criteria.

Chalcedonian Critique of Contextual Ecclesiologies

In this section, we evaluate two contextual ecclesiologies in light of the incarnational logic that Barth employed. On the one hand, Donald McGavran's Church Growth Movement and its much-maligned homogenous unit principle will be criticized for its ebionitic ecclesiology. On the other hand, much of the contemporary argument for multiracial churches will be revealed for its docetic weaknesses.

In each of these cases, we are dealing with theological abstractions. A concept is considered "abstract" when "it is formulated without reference to the nexus of active relations in which God and humanity have their respective modes of being," when it misses the nature of God's gracious and sovereign activity.[73] The concerns that these theological abstractions are seeking to address might not be necessarily evil or even wrong, but their problem lies in an improper relationship with revelation. In a sense, they are a form of natural theology, asserting a kind of autonomy or authority that the lordship of Christ does not allow. Ultimately, theological abstractions are incidents of idolatry and violations of the first commandment.[74]

Throughout the discussion, Barth's ecclesiology will be critically

71. Ibid., 899–90.
72. Ibid., 899.
73. George Hunsinger, *How to Read Karl Barth: The Shape of His Theology* (New York: Oxford University Press, 1991), 32.

appropriated and engaged. As stated above, our goal is not to simply follow Barth as a teacher, but to be in serious conversation with him as we develop ideas for our own contexts.

Homogeneous Unit as an Abstraction

The Church Growth Movement began with the missiological insights and leadership of Donald McGavran, who spent a little over thirty years in India and later served as the founding dean of Fuller Theological Seminary's School of World Missions.[75] McGavran initially focused on international missionaries. However, with C. Peter Wagner and Fuller's new Doctor of Ministry degree in the mix, whole generations of church leaders were exposed to Church Growth Movement concepts, applying them to their contexts in North America.

While the movement and its various ideas have lost much of their appeal, having been critiqued and even dismissed as *passé* in recent years, its global impact should not be minimized. It should be noted that even in Donald McGavran's *Understanding Church Growth,* his ideas were never really systematized or articulated with theological rigor.[76] Moreover, currently, few have actually read the primary sources but have merely attacked a strawman version of these ideas. Our hope is to give McGavran's proposals a fair and clear analysis. We will organize the discussion in three parts: an orientation toward numerical growth, a strategy rooted in people movements, and the colonial origins of these concepts.

First, numerical growth frames the orientation of this movement, which is appropriately named "church growth." During his time in India, McGavran came to believe that much of missions work had been reduced to social justice at the expense of evangelism.[77] While still affirming all these social development works, McGavran wanted to

74. See Karl Barth, "The First Commandment as an Axiom of Theology," in *The Way of Theology in Karl Barth*, ed. H.M. Rurnscheidt (Allison Park, PA: Pickwick, 1986).
75. Gary L. McIntosh, "Introduction: Why Church Growth Can't Be Ignored," in *Evaluating the Church Growth Movement*, ed. Gary L. McIntosh (Grand Rapids, MI: Zondervan, 2004), 13–14.
76. Donald A. McGavran, *Understanding Church Growth*, 3rd ed., rev. and ed. C. Peter Wagner (Grand Rapids, MI: Eerdmans, 1990).
77. McIntosh, "Introduction," 12.

recover evangelism, and furthermore, to apply pragmatic and scientific research to this task. Through careful observation, he realized that some churches were more effective at evangelism, and thus grew, whereas others floundered and were stunted.

How are we to evaluate theologically this pragmatic bias toward numerical growth? In one sense, the liberal truncation of mission as simply social works was rightly rejected. Barth understood witness in a dialectical unity of word and action.[78] While both are valued equally and cannot be separated, there is an irreversible order in which word takes precedence.

> The example of the life action of Jesus Himself, the direction given to His disciples according to the Gospels, the indications at least which we are given of its work, and finally the Pauline description of the ministry of the community, all tell us plainly that two great and distinctive elements must always be present in it independently and yet in concert, namely, the elements of word and deed. The right order is that it should first speak. But with the same seriousness and emphasis it has also to act in correspondence with its word. In this unity and differentiation it represents what it is its task to represent to the world, namely, the likeness of the kingdom of God.[79]

Also, regarding the usage of insights from outside the Bible and the church, Barth notes that God can and does speak in the world as well, and that these sources are helpful when they "illumine, accentuate or explain the biblical witness in a particular time and situation."[80]

On the contrary, Barth rejects as unhealthy this seeking to "grow only or predominantly in this horizontal sense" and believes that it will lead to temptations and distortions of the gospel.[81] As the community grows spiritually, it will grow extensively as well.

While this order is correct, however, Barth fails to see that the lack of numerical growth could also be a sign of sloth or unfaithfulness. Increased numbers might arise out of unfaithfulness to the gospel, but lack of numbers is no proof of faithfulness. Thinking in term of

78. Barth, *CD* IV/3.2, 863.
79. Ibid., 864.
80. Barth, *CD* IV/3.1, 115.
81. Barth, *CD* IV/2, 646.

Chalcedonian errors, the spiritual can be docetically emphasized while the numerical is erroneously ignored. In this vein, McGavran's numerical orientation is seriously problematic, but Barth's views are open to distortions as well.

Second, the theoretical heart of the Church Growth Movement is the concept of people movements. What McGavran saw on the field was that mission stations were extracting converts from their own communities and treating them as individuals without communal ties. This perspective of Western individualism obscured the fact that in other parts of the world, people are communal and make communal decisions, as seen even in the Bible.[82] These communal relationships are natural bridges for the gospel to spread, and the mission station approach was breaking them all.[83] Within this setting, the idea of a homogeneous unit emerged. In the context of India, where McGavran served, he saw how an endogamous community was, in a sense, a homogeneous unit.[84]

McGavran should be commended for highlighting the distortions of Western individualism in the evangelism of non-Western people, especially in places where Christianity is already seen as a foreign religion. As Barth stressed, these non-Western churches should correspond to people's "environment and history and language and customs and ways of life and thoughts."[85] People exist in their particularity, as Barth clearly affirms. As we explored in chapter 2, gospel and contexts exist in an ordered and reciprocal relationality. Every church must take its particularity seriously, without losing its universality. The idea of the homogenous unit understands that modern national identities are artificial and often meaningless since the internal diversity of cultures and ethnic groups within a nation may be ignored.[86]

82. Donald A. McGavran, *The Bridges of God: A Study in the Strategy of Missions* (London: World Dominion, 1955), 8–10.
83. Ibid., 56.
84. Donald A. McGavran, *Ethnic Realities and the Church: Lessons from India* (Pasadena, CA: William Carey Library, 1979), 56.
85. Barth, *CD* IV/1, 671.
86. While there are limitations to applying this Indian insight of "people movement" widely to the US context, tribal identities and endogamous practices are practiced within some ethnic

Christianity should not cause the destruction of a community's culture and identity, nor should it be disconnected from them, even as it judges and redeems them. As Barth asserts, the integrity of the local context should be protected in missions.[87] Also, regarding endogamy, the gospel does not dictate whom we marry, nor does it judge ethnically mixed marriages to be of higher value.[88]

However, the dangers of homogeneity are clear. Essentializing or absolutizing a people's boundaries would, however unintentional, inevitably lead to a culturally captive church, one that violates its catholicity.[89] Cultural identity would become an abstraction, an idol that determines the gospel's authenticity for the community. We pointed out in chapter 1 that the boundaries of cultural identity are "reversible, fluid and removable," as Barth argues in *CD* III/4, §54.

The ecclesial corollary of this anthropological abstraction is that the church becomes a function of the community, and thus, simply exists for itself and not for the world. Barth exhorts every church to ask these questions and examine itself:

> Does it exist only as a kind of respectable local, regional or national tradition valued and cherished by certain circles and sections? Or as one of the instruments of the power of society or the ruling class in society?[90]

Moreover, the church would be complicit in perpetuating racist divisions and dynamics.[91] Thus, no faithful church can be exclusive, rejecting the other and ignoring its vocation to the world.

communities. See Jerry Z. Park, "Ethnic Insularity among 1.5- and Second-Generation Korean-American Christians," *Development and Society* 42, no. 1 (June 2013): 113–36.

87. Barth, *CD* IV/3.2, 875.
88. This point regarding marriage differs from the views of the Unification Church. "Sun Myung Moon is famous for holding mass weddings. He teaches that these couples are to be called 'Blessed Couples.' He encourages marriages of mixed races and nations to help bring unity between warring races and nations. He has personally matched many thousands of couples and now encourages parents to match their children. He teaches that the key to world peace is for these Unificationist couples to be exemplary families that will be model families who live by God's laws" (Jon Quinn, *Practical Plan for World Peace: Unificationism-The Teachings of Sun Myung Moon* [Principled Publications, 2009], 14). Surely racial reconciliation would be easier if interracial marriages were valued more highly or simply highly within Christianity. However, no such doctrine exists and endogamy is nowhere condemned.
89. Barth, *CD* IV/1, 703.
90. Ibid., 703.
91. Barth, *CD* IV/3.2, 899.

Third, the roots of the Church Growth Movement in its colonial context must be recognized. McGavran was concerned about the problem of Christianity being perceived as a foreign religion. The mission station approach extracted converts from their culture and too often resulted in missions being an expression of cultural colonialism.[92] McGavran argues that this approach arose out of "the individualistic background typical of much Protestantism in the eighteenth and nineteenth centuries."[93] Therefore, the problem was the imposition of Western Christianity and its standards upon a different cultural context. McGavran's exegesis of Matthew 28:19–20, and his separation of discipline from perfecting must be framed within this colonial context.[94]

The importance of contextualization in general has been noted, and specifically, chapter 2 observed that Barth's actualistic ontology demands that the living God be encountered where people are. So, McGavran's insights about the methodological colonialism expressed in some missions work, and the ways that this colonialism was expressed through Western individualism and Western standards that defined what a convert is, should be welcomed.

However, McGavran's exegesis, including its discipline-perfecting distinction, is highly problematic. Also, because of the broad focus on numerical growth, his strategy becomes open to "the temptation to win them by diluting the wine with a little water," as Barth warns.[95]

In sum, the Church Growth Movement's ecclesiology struggles with ebionitic distortions. Barth's christological logic clearly places the emphasis on the theological basis of the church. This asymmetry stresses that "Jesus Christ is the community," but "the community is not Jesus Christ."[96] Barth goes on to explain that in the relationship between the Jesus Christ and the community, the "sequence and order are all-important."[97] Along this line of thought, the sociological, visible,

92. McGavran, *The Bridges of God*, 46.
93. Ibid., 46.
94. Ibid., 14–16.
95. Barth, *CD* IV/2, 647.
96. Ibid., 655.
97. Ibid.

human dimensions continually take precedence in McGavran's thought, whether in discussions of numerical growth or cultural contexts.

Multiracism as an Abstraction

The heyday of the Church Growth Movement has passed, and a multiracial ecclesiology has become the new reigning paradigm. While it cannot be denied that the gospel must break down walls of racial hostility, and Barth himself argues for multiracial churches, we will present the case that multiracialism or a multiracial agenda can also become a theological abstraction if it becomes an ecclesiological shibboleth, or a fifth mark of the church, which insists that all true churches must be multiracial. Three main points guide our argument: the black–white binary paradigm, the language of segregation, and the issue of culture.

First, this multiracial ecclesiology establishes race relations primarily in terms of a black–white binary. Race becomes not just "*an* important issue for the Church today" but, for many, "*the* most important problem."[98] In their influential book, Michael O. Emerson and Christian Smith highlight the great divergence of perspectives on race among white and black evangelical Christians.[99] They note that the "United States is of course not just composed of two groups, one black and one white" and but that fact does not impact the binary paradigm that they use to interpret every kind of racial and ethnic diversity in America.[100] This binary paradigm is the reason for focusing on specifically "multiracial" diversity in terms of race as defined mostly by skin color. For example, pan-Asian churches, which are "multiethnic" churches in a technical sense, are of little significance for this paradigm.[101]

98. J. Daniel Hays, *From Every People and Nation: A Biblical Theology of Race* (Downers Grove, IL: InterVarsity, 2003), 17.
99. Michael O. Emerson and Christian Smith, *Divided by Faith: Evangelical Religion and the Problem of Race in America* (New York: Oxford University Press, 2000).
100. Ibid., 163.
101. Curtiss Paul DeYoung, Michael O. Emerson, George Yancey, and Karen Chai Kim, *United by Faith:*

The vestiges of slavery, the struggles of the Civil Rights Movement, and continuing injustices in the historic black–white racial divide impact all peoples in the USA. Asian Americans, Hispanic Americans, and others inherit and participate in these realities, regardless of their awareness or appreciation of the issues. The Civil Rights Movement and the resulting Civil Rights Act of 1964, and the closely related Immigration and Nationality Act of 1965, are concrete connection points for all these communities to this historic binary paradigm.

However, as we discussed in the previous chapter, when this binary paradigm is portrayed in a totalizing way as the one into which all others must fit, it becomes procrustean and oppressive.[102] Asian Americans have long decried this racial reduction of their identity, wherein their internal ethnic and cultural diversity is disregarded or summarily ignored.[103] Moreover, how should the church evaluate how pressing the question of race is? More importantly, what shape should this issue take, since different people struggle with it differently? Is it proper to make race *the* important issue for the church today, even a *status confessionis* issue? Within the context of slavery, segregation, civil rights, or apartheid, indeed race can rise to that level, and rightly so. However, over the years, other concerns have also been identified as *status confessionis* issues, such as women's ordination, biblical inerrancy, and most recently, homosexuality. The task of discerning these concerns is itself complex and fraught with dangers as well.

Second, directly connected with this binary paradigm is the use of the word "segregation" to refer to racial and ethnic diversity in churches. Martin Luther King Jr.'s oft-quoted maxim from the 1960s that "eleven o'clock on Sunday morning is the most segregated hour in

The Multiracial Congregation as an Answer to the Problem of Race (New York: Oxford University Press, 2004), 121–22.

102. In chapter 3, we discuss Victor Anderson's critiques of how ontological blackness is a form of "cultural idolatry." See Victor Anderson, *Beyond Ontological Blackness: An Essay on African American Religious and Cultural Criticism* (New York: Continuum, 1995). J. Kameron Carter extends this idea, calling this kind of racial discourse a theological abstraction, see J. Kameron Carter, *Race: A Theological Account* (New York: Oxford University Press, 2008), 192.

103. For example, Lee lists this "invalidation of interethnic differences" as one of the micro-aggressions that Asian Americans face (Sang Hyun Lee, *From a Liminal Place: An Asian American Theology* [Minneapolis, MN: Fortress Press, 2010], 19).

America" is repeated even today. The quote and King's context point to a time in which segregation meant white exclusivity and systemic power in churches. Black Americans were excluded from white churches, as well as from other segregated institutions. Is that what is happening today? What is the power that segregates, and what is the form of oppression?[104]

In the post-1965 Immigration Act era, which King's work brought about, immigrants brought and are still bringing their churches with them.[105] So, to call the existence of these churches instances of segregation is problematic. By this logic, a Korean church in Korea is fine, but if it immigrates to America, then it is a segregated church and therefore "an abomination" and a rejection of the gospel.[106] Such imposition of the binary paradigm is an oppressive expression of power by both black and white Americans over newer immigrants.[107] Degrading a church of a minority group in such a way, when being a part of a multiracial church so often means cultural assimilation, is an act of cultural colonialism and also a denial of the gospel.

Barth's ecclesiology simply does not articulate the way the ecumenical diversity that he affirms intersects with his call for fellowship across identity boundaries, especially in terms of cultural and ethnic backgrounds. Moreover, his German/Swiss context does not correspond neatly with the globalizing context we face in the USA. Therefore, while Barth's conceptual rubric for his christological logic is helpful, the relevance of its particular applications is limited.

104. The problem with a civil rights or apartheid projection upon ethnic churches has to do with the directionality of power and oppression. D. J. Bosch, J. N. J. Kritzinger, P. G. J. Meiring, and W. A. Saayman, "Debate with Donald McGavran: From D. J. Bosch, J. N. J. Kritzinger, P. G. J. Meiring, W. A. Saayman, South Africa: Department of Missiology, University of South Africa, Pretoria," in *Evangelistically Yours: Ecumenical Letters on Contemporary Evangelism*, ed. Raymond Fung (Geneva: WCC Publication, 1992), 147ff.

105. Hanciles provides examples of African churches in the West, but there are examples from Asian and Hispanic churches as well. Many of these immigrants are Christians and therefore bring their own versions of Christianity and church with them. See Jehu Hanciles, *Beyond Christendom: Globalization, African Migration and the Transformation of the West* (Maryknoll, NY: Orbis, 2009); and M. Daniel Carroll R., *Christians at the Border: Immigration, the Church, and the Bible* (Grand Rapids, MI: Brazos, 2014).

106. DeYoung et al, *United by Faith*, 113.

107. Andrew Sung Park, "Church and Ministry," in *Journeys at the Margin: Toward an Autobiographical Theology in American-Asian Perspective*, ed. Peter C. Phan and Jung Young Lee (Collegeville, MN: Liturgical Press, 1999), 162.

Of course, an immigrant church in the USA will need to engage with its new neighbors in its new context. However, using the word "segregation" or citing an anachronistic quote only adds confusion; carrying on the conversation on those terms is not constructive.

Third, within this binary paradigm, the issue of culture is generally marginalized, as though diversity were only about ethnocentricity and identity politics. Hays's "biblical theology of race" falls prey to this error. Hays concludes his study with an affirmation of the equal value of races and ethnic groups, out of which God creates a people. However, he fails to articulate the theological import of their cultures. Are these anything more than just "cultural baggage" that leads only to racial divisions, as he calls them?[108] What Hays fails to understand is that Christ and the gospel are always expressed in a cultural context. There is no pure expression of the gospel, no such a thing as a gospel without "cultural baggage."

Regarding this issue of culture, *United by Faith,* by Curtis Paul DeYoung and colleagues, presents perhaps one of the more sophisticated cases for multiracial churches, calling for not just superficial diversity, but a deep "*transformation* of congregational culture" whereby various cultures come together to create "a new hybrid culture."[109] The problem here is that the majority of the churches that claimed to be multiracial in these authors' study functioned within an assimilationist culture, with the majority group dominating. The authors do not recognize that if the majority group is white, then the church culture would reinforce the "honorary white" and "model minority" tropes that Asian Americans struggle against.[110] Thus, unless the church culture is actually "strictly egalitarian" in terms of racial and ethnic diversity, it would be oppressive to the minorities.[111]

Moreover, this idea of "a new hybrid culture" fails to take seriously

108. Hays, *From Every People and Nation*, 205.
109. DeYoung et al., *United by Faith*, 168.
110. See Mia Tuan, *Forever Foreigners or Honorary Whites? The Asian Ethnic Experience Today* (New Brunswick: Rutgers University Press, 1999).
111. DeYoung et al., *United by Faith*, 168.

cultural particularities. As quoted above, Barth takes as a given respect for people's ethnic, racial, or cultural particularities.[112] But, how would these particularities be respected if their integrity were not recognized? Barth's mistake is assuming that this givenness is a simple matter that only requires a mere acknowledgement with no actual discussion or further engagement.

Whether taking people's particularities as "cultural baggage" or advocating for "a new hybrid culture," multiracial ecclesiology can presuppose a "colorless theology" that assumes a melting pot view of American culture, as Wagner warned.[113] There actually is a need for contextualization to occur within various ethnic and cultural groups, even as their boundaries are fluid.[114] Just because cultural heritage is no longer meaningful to many whites and blacks does not mean that it is merely "baggage" to others. If a multiracial church is simplistically and naively understood to be "a sneak preview of heaven," then it is no better than an ethnocentric church, except for its pharisaic arrogance and judgmental attitude toward other "less diverse" churches.[115]

To summarize, whereas the Church Growth Movement's distortions leaned toward ebionitism, the multiracial ecclesiology tends toward docetism. Whether through the creation of a new culture or through colorblindness, universalizing themes are stressed at the expense of the concrete particularities of people. Whereas human community and diversity loomed large in Church Growth ecclesiology, the divine Christ and the press toward spiritual unity overwhelm multiracial ecclesiology. The Chalcedonian differentiated unity is vulnerable on both sides. Therefore, it is crucial that each side recognize the beam in its own eye before judging the other. More importantly, they both must recognize that neither essentializing particularity nor superficial unity leads to "a sneak preview of heaven." Rather, all churches must

112. Barth, *CD* IV.3.2, 899.
113. C. Peter Wagner, *Our Kind of People: The Ethical Dimensions of Church Growth in America* (Atlanta, GA: John Knox, 1979), 83.
114. Wagner, *Our Kind of People*, 92.
115. DeYoung et al., *United by Faith*, 176.

continually be formed and reformed in the likeness of Christ in his human–divine unity.

These two examples clarify the dangers of contextual ecclesiologies. In each case, Barth's christological logic provides an overall framework for theologically evaluating its contributions and weaknesses. Now, we turn to the final section, in which Asian American ecclesiologies are outlined.

Asian American Ecclesiologies

In this section, we discuss Asian American ecclesiologies while engaging with the four aspects of the AAQ, applying each one similarly to the way it was applied to the engagement of culture in the previous chapter. Corresponding to each of these aspects, four ecclesiological proposals are offered: *contextual community* for Asian heritage, *transitional community* for migration experience, *missional community* for American culture, and *liberational community* for racialization.[116]

As Barth stated, these ecclesiologies are for churches that already exist and not for vague, platonic ideals. Just as their identities are hybrid, complex, and dynamic, Asian Americans exist in diverse ecclesial communities, from ethnic churches to multiracial churches, and everything in between. Using Barth's Chalcedonian logic, the section above showed that the asymmetric, differentiated union between the divine, invisible, universal dimension and the human, visible, particular dimension is a challenge to embody, and is vulnerable to various abstractions. Given these complexities and difficulties, it just is not the case that one ecclesial expression is more biblical than others. Rather, they witness to different dimensions of the eschatological vision of affirming the church in its unity-in-diversity.

For each of these four ecclesiologies, we will propose a theological

116. Yoder stresses the social shape of moral judgment. In that light, the kind of cultural or contextual discernment described in the previous chapter occurs in the communal life of worship and discipleship, not in individuals by themselves. See John Howard Yoder, "How H. Richard Niebuhr Reasoned: A Critique of Christ and Culture," in *Authentic Transformation: A New Vision of Christ and Culture*, ed. Glen H. Stassen, D. M. Yeager, and John Howard Yoder, 31–90 (Nashville: Abingdon, 1996), 71–77.

basis, a formational dialectic, and a missional calling. These three elements reflect Barth's triadic doctrine of reconciliation of justification, sanctification, and vocation as related to his ecclesiology of the gathering, upbuilding, and sending of the community. The *theological basis* will affirm the church as a theological reality and not simply a sociological one. In terms of christological logic, this reflects the asymmetry and precedence of Jesus Christ over the community. No contextual, political, or sociological reasoning establishes the church, even as these surely are incorporated into the church's being in the world. A *formational dialectic* will ensure that there is no separation or fusion of the theological and the contextual. Docetic and ebionitic temptations are the main concern here. Finally, *missional calling* refers to the participation of the community in the mission of Jesus Christ, a missional existence for the sake of the world. In each of the four ecclesiological proposals, this missionality is one of the critical elements that keep the community from merely devolving into a self-serving human institution.

Contextual Community

Throughout this work, we have made it clear that the Asian heritage is diverse and living, meaning that it is continually developing and growing. Moreover, the Asian American communities' appropriation of and engagement with this heritage is complex. Nevertheless, if the gospel is to become deeply transformative in Asian American contexts, the Asian heritage must be explicitly and consciously engaged theologically.[117] This dynamic, with the grammar of this theological engagement, was the topic of the previous chapter. The point that must be made here is that this engagement occurs in a community, not in isolation. All theology is "autobiographical," but if it is not to

117. For examples of Asian American spirituality and discipleship, see Jeanette Yep et al., *Following Jesus without Dishonoring Your Parents* (Downers Grove, IL: InterVarsity, 1998). For examples of Asian American church life and ministry, see Peter Cha, S. Steve Kang, and Helen Lee, eds., *Growing Healthy Asian American Churches: Ministry Insights from Groundbreaking Congregations* (Downers Grove, IL: InterVarsity, 2006).

be a narcissistic ideology, it must reside in its proper context, the community of God.[118]

Contextualization means critiquing a context just as much as it does redeeming or transforming it for kingdom purposes. Ultimately, it means receiving God's Word in its particularity, as discussed in chapter 2. Engaging the Asian heritage consciously and explicitly means that it is not lost, ignored, or denied. Rather, it must be recalled, studied, and understood. This task is particularly challenging to Asian Americans because of migration patterns as well as the racist Orientalist forces that push us toward self-hatred and white assimilation.[119] These sociological realities are intertwined with strong theological rubric for the church being a *contextual community*.

Of course, depending on the ecclesial expression, from ethnic church to multiracial churches, this cultural engagement presents different kinds of challenges. The formational dialectic can be described as follows. On the one hand, in ethnic churches, the temptation is to allow the gospel become a function of the cultural heritage and family life. When churches confuse the gospel with culture, being accepted in the church is defined by one's ability to embody the culture. Put in another way, being a good Christian means being a good Asian.[120] What follows closely is an essentializing of cultural heritage, which then becomes an idol and a lord for the community. However, these distortions often occur precisely because the heritage is not explicitly and consciously engaged, but rather, remains implicitly and unconsciously influential. The point of theological engagement is not a christening and rigid preservation of an ethnic group's heritage, but rather, a more genuine and deeper embodiment of the gospel in the group's immediate situation.

On the other hand, in multiracial churches or even in pan-Asian

118. See the essays in this volume about the autobiographical nature of Asian American theology. Phan and Lee, *Journeys at the Margin*.

119. On this topic of Asian American self-hatred as related to marginalization and assimilation, see, for example, Lee, *From a Liminal Place*, 32.

120. This culture-gospel fusion is also one of the reasons why the second generation leaves the immigrant church. See Helen Lee, "Silent Exodus: Can the East Asian Church in America Reverse the Flight of Its Next Generation?" *Christianity Today*, August 12, 1996.

churches, this heritage is often ignored or even denied because everyone is supposed to be "American," a product of the colorless melting pot. The theological problem here is that the gospel remains superficial, and so, is unable to become deeply transformative in the lives of Asian Americans. Again, engaging cultural heritage is primarily a theological concern, not a sociological or even an anthropological one.

The particular missional calling of the Asian American church as a *contextual community* is to reach out to the family. The family is where the heritage most often resides. Western theology, captive to individualism, ignores the family as a theological category and a mission field. Yet, for the Asian American community, with its Confucian and Hindu heritages for example, unless the family systems dynamic is brought under the lordship of Christ, the gospel will remain on the surface.

Along with the family, the *contextual community* is called to discern, locate, and reach out to the segments of its own ethnic community or wider society that would be marginalized by their own Asian heritage. The people who have taboo status or are ethnic enemies based on cultural or historical heritage should be especially attended to. Unless these boundaries are crossed, heritage becomes the ultimate lord of the community, and the reconciliation that the gospel offers remains rejected.

Finally, the church as a *contextual community* is called to the task of missions back in the countries of origin, especially if the country is mostly unreached. Or if the country of origin has a robust Christian community, the Asian American communities and their originating communities in Asia can share and sharpen each other's theological insights regarding gospel–cultural heritage engagement.

Transitional Community

Affirming the church's particularity also leads us to affirm Asian American ecclesial situations as *transitional communities.*[121] Again, the theological basis of this *transitional community* lies in the living God—or in Barthian terms, in actualistic ontology. In his ethics, Barth rejects casuistry and abstract morals for the concrete command of God. God cannot be reduced to spiritual principles that are applied universally. Rather, God's command and call must be heard where we are, again and again.

Asian Americans encounter God in the particular situation and challenges of migration and the postmigration experience. Hybridity, identity formation, assimilation, and acculturation are just some of the themes that must be dealt with as individuals and as a community during this transitional and intergenerational experience. This community lives in marginality or liminality, not wholly belonging to Asia or America. Many members of the first generation often feel as if they were pilgrims or exiles in a foreign land while their offspring in later generations are made to feel like foreigners by others.[122] It is not so much that these experiences can be revelatory, although such things are possible, but rather, that we must listen to God's voice in the midst of them.

The formational dialectic of the Asian American church as a *transitional community* could, on the one hand, lead to the gospel becoming a function of the community as it focuses on its ethnic or racial identity. Whereas with the contextual community, the issue is cultural heritage, the concern here is identity. The danger is that the ethnic church could likewise become merely a community center for the activities and social life of the immigrant community. An ethnically-based expression of Christianity can further separate that

121. This idea of transitional community resonates closely with conceptualization of the church as a "resident alien" community, as articulated by Hauerwas and Willimon. However, because of the racist themes of orientalization and "perpetual foreigners" that Asian Americans face, the use of this idea is complicated and potentially oppressive. See Stanley Hauerwas and William H. Willimon, *Resident Aliens: A Provocative Christian Assessment of Culture and Ministry for People Who Know That Something Is Wrong* (Nashville, TN: Abingdon, 1989).

122. For the experience of being in exile, see Sang Hyun Lee, "Called to Be Pilgrims: Toward an Asian-American Theology from the Korean Immigrant Perspective," in *Korean American Ministry: A Resource Book*, ed. Sang Hyun Lee (Princeton, NJ: Consulting Committee on Korean-American Ministry of the Presbyterian Church, 1987). Also, for how the theme of exile functions in multiple and changing ways in the Asian American community, see Roy I. Sano, "Shifts in Reading the Bible: Hermeneutical Moves among Asian Americans," in *Semeia 90-91: The Bible in Asian America*, ed. Tatsiong Benny Liew, 105–18 (Atlanta, GA: Society for Biblical Literature, 2002).

community from mainstream society, causing it to live purely within a subcultural enclave.

On the other hand, the church can function as a way to affirm the efforts of members of that ethnic group to achieve acceptance into mainstream society, thereby enforcing the model minority trope. This assimilationist dynamic can occur in pan-Asian churches, but especially for the ethnic minority members of multiracial churches that are predominately white.[123] In a sense, the church becomes coopted into the service of identity politics, whether for the immigrant community or the dominant culture.

Being a true *transitional community* means resisting the temptation toward grasping power and security either in the Asian American subculture or in the dominant culture. Instead, the church can live out its Chalcedonian reality by faithfully affirming the precedence of its spiritual identity and the hybridity of its embodied identity. Jung Young Lee argued that this *transitional community* is to live beyond the two centers of subculture and dominant culture. "*To transcend or to live in-beyond does not mean to be free of the two different worlds in which persons exist, but to live in both of them without being bound by either of them.*"[124]

The particular missional calling of this *transitional community* is to reach out in service to the larger immigrant and postimmigrant communities in their struggles. As it serves recent immigrants with their various experiences of displacement, the church as a *transitional community* is called to support and guide them toward finding their secure base in God. Depending on the situation, Asian Americans in many postimmigrant generations might still find themselves in need of such a service as well.

While ethnic churches direct this work of service toward those of same ethnic heritage, the true calling of the Asian American church as a *transitional community* is to serve other ethnic Asian immigrants as well as immigrants of other races. Numerous times in Deuteronomy, God commands the Israelites to remember their experience of slavery

123. Russell Jeung, *Faithful Generations: Race and New Asian American Churches* (New Brunswick: Rutgers University Press, 2005), 161.
124. Lee, *Marginality*, 63.

that they might use it as a resource for extending mercy to others.[125] In the same sense, remembering the family experience of migration can lead the Asian American community into the service of any immigrant community. For example, the undocumented immigration issue that currently pertains, especially to the Hispanic community, should be of concern to the Asian American church as *transitional community.*

Missional Community

Missional community here implies a church that engages the American culture in its multicultural diversity and post-Christendom reality. Many studies from various perspectives have been written on engaging the American context as a mission field, The Missional Church Movement has taught us that Western culture is now post-Christian and must be engaged with the gospel anew.[126] Calling for a "continuing conversion of the church," Darrell Guder argues for an ongoing process through which God through the Word continually confronts the church. This process leads the church to avoid cultural truncation of the gospel.[127] The theological basis of the Asian American church as a *missional community* is the principle of *ecclesia reformata semper reformanda secundum verbum Dei*, and more fundamentally, the *missio Dei.*

The formational dialectic here is the tension between sacralization and secularization, which Barth explored in *CD* IV/2. As a hybridic people, Asian Americans share these tensions and dangers with the rest of the Christians in America. Depending on the personal and regional differences in acculturation or degree of assimilation, the diversity of types of North American cultural engagement is as broad as the rest of North America.

Just as the dangers of becoming *of* the world or failing to remain fully *in* the world are as common to Asian Americans as to other Americans, so the missional calling of the church as a *missional community* is shared

125. Deuteronomy 5:15, 15:15, 24:22.
126. See Darrell L. Guder. ed., *Missional Church: A Vision for the Sending of the Church in North America* (Grand Rapids, MI: Eerdmans, 1998).
127. Darrell L. Guder, *The Continuing Conversion of the Church* (Grand Rapids, MI: Eerdmans, 2000), 73–96.

as well. This calling begins with engaging the American context missiologically, identifying, for example, how Christianity has become commodified for private consumption without a public witness. More concretely, this calling also means awakening every Christian to be a kingdom witness, rather than a self-serving consumer.[128]

Also, the calling to engage the American context missiologically means reaching out to the neighborhood.[129] It is important that ethnic and pan-Asian churches actually see themselves in a mission field and think missionally about the local neighborhood. It is possible that even with all the evangelism and service, because of racism toward Asian Americans, non-Asians might not join their church.[130] However, as Barth stressed, numerical growth should not be thought of as the bottom line.

Furthermore, engaging American culture means becoming culture makers, not just cultural critics or cultural engagers.[131] As Barth discusses in *CD* III/4 in his doctrine of creation, culture is a task given by God. This task of culture making is especially important for Asian Americans because Asian American representation in American culture is either blatantly racist or reductionist most of the time. Creating a culture that represents the full humanity and dignity of Asian Americans is a task given by God the Creator, revealed in Jesus Christ. In this sense, churches as *missional communities* can and should support good culture, produced to the end of supporting Asian Americans.

Liberational Community

Finally, addressing the experience of Asian American racialization, the Asian American church is called to be a *liberational community*. The racism that Asian Americans face is multileveled and multifaceted.[132]

128. Alan Roxburgh and Fred Romanuk, *The Missional Leader: Equipping Your Church to Reach a Changing World* (San Francisco, CA: Jossey-Bass, 2006).
129. Alan J. Roxburgh, *Missional: Joining God in the Neighborhood* (Grand Rapids, MI: Baker Books, 2011).
130. Jeung, *Faithful Generations*, 156.
131. Andy Crouch, *Culture Making: Recovering Our Creative Calling* (Downers Grove, IL: InterVarsity, 2008).
132. Lee, *From a Liminal Place*, 11–21.

"Honorary white" and "perpetual foreigner" motifs bind Asian Americans between the rock and the hard place of assimilation or rejection. Individuals operating within racist structures based on "model minority" assumptions often indiscriminately combine Asian Americans with different ethnic heritages and ignore the great internal divergences in socioeconomic status that exists among them. Mundane micro-aggressions, such as questions like "where are you from?" harass and continue to cast Asian Americans as "the other." In the face of such situations, the theological basis for a *liberational community* is that because Jesus Christ "is the kingdom of God," based on the doctrine of *totus Christus*, "the kingdom of God is the community."[133] Justice and justification, the state and the church, both belong to Christ's kingdom, meaning that justice is the work of the church.[134] The *liberational community* witnesses to this truth and seeks to embody it in its life. The church is called to diaconal and prophetic services, as stated above.

In terms of formational dialectic, the danger is, on the one hand, for the church to become solely a refuge from oppressive racism. This theme of church as refuge is a very common one in Asian American theology and for good reasons.[135] However, the problem is that often in this model, the church becomes a quietistic escape from the realities of American society or a nationalistic escape to ethnocentricity. The church as refuge is ultimately a self-servicing community that quickly becomes even more inwardly focused when aggravated by issues of culture and migration, as discussed above.

On the other hand, the church could become a function of a political agenda. Here, the problem is that instead of a radical diastasis between God and creation, as Barth rightly maintained, the division resides between the victims and the oppressors. However, such a division is arbitrary, fluid, and limited since so often victims are oppressors in different contexts and oppressors are victims in others. Without

133. Barth, *CD* IV/2, 656.
134. David Haddorff "Introduction: Karl Barth's Theological Politics," in *Community, State, and Church* by Karl Barth (Eugene, OR: Wipf and Stock, 2013), 32.
135. See for example, Lee, *From a Liminal Place*, 128.

denying that there are injustices and victims, the church can never make such an ontological division. In Christ, God has reconciled the world to himself. Therefore, justice can never mean dividing humanity into the categories of victims and oppressors.

The ethnic church and the pan-Asian church are both vulnerable to these dangers. Multiracial churches have the potential to be such authentically liberational communities, but only if they are not colorblind, simply ignoring racial differences or limiting themselves to a black–white binary paradigm of justice.

The missional calling of the *liberational community* is to bring healing to the hurts of racism and to fight injustices. This healing begins with racist oppression being named and judged by the gospel, and it continues with the gospel affirming the dignity and humanity of Asian Americans.

Moreover, this *liberational community* must seek fellowship with other racial or ethnic churches. Deep fellowship with other churches would keep Asian American churches from devolving into a racially defined club that is more and more controlled by its own needs and wants than by the claims and demands of the kingdom.

Also, Asian Americans must own up to their complicity in North American structural racism, as well as their own individual racism. In this sense, becoming a *liberational community* means recognizing and mobilizing against historic black–white racism as well. They must become "households of mercy and justice," not only involved in incarnational ministry to other minorities, but also recognizing and fighting systemic racism in America.[136]

Conclusion

As they have in the previous chapters, the riches of Barth's theology have provided much creative fodder here. Barth developed his ecclesiology in a context much different from the contemporary

136. See Soong-Chan Rah, "Households of Mercy and Justice," in *Growing Healthy Asian American Churches: Ministry Insights from Groundbreaking Congregations*, ed. Peter Cha, S. Steve Kang and Helen Lee, 183–200 (Downers Grove, IL: InterVarsity, 2006).

globalized situation in the USA, especially from the perspective of Asian Americans. However, the wisdom of this modern-day "Church Father" crosses the boundaries of time and space to teach and stimulate the development of theology that takes the contextual particularity seriously.

In this chapter, we proposed Asian American ecclesiologies drawn from various insights from Barth. To understand key features, we reviewed the development of his ecclesiology culminating in his doctrine of election, which allowed him to bring together the divine–human diastasis and also fully affirm the human side. More formally, Barth's christological ecclesiology provides a way to unite and order the divine and human dialectic by using Chalcedonian categories. Understanding how churches can be docetic and ebionitic helped to clarify the relationship between the universal and particular dynamic of the church. Also, Barth's conviction that a theological basis must take precedence over any sociological basis explained the asymmetry in the christological logic. Then, the gathering, upbuilding, and sending of the community was discussed in the overall context of the doctrine of reconciliation with its triadic modes. The goal was not so much a comprehensive or exhaustive analysis of Barth's ecclesiology, but rather, a description of salient features and relevant insights for the construction of Asian American ecclesiologies.

To demonstrate how Barth's Chalcedonian logic functions as an analytical tool, two contextual ecclesiologies were assessed. Church Growth Movement ecclesiology with its theological abstraction of homogeneity was open to the distortion of ebionitism, allowing the context to become a captivity and losing the key asymmetry between the human and divine. Multiracial ecclesiology with its abstraction of diversity was vulnerable to the error of docetism, ignoring human contextual particularity.

Finally, Barth's christological logic and the triadic aspects of gathering, upbuilding, and sending of the community were all employed to envision Asian American churches as *contextual, transitional, missional,* and *liberational* communities corresponding to the four aspects of the AAQ. Keeping various ecclesial expressions in mind, from ethnic churches to multiracial ones, these four dialectical ecclesiological views highlighted different strengths and weaknesses of the Asian American church.

Conclusion

Seen in the light of our globalized Christianity, where the need for faithfully engaging with the context is greater than ever, the question of Barth's contextuality is not only crucial for Barthian scholarship, but for the future of theology. What we find in Barth is an example of continual struggles against every kind of Babylonian captivity to preserve the freedom of God's Word. His theology is truly a fine example of a *theologia reformata et semper reformanda secundum verbum dei*, a theology that is continually converted by encountering the Word of God. Here lies the heart of Barth's enduring legacy and challenge for the global church.

Because Barth is considered a modern church father, those who appreciate his theology can easily become intimidated by his genius and become Barthians, rather than simply learning from him. However, we have noted in the Introduction that Barth shows us a way to learn from him and move beyond him. Our task is to do theology *after* Barth, in the sense of *according* to Barth, learning from his wisdom, and in the sense of taking seriously our present situation.[1] For example, as we have noted above, Barth frankly is not theologizing for our globalized, multicultural, multiethnic context and its struggles of race, ethnicity, and culture.

Reviewing more closely the path of our work, along with this idea of theologizing *after* Barth, we began in the Introduction with some

1. Gunter Thomas, Rinse H. Reeling Brouswer and Bruce McCormack, eds., *Dogmatics after Barth* (Leipzig: CreateSpace, 2012), vii–viii.

evidences of Barth's contextual awareness and engagement. Barth distinguished between a theology that engages the context, and contextual theology that he believed was too limited and determined by the context. Acknowledging this critical insight, we sought to develop a Barthian contextual methodology to engage with the Asian American context. Therefore, although Asian American theological works were interacted with throughout the work, our primary focus was the Asian American context itself.

In chapter 1, we set out to propose a new way of defining the context. Looking to Barth's affirmation of the Jewish flesh of Christ and also his articulation of the fluidity of identity boundaries, we constructed a concrete, and yet, nonessentialist approach to framing the context. The concrete implication for the Asian American context was the development of the Asian American Quadrilateral (AAQ) as a defining rubric. This rubric ordered the multidimensions of the Asian American experiences in a way that was dynamic and comprehensive.

After this context definition, chapter 2 offered a contextual logic in the actualism of Barth's reasoning. Barth's actualism and his *Realdialektik* placed contextual logic at the very heart of the theological enterprise, and also Christian life, because ultimately Barth was stating that God revealed in Jesus Christ is alive and with us here and now. In what we have defined as double particularity, revelation and context are related in an asymmetric way with revelation taking the precedence. For the Asian American context, this contextual logic meant that God's presence and actions are to be addressed and discerned in three levels of theological reflection: the methodological, the communal, and the personal. This seemingly simple distinction supported our avoidance of essentialism, ethnic monopolizing, as well as contextual captivity.

The contextual logic of chapter 2 meant that we must take seriously our context here and now, as well as revelation there and then. Just how we take the context seriously is explained in chapter 3, with a dialectical grammar that comes from Barth's doctrine of reconciliation. This doctrine of reconciliation is the unfolding of Barth's understanding of *participatio Christi*, which in turn, is rooted in his universal and christological revision of the doctrine of election. Here, Barth argues that God elects all humanity to be *de jure* united with Christ. Barth elaborates the substance of this christological participation in his triadic doctrine of reconciliation (justification, sanctification, and vocation). We argued that this triadic doctrine could serve as a grammar for engaging with culture in a dynamic, multifaceted, and nimble fashion. A glimpse of this grammar's capabilities was demonstrated in some *ad hoc* examples from each area of the AAQ.

In the final chapter, we sought to construct an ecclesiology for a community in which this kind of cultural engagement would occur. Using Barth's Chalcedonian pattern as a guide for avoiding the abstractions of the homogenous unit principle and of multiracism, we envisioned the church as a contextual, transitional, missional, and liberational community. These fourfold aspects of the community should not only be present in all Asian American churches, but also in all churches with Asian Americans as members.

This work has focused on methodological discussions, offering something of a contextual prolegomena. As Barth has shown in his *Church Dogmatics*, the prolegomena itself should already be determined by God's revelation. While sensitive to sociological and cultural insights, we have endeavored to follow Barth by constructing a theological basis for contextuality, asserting that God is alive and active, here and now. This theological move allows for the affirmation of contextuality, while still keeping God's revelation the main subject of our theological reflections. This focus and emphasis on revelation is not for the sake of some theological conservatism, but rather, about ecclesial rootedness. Our faith communities are ultimately seeking to be faithful disciples of Christ; thus, contextuality is meaningful only as it supports and enhances that task. Our conviction is that this communal faithfulness requires these communities to address the issues and concerns of contextuality. Without keeping this communal life in the forefront, theology would be for naught, becoming a much maligned ivory tower exercise.

To continue the trajectory of this work, more research is needed for engaging with the various elements within each of the four spheres of the AAQ with this new triadic grammar. For example, under the Asian heritage, Buddhism, Taoism, Shinto, shamanism, animism, Hinduism, and other traditions will have to be engaged in an archetypical, as opposed to stereotypical, way—as we proposed in chapter 1. Regarding migration, how could various themes of exile and exodus interact in a triadic manner with the experience of the various generations and their members' understandings of identity? Within the broader American society, what are the contributions and the challenges that Asian American communities bring and what is the church's mission in this collage? Within the sphere of racialization, what is the role of Asian Americans in opposing structural racism, even as we suffer under a perpetual foreigner status and model minority myth? These are examples of the kind of questions that must be asked and researched, all with the praxis of the community in mind.

To see the significance of this book in the life of the church, which, according Barth, is the *telos* of any theological work, we must begin to train Asian American faith communities to use the proposed method to critically reflect upon their life in Christ at the communal and personal levels. Whether in systematic theology, practical theology, sermons, Bible studies, or practices of missions, this book will prove its worth in its usefulness to these various theological tasks.

Asian American Christians are on the cusp of becoming a significant force in American religious landscape.[2] For the task of equipping the Asian American church, Barth's two criteria about: 1) seeking to be free from all Babylonian captivities, and 2) not being morose or boring, provide an important insightful warning and some joyful inspiration for the task. Also, his two suggestions about: 3) being authentic to ourselves, while also 4) remembering the universal church, further help to frame the way to proceed courageously and cautiously. These four exhortations of Barth summarize the general ethos of this whole

2. Helen Lee, "Asian Americans: Silent No More," *Christianity Today*, October 2014, 38.

book. These are lessons that every theologian in the global church should take to heart.

Bibliography

Karl Barth

Primary Sources

Against the Stream: Shorter Post-War Writings, 1946-52. Edited by Ronald Gregor Smith and translated by Stanley Godman. London: SCM, 1954.

The Christian Life: Church Dogmatics IV, Part 4: Lecture Fragments. Translated by Geoffrey W. Bromiley. Grand Rapids, MI: Eerdmans, 1981.

The Church and the Churches. Grand Rapids, MI: Eerdmans, 1936.

The Church Dogmatics. 14 vols. Edited by Geoffrey W. Bromiley and Thomas F. Torrance and translated by G. T. Thomson et al. Edinburgh: T&T Clark, 1956–1975.

Community, State, and Church. Edited and translated by Will Herberg. Eugene, OR: Wipf and Stock, 2013.

The Epistle to the Romans. Translated by Edwyn Hoskyns. London: Oxford University Press, 1968.

Evangelical Theology: An Introduction. Translated by Foley Grover. Grand Rapids, MI: Eerdmans, 1963.

The Göttingen Dogmatics: Instruction in the Christian Religion. Translated by Geoffrey W. Bromiley. Grand Rapids, MI: Eerdmans, 1991.

The Humanity of God. Translated by John Newton Thomas and Thomas Wieser. Richmond, VA: John Knox, 1960.

Letters, 1961-1968. Edited by Jürgen Fangmeier and Hinrich Stoevesandt.

Translated and edited by Geoffrey W. Bromiley. Grand Rapids, MI: Eerdmans, 1981.

"No Boring Theology! A Letter from Karl Barth." *The South East Asian Journal of Theology* 11 (Autumn 1969): 3–5.

On Religion: The Revelation of God as the Sublimation of Religion. Translated and introduced by Garrett Green. New York: T&T Clark, 2006.

Protestant Theology in the Nineteenth Century. New ed. Translated by Brian Cozens and John Bowden. London: SCM, 2001.

Theology and Church: Shorter Writings 1920-1928. Translated by Louise Pettibone Smith. New York: Harper and Row, 1962.

The Theology of John Calvin. Translated by Geoffrey W. Bromiley. Grand Rapids, MI: Eerdmans, 1995.

The Theology of the Reformed Confessions. Translated and annotated by Darrell L. Guder and Judith J. Guder. Louisville, KY: Westminster John Knox, 2002.

Unterricht in der christlichen Religion, III: Die Lehre von der Versöhnung / Die Lehre von der Erlösung. Edited by Hinrich Stoevesandt. Zürich: Theologischer Verlag Zürich, 2003.

The Way of Theology in Karl Barth. Edited by H.M. Rurnscheidt. Allison Park, PA: Pickwick, 1986.

The Word of God and Theology. Translated by Amy Marga. London: T&T Clark, 2011.

and Emil Brunner. *Natural Theology: Comprising "Nature and Grace" by Professor Dr. Emil Brunner and the Reply "No!" by Dr. Karl Barth.* Translated by Peter Fraenkel. London: The Centenary, 1946.

Secondary Sources

Anderson, Clifford Blake. "Jesus and the 'Christian Worldview': A Comparative Analysis of Abraham Kuyper and Karl Barth," *Cultural Encounters* 2, no. 2 (2006): 66–69.

Beintker, Michael. "Der Römerbrief von 1919," in Gerhard Sauter (ed.), *Verkündigung und Forschung: Beihefte zu "Evangelische Theologie,"* 2 (1985).

Bender, Kimlyn J. *Karl Barth's Christological Ecclesiology.* Burlington, VA: Ashgate, 2005.

Busch, Eberhard. *The Great Passion: An Introduction to Karl Barth's Theology.* Translated by Geoffrey W. Bromiley. Grand Rapids, MI: Eerdmans, 2004.

_____. *Karl Barth: His Life from Letters and Autobiographical Texts.* Translated by John Bowden. Minneapolis, MN: Fortress Press, 1977.

_____. *Meine Zeit mit Karl Barth: Tagebuch 1965-1968.* Göttingen: Vandenhoeck und Ruprecht, 2011.

Capper, John Mark. "Karl Barth's Theology of Joy." PhD diss., Cambridge University, 1998.

Chung, Paul S. *Karl Barth: God's Word in Action.* Eugene, OR: Cascade, 2008.

Congdon, David W. "Dialectical Theology as Theology of Mission: Investigating the Origins of Karl Barth's Break with Liberalism." *International Journal of Systematic Theology* 10, no. 4 (October 2014): 390–413.

DeCou, Jessica. *Playful, Glad, and Free: Karl Barth and a Theology of Popular Culture.* Minneapolis, MN: Fortress Press, 2013.

_____. "'Serious' Questions about 'True Words' in Culture: Against Dogmatics IV.3 as the Source for Barth's Theology of Culture." Paper presented at the Karl Barth Society of North America Panel at the annual meeting of the American Academy of Religion/Society for Biblical Literature, San Francisco, 2011.

Flett, John G. *The Witness of God: The Trinity,* Missio Dei, *Karl Barth and the Nature of Christian Community.* Grand Rapids, MI: Eerdmans, 2010.

Gorringe, Timothy J. *Karl Barth: Against Hegemony.* Oxford: Oxford University Press, 1999.

Hunsinger, George. *Disruptive Grace: Studies in the Theology of Karl Barth.* Grand Rapids, MI: Eerdmans, 2000.

_____. *For the Sake of the World: Karl Barth and the Future of Ecclesial Theology.* Grand Rapids, MI: Eerdmans, 2004.

_____. *How to Read Karl Barth: The Shape of His Theology.* New York: Oxford University Press, 1991.

Johnson, William Stacy. *The Mystery of God: Karl Barth and the Postmodern Foundations of Theology.* Louisville, KY: Westminister John Knox, 1997.

Jüngel, Eberhard. *God's Being Is in Becoming: The Trinitarian Being of God in the Theology of Karl Barth.* Translated by John Webster. Grand Rapids, MI: Eerdmans, 2001.

_____. *Karl Barth: A Theological Legacy*. Translated by Garrett E. Paul. Philadelphia, PA: Westminster, 1986.

Lindsay, Mark R. *Covenanted Solidarity: The Theological Basis of Karl Barth's Opposition to Nazi Antisemitism and the Holocaust.* New York: Peter Lang, 2001.

Mangina, Joseph L. *Karl Barth: Theologian of Christian Witness.* Louisville, KY: Westminster John Knox, 2004.

Marquardt, Friedrich-Wilhelm. *Theologie und Sozialismus: Das Beispiel Karl Barths.* Munich: Chri. Kaiser, 1972.

McCormack, Bruce L. *Karl Barth's Critically Realistic Dialectical Theology: Its Genesis and Development, 1909-1936.* Oxford: Clarendon, 1995.

_____. *Orthodox and Modern: Studies in the Theology of Karl Barth.* Grand Rapids, MI: Baker, 2008.

_____. Review of *Karl Barth: Against Hegemony* by Timothy Gorringe. *Scottish Journal of Theology* 55, no. 2 (2002): 233–52.

_____. "A Scholastic of a Higher Order: The Development of Karl Barth's Theology, 1921-31." PhD diss., University of Michigan, 1989.

Metzger, Paul Louis. *The Word of Christ and the World of Culture: Sacred and Secular through the Theology of Karl Barth.* Grand Rapids, MI: Eerdmans, 2003.

Moseley, Carys. *Nations and Nationalism in the Theology of Karl Barth.* New York: Oxford University Press, 2013.

Neder, Adam. *Participation in Christ: An Entry into Karl Barth's* Church Dogmatics. Louisville, KY: Westminster John Knox, 2009.

Nimmo, Paul T. *Being in Action: The Theological Shape of Barth's Ethical Vision.* New York: T&T Clark, 2007.

Palma, Robert J. *Karl Barth's Theology of Culture.* Allison Park, PA: Pickwick, 1983.

Sonderegger, Katherine. *That Jesus Christ Was Born a Jew: Karl Barth's Doctrine of Israel.* University Park, PA: Pennsylvania State University Press, 1992.

Stroud, Dean G., ed. *Preaching in Hitler's Shadow: Sermons of Resistance in the Third Reich.* Grand Rapids, MI: Eerdmans, 2013.

Thomas, Günter, Rinse H. Reeling Brouwer, and Bruce McCormack, eds. *Dogmatics after Barth: Facing Challenges in Church, Society and the Academy.* Leipzig: CreateSpace Independent Publishing, 2012.

Torrance, Thomas F. *Karl Barth: An Introduction to His Early Theology, 1910-1931.* London: SCM, 1962.

_____. *Karl Barth, Biblical and Evangelical Theologian.* Edinburgh: T&T Clark, 1990.

Vahanian, Gabriel. "Karl Barth as Theologian of Culture." *Union Seminary Quarterly Review* 28, no. 1 (1972): 37–49.

Villa-Vicencio, Charles, ed. *On Reading Karl Barth in South Africa.* Grand Rapids, MI: Eerdmans, 1988.

Webster, John, ed. *The Cambridge Companion to Karl Barth.* New York: Cambridge University Press, 2000.

_____. *Karl Barth.* 2nd ed. New York: Continuum, 2004.

Wood, Ralph C. *The Comedy of Redemption: Christian Faith and Comic Vision in Four American Novelists.* Notre Dame, IN: University of Notre Dame Press, 1988.

Ziegler, Philip G. Review of *The Word of Christ and the World of Culture: Sacred and Secular through the Theology of Karl Barth,* by Paul Metzger, *Scottish Journal of Theology* 59, no. 1 (2006): 113–16.

Other Sources

Abelmann, Nancy, and John Lie. *Blue Dreams: Korean Americans and the Los Angeles Riots.* Cambridge, MA: Harvard University Press, 1997.

Anderson, Ray S. *The Shape of Practical Theology: Empowering Ministry with Theological Praxis.* Downers Grove, IL: InterVarsity Academic, 2001.

Anderson, Victor. *Beyond Ontological Blackness: An Essay on African American Religious and Cultural Criticism.* New York: Continuum, 1995.

Bantum, Brian. *Redeeming Mulatto: A Theology of Race and Christian Hybridity.* Waco, TX: Baylor University Press, 2010.

Berthrong, John H. *All Under Heaven: Transforming Paradigms in Confucian-Christian Dialogue.* Albany, NY: State University of New York Press, 1994.

Bevans, Stephen B. *Models of Contextual Theology.* Rev. and expanded ed. Maryknoll, NY: Orbis, 2002.

Bonhoeffer, Dietrich. *Dietrich Bonhoeffer Works.* Vol. 4, *Discipleship.* Edited by Geffrey B. Kelly and John D. Godsey and translated by Barbara Green and Reinhard Krauss. Minneapolis, MN: Augsburg Fortress Press, 2001.

_____. *Dietrich Bonhoeffer Works.* Vol. 15, *Theological Education Underground, 1937-1940.* Edited by Victora J. Barnett and translated by Victora J. Barnett and Claudia D. Bergmann. Minneapolis, MN: Augsburg Fortress Press, 2011.

Bosch, David. *Transforming Mission: Paradigm Shift in the Theology of Mission.* Maryknoll, NY: Orbis, 1991.

Branson, Mark Lau, and Juan Martínez. *Churches, Cultures, and Leadership: A Practical Theology of Congregations and Ethnicities.* Downers Grove, IL: InterVarsity Academic, 2011.

Browning, Don S. *Fundamental Practical Theology: Descriptive and Strategic Proposals.* Minneapolis, MN: Augsburg Fortress Press, 1991.

Calvin, John. *Institutes of the Christian Religion.* Library of Christian Classics 20-21. Philadelphia, PA: Westminster, 1960.

Carter, J. Kameron. *Race: A Theological Account.* New York: Oxford University Press, 2008.

Cha, Peter, S. Steve Kang, and Helen Lee, eds. *Growing Healthy Asian American Churches: Ministry Insights from Groundbreaking Congregations.* Downers Grove, IL: InterVarsity, 2006.

Chan, Simon. "The Future of Global Theology from an Asian Perspective," A guest lecture at Fuller Theological Seminary at the release of the *Global Dictionary of Theology*, Pasadena. October 23, 2008.

Charry, Ellen T. *By the Renewing of Your Minds: The Pastoral Function of Christian Doctrine.* New York: Oxford, 1997.

Ching, Julia. *Confucianism and Christianity: A Comparative Study.* New York: Kodansha International, 1977.

Chuang, DJ. "Nine Things about Asian American Christianity." *The Exchange: A Blog by Ed Stetzer,* November 7, 2013. http://www.christianitytoday.com/edstetzer/2013/november/9-things-about-asian-american-christianity.html.

Carroll R., M. Daniel. *Christians at the Border: Immigration, the Church, and the Bible.* Grand Rapids, MI: Brazos, 2014.

Crisp, Oliver and Fred Sanders (eds). *The Voice of God in the Text of Scripture.* Grand Rapids, MI: Zondervan, 2016.

Crouch, Andy. *Culture Making: Recovering Our Creative Calling.* Downers Grove, IL: InterVarsity, 2008.

DeYmaz, Mark. *Building a Healthy Multi-Ethnic Church: Mandate, Commitments, and Practices of a Diverse Congregation.* San Francisco, CA: Jossey-Bass, 2007.

DeYoung, Curtiss Paul, Michael O. Emerson, George Yancey, and Karen Chai

Kim. *United by Faith: The Multiracial Congregation as an Answer to the Problem of Race.* New York: Oxford University Press, 2004.

Ecklund. Elaine Howard. *Korean American Evangelicals: New Models for Civic Life.* New York: Oxford University Press, 2008.

Edwards, Jonathan. *Works of Jonathan Edwards,* Vol. 8. *Ethical Writings.* Edited by Paul Ramsey. New Haven, CT: Yale University Press, 1970.

Emerson, Michael O., and Christian Smith. *Divided by Faith: Evangelical Religion and the Problem of Race in America.* New York: Oxford University Press, 2000.

Falicov, Celia Jaes. *Latino Families in Therapy.* 2nd ed. New York: Guilford, 2013.

Fällman, Fredrik. *Salvation and Modernity: Intellectuals and Faith in Contemporary China,* rev. ed. Lanham, MD: University Press of America, 2009.

Fong, Ken Uyeda, *Pursuing the Pearl: A Comprehensive Resource for Multi-Asian Ministry.* Valley Forge, PA: Judson, 1999.

Freire, Paulo. *Pedagogy of the Oppressed.* 30th anniversary ed. New York: Continuum, 2002.

Friedman, Edwin. *Generation to Generation: Family Process in Church and Synagogue.* New York: Guilford, 1985.

Fruchtenbaum, Arnold G. *Israelology: The Missing Link in Systematic Theology.* Tustin, CA: Ariel Ministries, 1994.

Fung, Raymond. *Evangelically Yours: Ecumenical Letters on Contemporary Evangelism.* Geneva: WCC Publications, 1992.

Gladney, Dru C. *Muslim Chinese: Ethnic Nationalism in the People's Republic.* Cambridge, MA: Harvard University Asia Center, 1996.

Goulbourne, Harry, ed. *Race and Ethnicity: Critical Concepts in Sociology.* New York: Routledge, 2001.

Grenz, Stanley J., and John R. Franke, *Beyond Foundationalism: Shaping Theology in a Postmodern Context.* Louisville, KY: Westminster John Knox, 2001.

Groome, Thomas H. *Sharing Faith: A Comprehensive Approach to Religious Education and Pastoral Ministry: The Way of Shared Praxis.* San Francisco, CA: Harper San Francisco, 1991.

Guder, Darrell L. *The Continuing Conversion of the Church.* Grand Rapids, MI: Eerdmans, 2000.

_____. *Missional Church: A Vision for the Sending of the Church in North America.* Grand Rapids, MI: Eerdmans, 1998.

Hanciles, Jehu. *Beyond Christendom: Globalization, African Migration and the Transformation of the West.* Maryknoll, NY: Orbis, 2009.

Harper, Brad, and Paul Louis Metzger, *Exploring Ecclesiology: An Evangelical and Ecumenical Introduction.* Grand Rapids, MI: Brazos, 2009.

Hauerwas, Stanley, and William H. Willimon. *Resident Aliens: A Provocative Christian Assessment of Culture and Ministry for People Who Know That Something Is Wrong.* Nashville, TN: Abingdon, 1989.

Haynes, Stephen R. *Reluctant Witnesses: Jews and the Christian Imagination.* Louisville, KY: Westminster John Knox, 1995.

Hays, J. Daniel. *From Every People and Nation: A Biblical Theology of Race.* Downers Grove, IL: InterVarsity, 2003.

Heitink, Gerben. *Practical Theology: History, Theory, Action Domains.* Grand Rapids, MI: Eerdmans, 1999.

Hollinger, David A. *Postethnic America: Beyond Multiculturalism.* New York: Basic Books, 2000.

Hopkins, Dwight N. *Introducing Black Theology of Liberation.* Maryknoll, NY: Orbis, 1999.

Hunsberger, George R. *Bearing the Witness of the Spirit: Lesslie Newbigin's Theology of Cultural Plurality.* Grand Rapids, MI: Eerdmans, 1998.

_____, and Craig Van Gelder. *The Church between Gospel and Culture: The Emerging Mission in North America.* Grand Rapids, MI: Eerdmans, 1996.

Hunsinger, Deborah Van Deusen. *Theology and Pastoral Counseling: A New Interdisciplinary Approach.* Grand Rapids, MI: Eerdmans, 1995.

Jennings, Willie J. *The Christian Imagination: Theology and the Origins of Race.* New Haven, CT: Yale University Press, 2010.

Jeung, Russell. *Faithful Generations: Race and New Asian American Churches.* New Brunswick: Rutgers University Press, 2005.

Joh, Wonhee Anne. *Heart of the Cross: A Postcolonial Christology.* Louisville, KY: Westminster John Knox, 2006.

Keller, Catherine, Michael Nausner, and Mayra Rivera, eds. *Postcolonial Theologies: Divinity and Empire.* St. Louis, MO: Chalice, 2004.

Keysser, Christian. *A People Reborn.* Translated by Alfred Allin and John Kuder. Pasadena, CA: William Carey Library, 1980.

Kierkegaard, Søren. *Attack upon "Christendom."* Translated by Walter Lowrie. Princeton, NJ: Princeton University Press, 1944.

Kim, Rebecca. *God's New Whiz Kids? Korean American Evangelicals on Campus.* New York: New York University Press, 2006.

Kinzer, Mark S. *Postmissionary Messianic Judaism: Redefining Christian Engagement with the Jewish People.* Grand Rapids, MI: Brazos, 2005.

Kirkpatrick, Lee A. *Attachment, Evolution, and the Psychology of Religion.* New York: Guilford, 2004.

Kraemer, Hendrik. *The Christian Message in a Non-Christian World.* New York: IMC 1947.

Kuyper, Abraham. *Abraham Kuyper: A Centennial Reader.* Edited by James D. Bratt. Grand Rapids, MI: Eerdmans, 1998.

Kwok, Pui-lan. *Postcolonial Imagination and Feminist Theology.* Louisville, KY: Westminster John Knox, 2005.

Kwon, Ho-Youn, Kwang Chung Kim, and R. Stephen Warner, eds. *Korean Americans and Their Religions: Pilgrims and Missionaries from a Different Shore.* University Park, PA: Pennsylvania State University Press, 2001.

Larsen, Timothy, and Daniel J. Treier, eds. *Cambridge Companion to Evangelical Theology.* Cambridge: Cambridge University Press, 2007.

Lee, Jung Young. *Marginality: The Key to Multicultural Theology.* Minneapolis, MN: Fortress Press, 1995.

_____. *The Trinity in Asian Perspective.* Nashville, TN: Abingdon, 1996.

Lee, Helen. "Asian Americans: Silent No More." *Christianity Today*, October 2014.

Lee, Sang Hyun. *From a Liminal Place: An Asian American Theology.* Minneapolis, MN: Fortress Press, 2010.

Legge, James. *Confucianism in Relation to Christianity: A Paper Read before the Missionary Conference in Shanghai, on May 11th 1877.* London: Trubner, 1877.

Liew, Tatsiong Benny, ed. *Semeia 90-91: The Bible in Asian America.* Atlanta, GA: Society for Biblical Literature, 2002.

Lindbeck, George A. *The Nature of Doctrine: Religion and Theology in a Postliberal Age.* 25th anniversary ed. Louisville, KY: Westminster John Knox, 2009.

Luther, Martin. *Luther's Works.* Vol. 31, *Career of the Reformer 1.* Edited by Harold J. Grimm and Helmut T. Lehmann. Minneapolis, MN: Fortress Press, 1957.

McClendon, James William Jr. *Biography as Theology: How Life Stories Can Remake Today's Theology*. Philadelphia, PA: Trinity International, 1990.

McConnell, Douglas C. "Confronting Racism and Prejudice in Our Kind of People." *Missiology: An International Review* 25 (October 1997): 388–404.

McGavran, Donald A. *The Bridges of God: A Study in the Strategy of Missions.* London: World Dominion, 1955.

_____. *Ethnic Realities and the Church: Lessons from India.* Pasadena, CA: William Carey Library, 1979.

_____. *Understanding Church Growth.* 3rd ed. Revised and edited by C. Peter Wagner. Grand Rapids, MI: Eerdmans, 1990.

Medina, Néstor. "Transgressing Theological Shibboleths: Culture as Locus of Divine (Pneumatological) Activity." Paper presented at the annual meeting of the Academy of American Religion/Society for Biblical Literature, Baltimore, 2013.

Min, Pyong Gap, ed. *Asian Americans: Contemporary Trends and Issues.* Thousand Oaks, CA: Pine Forge, 2005.

Moltmann, Jürgen. *Experiences in Theology: Ways and Forms of Christian Theology.* Translated by Margaret Kohl. Minneapolis, MN: Fortress Press, 2000.

Nakka-Cammauf, Viji, and Timothy Tseng, eds. *Asian American Christianity: Reader.* Castro Valley, CA: Institute for the Study of Asian American Christianity, 2009.

Neville, Robert Cummings. *Boston Confucianism: Portable Tradition in the Late-Modern World.* Albany, NY: State University of New York Press, 2000.

Newbigin, Lesslie. *Context and Conversion.* London: Church Missionary Society, 1978.

_____. *Foolishness to the Greeks: The Gospel and Western Culture.* Grand Rapids, MI: Eerdmans, 1986.

_____. *The Gospel in a Pluralist Society*. Grand Rapids, MI: Eerdmans, 1989.

_____. *The Open Secret: An Introduction to the Theology of Mission.* Grand Rapids, MI: Eerdmans, 1995.

Ng, David, ed. *People on the Way: Asian North Americans Discovering Christ, Culture, and Community.* Valley Forge, PA: Judson, 1996.

Park, Jerry Z. "Ethnic Insularity among 1.5- and Second-Generation Korean-American Christians." *Development and Society* 42, no. 1 (June 2013): 113–36.

Park, M. Sydney, Soong-Chan Rah, and Al Tizon, eds. *Honoring the Generations: Learning with Asian North American Congregations.* Valley Forge, PA: Judson, 2012.

Phan, Peter. *Christianity with an Asian Face.* Maryknoll, NY: Orbis, 2003.

_____, and Jung Young Lee, eds. *Journeys at the Margin: Toward an Autobiographical Theology in American-Asian Perspective.* Collegeville, MN: The Liturgical, 1999.

Quinn, Jon. *Practical Plan for World Peace: Unificationism: The Teachings of Sun Myung Moon.* N.p.: Principled Publications, 2009.

Rah, Soong-Chan. *The Next Evangelicalism: Freeing the Church from Western Cultural Captivity.* Downers Grove, IL: InterVarsity, 2009.

Reilly, Kevin, Stephen Kaufman, and Angela Bodino, eds. *Racism: A Global Reader.* Armonk, NY: M.E. Sharpe, 2003.

Reisacher, Evelyn A. "The Processes of Attachment between the Algerian and French within the Christian community in France." PhD diss. Fuller Theological Seminary, 2001.

Roberts, J. Deotis. *Liberation and Reconciliation: A Black Theology*, 2nd ed. Louisville, KY: Westminster John Knox, 2005.

Roxburgh, Alan J. *Missional: Joining God in the Neighborhood.* Grand Rapids, MI: Baker, 2011.

_____, and Fred Romanuk. *The Missional Leader: Equipping Your Church to Reach a Changing World.* San Francisco, CA: Jossey-Bass, 2006.

Said, Edward W. *Orientalism*, 25th anniversary ed. New York: Vintage, 1994.

Schleiermacher, Friedrich. *The Christian Life*, 2nd ed. Translated by H. R. Mackintosh. Philadelphia, PA: Fortress Press, 1976.

Schreiter, Robert J. *Constructing Local Theologies.* Maryknoll, NY: Orbis, 1985.

Sedmak, Clemens. *Doing Local Theology: A Guide for Artisans of a New Humanity.* Maryknoll, NY: Orbis, 2002.

Shin, Gi-Wook. *Ethnic Nationalism in Korea: Genealogy, Politics, and Legacy.* Stanford, CA: Stanford University Press, 2006.

Siegel, Daniel J. *The Developing Mind: How Relationships and the Brain Interact to Shape Who We Are.* 2nd ed. New York: Guilford, 2012.

Song, Choan-Seng. *Theology from the Womb of Asia.* Maryknoll, NY: Orbis, 1986.

_____. *Third-Eye Theology: Theology in Formation in Asian Setting*. Rev. ed. Maryknoll, NY: Orbis, 1991.

Stassen, Glen H., D. M. Yeager, and John Howard Yoder, *Authentic Transformation: A New Vision of Christ and Culture*. Nashville, TN: Abingdon, 1996.

Steinberg, David I., ed. *Korea's Changing Roles in Southeast Asia: Expanding Influence and Relations*. Singapore: Institute of Southeast Asian Studies, 2010.

Tan, Jonathan Y. *Introducing Asian American Theologies*. Maryknoll, NY: Orbis, 2008.

Tanner, Kathryn. *Theories of Culture: A New Agenda for Theology*. Minneapolis, MN: Fortress Press, 1997.

Tillich, Paul. *Systematic Theology*. Vol. 1. Chicago: University of Chicago Press, 1951.

Tracy, David. *The Analogical Imagination: Christian Theology and the Culture of Pluralism*. New York: Crossroad, 1989.

Tran, Jonathan. "The New Black Theology: Retrieving Ancient Sources to Challenge Racism." *The Christian Century*. Jan 26, 2012. http://www.christiancentury.org/article/2012-01/new-black-theology.

Tuan, Mia. *Forever Foreigners or Honorary Whites? The Asian Ethnic Experience Today*. New Brunswick: Rutgers University Press, 1999.

Vines, Stephen. "China's Black Pop Idol Exposes Her Nation's Racism." *The Observer*, November 1, 2009. http://www.guardian.co.uk/world/2009/nov/01/lou-jing-chinese-talent-show.

Volf, Miroslav. *Exclusion and Embrace: A Theological Exploration of Identity, Otherness, and Reconciliation*. Nashville, TN: Abingdon, 1996.

Wagner, C. Peter. *Our Kind of People: The Ethical Dimensions of Church Growth in America*. Atlanta, GA: John Knox, 1979.

Walls, Andrew F. *The Cross-Cultural Process in Christian History: Studies in the Transmission and Appropriation of Faith*. Maryknoll, NY: Orbis, 2002.

_____. *The Missionary Movement in Christian History: Studies in the Transmission of Faith*. Maryknoll, NY: Orbis, 1996.

Weiner, Michael. *Japan's Minorities: The Illusion of Homogeneity*. New York: Routledge, 1997.

Wyschogrod, Michael. *Abraham's Promise: Judaism and Jewish-Christian Relations.* Grand Rapids, MI: Eerdmans, 2004.

_____. *The Body of Faith: God in the People Israel.* Lanham, MD: Jason Aronson, 1996.

Yang, Huilin, and Daniel H. N. Yeung, eds. *Sino-Christian Studies in China.* Newcastle: Cambridge Scholars, 2006.

Yao, Xinzhong. *An Introduction to Confucianism.* New York: Cambridge University Press, 2000.

_____. *Confucianism and Christianity: A Comparative Study of Jen and Agape.* Brighton: Sussex Academic, 1997.

Yep, Jeanette, and Peter Cha. *Following Jesus without Dishonoring Your Parents.* Downers Grove, IL: InterVarsity, 1998.

Yong, Amos. *The Future of Evangelical Theology: Soundings from the Asian American Diaspora.* Downers Grove, IL: InterVarsity Academic, 2014.

Yoo, David, and Russell Leong, ed. *New Spiritual Homes: Religion and Asian Americans.* Honolulu: University of Hawaii Press, 1999.

Young, John D. *Confucianism and Christianity: The First Encounter.* Hong Kong: Hong Kong University Press, 1983.

Index